EXaminations

TOM KESSENICH

National Library of Canada Cataloguing in Publication

Kessenich, Tom
 Examinations : an unauthorized look at seasons 6-9 of
The X-files : featuring the reviews of Unbound I /
Tom Kessenich.
 ISBN 1-55369-812-6
 1. X-files (Television program) I. Title.
PN1992.77.X34K48 2002   791.45'72   C2002-903684-4

TRAFFORD

This book was published *on-demand* in cooperation with Trafford Publishing.
On-demand publishing is a unique process and service of making a book available for retail
sale to the public taking advantage of on-demand manufacturing and Internet marketing.
On-demand publishing includes promotions, retail sales, manufacturing, order fulfilment,
accounting and collecting royalties on behalf of the author.

Suite 6E, 2333 Government St., Victoria, B.C. V8T 4P4, CANADA

Phone	250-383-6864	Toll-free	1-888-232-4444 (Canada & US)
Fax	250-383-6804	E-mail	sales@trafford.com
Web site	www.trafford.com	TRAFFORD PUBLISHING IS A DIVISION OF TRAFFORD HOLDINGS LTD.
Trafford Catalogue #02-0625		www.trafford.com/robots/02-0625.html

10   9   8   7   6   5   4   3   2

TABLE OF CONTENTS

3

AND SO IT BEGAN

The year was 1993. Bill Clinton was the President, the Dallas Cowboys were still "America's Team," Whitney Houston was promising to "Always Love You," and Steven Spielberg was painting an exquisite picture of a horrifying period in mankind's history with his cinematic masterpiece, "Schindler's List."

Meanwhile, a television series called "The X-Files" was about to leave an imprint on me - and millions of others - that would last a lifetime.

I was a sportswriter for a newspaper in Wisconsin at the time and when I wasn't busy chronicling the Green Bay Packers' return to prominence, I was working the sports desk on Friday nights, proofreading stories and putting the sports section to bed. Long after work had ended and before I was prepared to call it a night, there was one weekly ritual left to accomplish to make the night complete.

Watching the latest episode of "The X-Files."

I had become hooked on the show immediately. With its unique blend of UFOs and the paranormal, plus the fascinating relationship between the two lead characters, it was a show unlike any other I had seen on television. And it soon became a show I refused to miss.

In the middle of the show's fifth season, I discovered the world of online fandom. Before long, I found newsgroups and message boards where other X-Philes (as fans of the show were called) were gathering. They broke down each episode's content, discussing such things as the potency of the mytharc, the true nature of Fox Mulder and Dana Scully's relationship and their ever-changing hairstyles.

The fan base featured many parts. There were the relationshippers whose focus was on Mulder and Scully's relationship, or the MSR as it was called (with a possible emphasis on romance). There were the noromos, who opposed a romance of any kind between the two lead characters, believing it would lead to the show's downfall. And there were fans who preferred one character over the other, ones who believed Mulder would never be good enough for Scully and those who believed Scully was a shrew who constantly held Mulder back.

In other words, this was one giant family. And when they welcomed me with open arms, I felt as if I had found an online home.

I soon began writing reviews using the pseudonym "Unbound I" and over time, those reviews garnered me a certain amount of acclaim within the fan community. That enabled me to form relationships with other fans as well as people within and connected to the television industry. As a fan, I continued to review and discuss the series. As a reporter, I succeeded in landing interviews with people connected with the show and gathered voluminous amounts of information about the series from a wide variety of sources.

As a fan, I had plenty to talk about with each passing episode. And as a reporter, the information I obtained was painting a fascinating look at what was

4

going on with the series I loved. Together, they helped me piece together the reasons why the show was such a success for as long as it was and what happened at the end that left a passionate fan base torn apart and often angry with the show's storytellers.

The deterioration of the fan base was shocking given how passionately it had been embraced by the staff at 1013 Productions (series creator Chris Carter's production company) when the show first went on the air. In the early days of the series, it was not uncommon for Carter to hang out in "X-Files" chat rooms and message boards, mingling with fans and entertaining their thoughts and ideas.

The writers playfully poked fun at the online fans' intense analysis of the series and the fans responded by helping turn the show from a cult hit into a full-blown critical success.

Over time, though, a divide began to occur between 1013 and the online fans. Never was that more apparent than in the final two seasons, when Carter sought to reinvent his series without Mulder and Scully at its core. Many members of the online community criticized the decision and predicted it would quickly lead to the show's demise.

It did not help matters that Carter and his chief collaborator the last four seasons, executive producer Frank Spotnitz, frequently questioned the online fan base, calling these viewers "hysterical" and "aggravating," and claiming the collective online voice of the fans had been "dumbed down" over time. Suddenly, the very fans who helped make this show such a success could not wait for it to come to an end.

As if that weren't enough, the online fan base itself began to splinter apart. There had always been a separation between the noromos and the shippers, but at the start of the eighth season, another significant division was born.

On one side of the fence stood fans who embraced the show's new direction and new main character (Agent John Doggett). On the other side of the fence were fans who had no interest in seeing the series reinvented without Mulder and Scully at its center.

Rancor often replaced reason as a once-powerful fan base became fractured and combative. When the series finally ended, many fans were more relieved than sad to see the show they once loved come to an end.

To quote the Grateful Dead, "What a long, strange trip it's been."

My purpose in writing this book is to take you through the concluding acts of this trip. Consider this book to be a journey as it guides you through the final four seasons of "The X-Files." Along the way, you will hear from some of the people who made the key story decisions on the series as well as thoughts and comments from many of the show's fans, whose passion for "The X-Files" made it such a resounding success.

At the book's core will be my episode reviews and essays. They are just the thoughts of one fan, but it is my hope they will strike a chord with each of you and serve as a written testimony of the powerful emotional resonance this wonderful series had on all those it touched.

For nine seasons, "The X-Files" provided thrills and drama unlike anything I had ever seen on television before. I doubt another show will come along that will be its equal and it will be the rare series which will inspire the type of devotion from its viewers this show enjoyed. It was an amazing ride, ones which began with such promise and ended with so much uncertainty. I hope you enjoy the ride as much as I did.

MOVIE REVIEW: "FIGHT THE FUTURE"

From a federal building in Dallas to a cornfield in Texas and all the way to Antarctica, Mulder and Scully go where The X-Files have never gone before. To the big screen. And what a rousing ride it turned out to be.

It's not uncommon for a television series to inspire a cinematic incarnation. But such inspirations typically come *after* the TV series has come to an end. "The X-Files," though, is not your ordinary television series, so leave it to Chris Carter to turn the formula upside down and deliver the cinematic exploits of Mulder and Scully while his series is still on the air.

"Fight The Future" bridges the fifth and soon-to-be sixth season in tremendous fashion by furthering the alien colonization and re-investing Mulder and Scully's quest into the paranormal and unusual. But most of all, it is a two-hour example of the significant and unique bond between these two characters which has served as the foundation on which this wondrous series has been built.

Shady characters (some new such as Dr. Alvin Kurtzweil and Strughold, the apparent leader of the Consorium, while others such as the Cigarette Smoking Man and the Well Manicured Man are quite familiar) and revelations about the role mankind plays in the alien colonization threat (turns out we're nothing more than "digestives for the creation of a new race of alien life forms." It sounds believable when the WMM says it, trust me) are window dressing for the centerpiece of Chris Carter's story here. The relationship between Mulder and Scully.

It's put to the test when Mulder and Scully take the fall for an explosion in a federal building in Dallas which kills a federal agent. Scully ponders quitting the FBI, but before she can turn in her agency scrubs, Mulder (thanks to a tip from old family friend Kurtzweil) has her back in Dallas as they pursue what may be an alien virus.

This virus has already claimed the life of a little boy, some firefighters and one of the Consortium doctors. Soon it will lead Mulder and Scully to another run-in with bees, another Scully abduction (this time by human forces) and the death of the Well Manicured Man, who before being offed in a car bomb politely gives Mulder many of the answers he has so desperately sought for the past five seasons.

Damn, those Brits are polite.

Well, he did withold the whereabouts of Mulder's sister. Then again, did anyone really think Carter would give up the show's holy grail when he still had more TV episodes to produce?

By the way, I realize the CSM is the show's resident villain, but the WMM has always struck me as being more sinister. I'm pretty sure it's the English accent and the fact he drives on the wrong side of the road.

Is that someone you'd trust?

Carter smoothly integrates his script with enough exposition about his characters and their back story to help educate those unfamiliar with his show. David Duchovny has a slightly intoxicated moment in a bar where he recounts his life story, all the way from Samantha's abduction to his aiming to blow the lid off a government conspiracy which will be "the shit storm of all time." Meanwhile, Gillian Anderson peppers a few moments here and there to let people know she's a medical doctor who was assigned to The X-Files to debunk Mulder's work.

That plan lasted about a half-hour before Mulder got her into an Oregon motel room and had her wide-eyed with interest as he told her his life story. One thing about Mulder, he's pretty damn persuasive.

If there is a problem, it's Carter's attempt to go the mytharc route on the big screen as a means to add more mass appeal to his television series. The mytharc has grown into a tangled web of clues and mysteries and even some of the most focused fans have begun to wonder if Carter isn't making up the story as he goes along. That seems to be the case here at times as we see the "black oil" suddenly evolve into an "Alien" ripoff, reducing its overall menace by rendering it into simply being another monster from outer space.

Carter would have been better served by serving up a stand-alone effort on the big screen, thus allowing first-time viewers to ease their way into the story without having their heads explode as they try to decipher what the aliens are doing next.

That's not to say the story doesn't work. It does. It works because Duchovny and Anderson prove to be even more glorious together on the big screen than they are when we invite them into our homes every Sunday night.

Duchovny's wry wit is on full display. Among the highlights are when he pokes fun at his droll reputation by showing Scully his "panic face," when he tells the cops he needs to see Kurtzweil (an OB/GYN) for a "pelvic examination" and his retort to Scully after he makes a driving decision in the middle of nowhere ("Five years together Scully, how many times have I been wrong? Never … not driving anyway"). Anderson loses out on the one-liners, but matches him with a quiet elegance that shows Scully is also at home on a much grander scale than we had ever seen her before.

Mulder and Scully are true cinematic figures. They are larger then life, yet it remains their humanity and the humor and tenderness by which they relate to one another that enables them to remain easily accessible. Nowhere is that more apparent than in a climactic moment in Mulder's hallway when Scully tells him she's headed off to Utah to root for the Jazz and check out this whole Mormon thing she's heard about.

Faced with the reality that Scully may leave him forever, Mulder bares his soul, revealing how Scully's presence in his life helped replace the missing part of his soul, taken the night his sister was abducted. "You've kept me honest and made me whole. I owe you so much Scully, and you owe me nothing."

Mulder's words strike at the heart of their relationship. Without her stabilizing influence, Mulder would have easily lost his way by now, lost adrift in a maze of endless dead ends and painful revelations.

Scully's decision to leave forces Mulder to reveal what Scully has needed to hear. In "The End," the appearance of another believer from the past (Diana Fowley) led Scully to question her place alongside Mulder. We see that contemplation continue again in the film as Scully wonders if Mulder would be better off without her, without her endless skepticism and need to prove his theories from a scientific perspective.

But Mulder's words reassure her that they truly belong with one another. They have grown together in so many ways that the idea of living without one another is unfathomable.

Also unfathomable (for noromos anyway) is the near kiss which is the high point of this scene. As Mulder and Scully draw close, their possible moment of passion is ended by a bee sting. Scully goes into shock as the alien virus begins to pour through her system. Soon, Mulder is shot, Scully is taken and Mulder has to head off to Antarctica to rescue her.

Needless to say, he does just that, avoiding some nasty "Aliens" in the process. Back in D.C., Scully provides evidence of the massive conspiracy to Blythe Danner before reminding Mulder that her place is alongside him no matter what ("If I leave now, they win."). Somewhere in Tunisa, there's a cornfield a poppin', the CSM and Strughold are a meetin' and the movie ends with a prophetic statement referring to Mulder's passionate quest to uncover "the truth."

"No man alone can fight the future."

Well, of course not. That's what Scully is for. She is "that which he holds dear." Among other things.

While not offering any real answers to the goings-on for the previous five seasons, Carter does prove his characters and their story are quite at home on the big screen. Whether this will lead to more "X-Files" films in the future remains to be seen. But "Fight The Future" proved Mulder and Scully are without a doubt big-screen material.

SEASON 6

The sixth season of "The X-Files" marked a dramatic shift with the series, not only in the tone of the episodes, but more importantly, the location where it was being produced.

After five critically acclaimed seasons in Vancouver, the show moved to Los Angeles for its sixth season. The move resulted in criticism from some fans and members of the media, who believed one of the series' most alluring attributes was its ability to utilize its unique Canadian locations. Moving to Hollywood, they reasoned, would rob the series of its sense of mystery and foreboding terror.

"The move to L.A. hurt," said Elizabeth B. Schillaci, a fan from Alabama who watched the series from its inception. "The whole series seemed different. Vancouver was such a perfect place to film a series like 'The X-Files.' It just gave the series a perfect, creepy, woodsy feel that I loved. L.A. had to manufacture that feeling."

"The most critical component in the downhill slide of 'The X-Files' (and the MSR) was the move from Vancouver," Jan Sellers Ashton, an Illinois fan since Season 2, said. "I understand why it happened. If I were (Duchovny) or anyone else connected to the show, I, too, would want to be where the industry is based. But the move precipitated weak writing; unfocused characterization and confused mythology; and, I hate to write this part, slippage in the acting done by (Duchovny and Anderson)."

Some fans also lamented the shift toward more lighter fare. "The X-Files" had long dotted its seasonal lineups with humorous episodes. Several of the best were written by Darin Morgan, who many TV insiders believe was the most essential element to the show's eclectic creative mix along with Duchovny.

Morgan left the series after the third season, leaving producer Vince Gilligan as the show's strongest source of light-hearted stories. Gilligan's fourth-season episode, "Small Potatoes" (featuring Morgan in an acting role) and his fifth-season effort, "Bad Blood," remain two of the series' most popular episodes among fans to this day.

So the ability to put a humorous twist on a familiar formula had been one of the show's strengths for quite some time. However, the sixth season saw a clear trend toward serving up numerous episodes of "X-Files Lite" as they were labeled within the fan community. The results were often mixed.

"I thought some of the episodes of Season 6 were some of the most imaginative," said Kaaren Perry, a fan from Los Angeles who started watching the show in its third season. "For instance, 'Triangle' was a huge endeavor and 'Field Trip' was a very unique episode and depicted the strength of the bond between Mulder and Scully."

"I liked the humorous aspect," said Valerie Martin, a fan from New York whose love affair with the show began with the pilot episode. "It was a nice change from all the seriousness of the past few seasons. It was also nice to watch the actors experiment with a new style."

Other fans weren't as taken with the light-hearted approach or its frequency during the season.

"In Season 6 they lost their X-Files touch," said Vanessa Griekspoor from Heerlen, The Netherlands, a fan since the third season. "Gone were the scary MOTW's and in came all the humorous episodes. Not that there is anything wrong with that, but it was a bit too much."

"The problem with Season 6 was that there were too many light stories," said Chris Neefus, a fan since the first season from Pennsylvania. "Although I love light stories, the whole reason people tuned in to the show for the first five seasons was to watch eerie and sometimes gory case files unfold, and see their two favorite characters solve them."

In other words, "The X-Files" wasn't really "The X-Files" anymore. At least not for some fans who believed the trend toward more light-hearted episodes was reflective of the show's creative decline.

"The writers were trying too hard to make the show whimsical and quirky, and they were failing miserably," said Courtney Smith, a Philadelphia-area fan who began watching after Season 2.

"I'd have been content to see the show go out (relatively) triumphant at the end of Season 5," added Joann Humby, a European fan since the beginning of the series. "The writing pool (after the fifth season) wasn't big enough. Many of the best left it, and there were too many 'yes men' in it. The L.A. move kept the show alive. Whether it deserved the stay of execution is a different matter."

The show's creative forces certainly understood the fans' trepidation with regard to influx of lighter episodes that were on display in the sixth season.

"My position is that humor could work in it," Duchovny said in an interview during the show's seventh season. "When we had (Glen) Morgan and (James) Wong, and when we had Darin Morgan, and we still have Vince Gilligan, they seem to be able to hold both a humorous whimsical element and a scary supernatural element.

"When they fall flat, they fall flat because they're too whimsical. (In the sixth season), just by coincidence, the writers just had four or five funny shows in a row. It probably has something to do with being in the sixth year of a show. You become self-referential. You start to wink at the audience. I think people got scared because they all happened to occur in one spate and people went, "Oh my God, it's Ally McBeal!"

"Ally McBeal" also had its fair share of romantic entanglements. And one of the greatest questions surrounding "The X-Files" after the film was released was whether Mulder and Scully would soon make the leap from partners in the basement of the FBI to partners in crime in the bedroom.

The near kiss in the film sparked intense debate among the show's fans about the nature of Mulder and Scully's relationship and where it was headed. Many fans openly lobbied for the relationship to deepen, while others viewed such a development as a sign of the show's apocalypse.

The fans weren't the only ones debating whether Mulder and Scully should become romantically involved. The writers at 1013 also pondered that subject, with some members of the show's creative team strongly opposing a romance.

In an online chat with fans before the sixth season began, Gilligan said he believed if Mulder and Scully went so far as to have a romantic relationship, it would remove the sexual tension that had become a significant, and electrifying, aspect of their relationship.

At no point in the sixth season was there a clear indication that anything romantic was happening between Mulder and Scully. However, one of the season's most prevalent themes was an examination of their relationship and its evolution, often by comparing and contrasting it with other couples.

"Triangle" provided a peak into Mulder's subconscious feelings for Scully and ended with his declaration of love. In "The Rain King," Mulder and Scully were constantly being misidentified as a couple and near the episode's conclusion, Scully has a revealing discussion with another woman about how friendship can suddenly develop into something more. And in "Arcadia," the relationship was turned on its head as Mulder and Scully went undercover posing as man and wife.

However, none of those episodes pushed the envelope quite as strongly as Duchovny did in "The Unnatural," which he also wrote and directed. The episode's final scene, which showed Mulder giving Scully a "birthday present" by teaching her how to play baseball, was equal parts witty, smart and sensual. And it served to drive this relationship forward in a powerful way.

Maybe they weren't "getting it on" as Mulder joked in "Arcadia," but the show's writers obviously weren't oblivious to the changing nature of the characters' relationship. The moment in the hallway in the film served notice there was something more happening, something more intimate than we'd already seen. Although 1013 was in no rush to get there, the writers weren't turning a blind eye to this development.

One development no one could ignore was the decline in the number of viewers tuning in to watch the show every week. The show had been steadily rising in popularity with an average of 16.9 million viewers watching the third season, 19.2 million watching the fourth and 19.8 million checking out Season 5.

In Season 6, however, that average dipped to 17.2 million. That decrease occurred despite the fact two episodes ("The Beginning" and "The Rain King") topped 20 million viewers. For whatever reason, the bloom was coming off the rose of "The X-Files" from a numbers perspective and the decline that began in

Season 6 would be a trend that would continue until the show's expiration three seasons later.

Although some fans were unhappy with the sixth season, I viewed it as a revelation. I enjoyed the fifth season, but found several episodes lacking and a few others quite mundane. Only rarely did I believe the series reached the glorious levels of the first four seasons.

One of my central problems with the fifth season was the inability to properly develop the idea of Mulder suddenly losing his faith and beginning to believe "the truths" he had long clung to were merely lies created to manipulate him. On the surface, this was a wonderful idea given how powerful Mulder's longing for the truth had always been and how that desperate need for the truth could be used to deceive him.

But while the idea was enticing, the execution was flawed. Mulder stopped believing merely on the word of one man he had no reason to trust. And instead of examining Mulder's loss of faith over the course of the season, it was glossed over until the time came (in "The Red and the Black") for him to suddenly regain what he had lost so he could become the show's resident "believer" again.

I would have much preferred to see Mulder's crisis of faith be a season-long story arc that took his character, and the series, to new heights.

Given that, I found much more to my liking in Season 6. Some episodes, such as "Drive" and "Monday," I consider to be under rated classics. Others such as "Milagro," "Tithonus" and "Field Trip" quickly became personal favorites and two (Carter's "Triangle" and Duchovny's "The Unnatural") were elevated to a prominent position among my selections of the most memorable episodes in the series' history.

It was an amazing season and it proved once again there was no other show on television quite like "The X-Files."

"THE BEGINNING"

A bright, sizzling ray of sun beats down upon 20-some million viewers. The sun is blinding, its brilliance fills up the screen. It's obvious we're not in Vancouver anymore.

Welcome to Los Angeles everyone, the new home of "The X-Files." And with that opening shot of the bright California sun, this really was "The Beginning" in many ways for the series as it begins its sixth season.

"The Beginning" was a pretty good premiere episode. I was quite pleased to see how Chris Carter took last season's finale and the movie and tied things together to get Season 6 off to a fresh start.

So we've seen the aliens and they are us? Nice twist at the end and again this builds upon what Well Manicured Man told Mulder in the movie.

13

Once again, Carter takes the standard mytharc and tweaks it a bit just to keep us guessing. At the same time, he offers up development and some insight into the movie aliens who I know bugged a lot of people. At least now we have an idea how they are tied in with the gray aliens and have seen the reason behind their vicious behavior: A defense mechanism during the early forms of gestation. Perfectly logical.

I was quite pleased with the layers that were tossed out for public consumption. I know a lot of fans don't like Diana Fowley and it would be wise for Mulder to not be quite so trustworthy of her, but although I'm beginning to have reservations about her character, I am still interested to see where Carter takes her and what future effect she has on Mulder and Scully.

And for all those worried about the jealousy angle, that seemed to be played down quite a bit although I was never opposed to it in the first place. It always seemed to me that Scully's reaction to Fowley was perfectly natural.

On that note, of course, Carter teased us with the opening shot of the near kiss and then didn't follow up - with the exception of that abrupt cut to Scully holding Mulder's hand in Phoenix. Not very subtle.

As far as Scully is concerned, I'm sure her rapid turn to skeptic again will frustrate a lot of people. At first it did me as well. But the scene with Gibson I believed was very revealing.

I think Scully does believe. I think she wants to believe. But it goes so far against her very nature that it makes it difficult to reconcile these feelings she has with what she has seen and how she can go about proving it scientifically, not just to her superiors, but to herself. So she attempts again to use science to back up what she knows to be true.

For someone who has lived her entire life a certain way and has suddenly been faced with a major revelation, it seems logical to me that she would turn to what she holds most dear to come to grips with what she now is forced to confront. This is her safety net. Her way of attempting to understand something she never thought possible. It's frustrating to Mulder, but as she said she has to be honest and he needs her to be honest to legitimize his work.

Some other side notes: I was glad to see the Cigarette Smoking Man working in line with Jeffrey Spender. Perhaps this will actually develop the character of Spender in a way that makes him an integral part of the storyline as opposed to being an overall nuisance.

Besides, the Consortium needs a fresh twist, in my opinion. Perhaps Spender can provide one. So what do we make of Skinner now? Is he a lost soul at the FBI as Mulder has become? What is his role in the future? I, for one, am interested to see what his fate will be as well.

The X-Files have been closed to Mulder and Scully. But of course, Mulder will not go down without a fight. His blatant disregard for authority is one of his most appealing characteristics. And that last scene with Scully convinces me she is inclined to believe there is something out there and the truth is something she could never have contemplated before.

"DRIVE"

I've seen Keanu Reeves and Fox Mulder is no Keanu Reeves. Thank God for that. And thank God for "Drive," which taps into the idea of "Speed," the hit movie starring Reeves, but pushes it in an excitingly different direction.

Vince Gilligan takes the basic premise of "Speed," (which featured a runaway bus set to explode if its velocity dipped below 55 miles per hour) and adds a wonderful X-Files twist. Here, Mulder is held captive by one Patrick Crump, who insists Mulder continue to drive west or else there's going to be hell to pay. Or more precisely, his exploding head all over the dashboard.

And here Mulder thought the brains of a dead limo driver in the film was all that could ruin the upholstery.

Gilligan is smart enough to know most people will pick up on the connection to "Speed." He diffuses that matter quickly having Mulder joke about "having seen this movie."

But "Drive" is more than just "The X-Files" meets "Speed." It's a fascinating character turn and adds another sinister layer to the idea of government paranoia which has been one of the show's strongest roots since its inception.

It's doubtful Patrick Crump was voted "Most Charming" by his high school graduation class. He's a redneck and a bigot and has an innate distrust of authority and the government.

Now that I think about it, he sounds a lot like some of the guys I knew when I was in high school. Crump, though, is quite a bit higher up the evolutionary ladder than many of them were.

But I digress.

What Crump is most of all, however, is a victim. And that is where he and Mulder connect. Crump has lost his wife and will soon lose his life, thanks to the insidious work of the government near the trailer park where they live.

Held hostage by Crump, Mulder's first instinct is survival. But after learning of Crump's tale, it becomes something stronger. It begins to strike at the heart of his life's work.

And this is why "Drive" excels. It takes a basic premise and integrates it masterfully into the fundamental themes and ideas of "The X-Files."

Mulder and Scully stumble onto the scene after catching a look at Crump's wife's head explode while surrounded by authorities on the local news. For Mulder, this looks too good to be true, especially since he and Scully are now off The X-Files and assigned to, as he calls it, "scut work."

Shit detail is more like it. Literally.

In a witty touch by Gilligan, he has Mulder and Scully begin by interviewing a farmer for his voluminous purchase of ammonium nitrate fertilizer, which could be used to make a cheap terrorist bomb. Mulder's curiosity (surprise, surprise) gets the better of him and before we know it, Crump has escaped from the cops and has a gun to Mulder's head, issuing one simple command:

"Drive."

The back-and-forth between Mulder and Crump serve as the backbone of the episode. David Duchovny and Bryan Cranston both do tremendous work, playing polar opposites with no interest in one another beyond mere survival. Crump's in no mood to bond, calling Mulder part of the "Jew FBI" and accusing him of being part of the government testing that infected he and his wife.

Grudgingly, though, a bond does form between the two men. Two men from vastly different social backgrounds, flung together by circumstance with one powerful thing in common.

A distrust of the government.

The depth of Gilligan's script becomes even more apparent as we see Crump and Mulder are actually very much alike. Both men are outcasts. Crump doesn't fit into the more elegant (or evolved) parts of society whereas Mulder does not fit in at the FBI. Both men are on the outside looking in.

For Mulder, Patrick Crump represents all that he once was a part of and as he pushes the car further and further west, his goal isn't just to keep Crump alive and expose whatever has happened to him. It's also to reconnect with what Kersh has taken from him, what those in authority at the FBI no longer want him to possess.

The passion to keep forging ahead into the unknown.

While Mulder is getting acquainted with the wrong side of the tracks, Scully is busy doing what she does best - searching for a scientific explanation for what is going on. And this is another reason why "Drive" works so well. It is fundamentally in tune with both of these characters.

Mulder's intuitive nature enables him to connect with Crump with the hope of keeping them both alive. Meanwhile, Scully's science is providing the answers to the problem they have encountered. They spend most of the episode apart, but they are completely in tandem, working together and utilizing their fundamental strengths to get to the heart of the matter.

Is this a great team or what?

Scully soon learns the Crumps were part of a government plan to test ELF waves which, when overloaded, could match the resonant frequency of the human skull. As Mulder notes, this could have serious weapons application as a form of "electrical nerve gas."

Mulder and Scully learn all this, but time runs out on Crump. All that's left is a smattering of blood on a backseat window as Mulder and Scully are left helpless to prevent his demise. As Mulder stares out at the vast ocean, he's left with the reality that there often is no justice in this world, only victims.

And in the end, that's all Patrick Crump was left to be. A victim. One Mulder may never forget. In an episode that was equally unforgettable.

"TRIANGLE"

"This is unbelievable."

Actually, this is pretty incredible. After hearing all of the gloom and doom over the creative direction "The X-Files" was heading in during last season and this summer after the movie came out, here was a powerful example of just how exciting this show can be. In my humble opinion, this was 60 minutes of "The X-Files" at its finest.

As much as I enjoy the mytharc, this to me was an example of what "The X-Files" can be. A wonderful blend of fantasy and reality with the viewer left to try and ascertain what is real and what is not. Was it all a dream? Was Mulder caught in a time warp of some kind? Does this kiss count as an actual kiss? How come The Lone Gunmen weren't on board the ship in 1939 or is that too frightening a question to ponder?

All of this was so much fun to watch. Granted, this was probably just Chris Carter's attempt to nail down some Emmy nods, but he certainly came up with a zinger in his quest to do so. The entire cast was in top form, the show was beautiful to behold (I loved the dissolve into the letterbox format and the cinematic feel the entire show had) and Mark Snow's music heightened the pace wonderfully.

And again, as was the case with "The Beginning," we clearly see the seeds that were planted in the movie continue to be dealt with in some fashion. In this instance, we have the kiss between Mulder and the 1939 version of Scully and his declaration of "I love you" to the real Scully at the end. Scully clearly believes this is a man lost in delirium, but Mulder's goofy grin on his face at the end displays a man who is finally beginning to deal with some pretty powerful feelings he has for his partner.

What Mulder has begun to realize is that it's not the length of the journey, it's the destination you arrive at that makes all the difference in the world.

As enjoyable as I found David Duchovny to be in this episode (spouting time travel ideas at the crew and being positively giddy at his discovery of where he has ended up at the start of the episode) I really enjoyed watching Gillian Anderson. Her 10-minute prowl through the FBI in search of someone to help her (beautifully filmed with a steadi-cam and some tremendous tricks in editing to make it look like one uncut take) was magical.

From her frustration with Skinner to her disgust with herself at trying to go to Kersh to her threats aimed at "that rat bastard" Spender and her quick dodge back into the elevator after being spotted by the unholy three (Kersh, the CSM and Spender) to her obvious delight with herself after finally being aided by Skinner (who gets a pretty nice thank you in return I might add) to ducking into the Lone Gunmen's getaway car (a Volkswagen? Classic), this was wonderful acting.

Gillian Anderson has long been one of the most interesting actresses on television. Her ability to run the gamut of emotions has made her presence a real strength on "The X-Files" and it has been quite enjoyable to watch her grow and mature as an actress over the past few years. Here, in 10 quick minutes, she puts forth a mini tour de force. Wonderful.

On top of all that, we learn a few things about the mytharc situation as well. Kersh is clearly in league with the CSM as is Fowley. No surprise to any of us here, but it will be interesting to see how Scully uses this newfound info which Mulder obviously is unaware of. And, one more thing, I loved the scene at the end when the two Scully's "walk through" each other and then stop and pause wondering what just passed through them. Great use of the split-screen in that entire closing segment by Carter.

I'm sure a lot of fans won't like this episode just as they dismissed "Post Modern Prometheus" last season. I'm sure there are many fans who like their "X-Files" more serious. But think about it, this was a class X Files case.

It was set in The Bermuda Triangle of all places and presented us with an opportunity for Mulder to seek out the truth behind the sudden re-appearance of a 1939 British ocean liner that had been presumed lost. Sounds like an X-File to me. And oh yeah, they had a lot of fun along the way and it was one hell of a ride.

Kudos to all involved for giving us one of the finest "X-Files" episodes in years. After watching this episode, I was reminded precisely why I love this show so much and why it ranks so far above any other drama on the air right now.

"Dreaming Is Free"

The great debate regarding "Triangle" seems to have drifted from the ramifications of the great declaration at the end to whether or not the entire episode was a dream or just portions were. Given all the "Wizard of Oz" references and even Chris Carter's own words saying he was intrigued by the idea that this was part of Mulder's subconscious at work, I think it's fair to say much of what we saw was indeed a dream.

But which parts?

Clearly, everything on board the ship in the 1939 time period could be stipulated as being a dream. I don't discount the alternate reality theory just because this is "The X-Files," after all, and there's no reason to think in their universe that couldn't happen. But let's assume the show is grounded in some form of reality we're all acquainted with. That means there are no alternate realities or time warps and what Mulder experienced on board the 1939 ship was his subconscious acting out.

This makes logical sense given the characteristics of the familar faces he sees there. The CSM as the ultimate evil leader, Spender as his lap dog, Skinner a possible double agent who is ultimately on his side, Kersh an unfamiliar friend or foe that Mulder has yet to get a handle on. And of course, Scully, his dream woman who is equal parts savvy, sassy, sexy and smart. And, most importantly, ultimately there to save him.

It even works given how he views himself: Flip, inquisitive, insightful, a man who can even win a fight once in awhile and ultimately cool under pressure

The dream theory even works when it comes to "The Kiss." That entire scene is darkly lit and the kiss itself is virtually filmed in total darkness. Given the fact Mulder has never kissed Scully before, this could be seen as his own trepidation and uncertainty as to what that experience might be like. As wonderful as he believes it has to be, he can't truly visualize it yet since it has yet to occur. And so he gives himself that pleasure subconsciously, but cannot bring himself to fully imagine what that experience must really be like.

Now the debate stretches to Scully's scene at the FBI as she goes on her lengthy journey to find help for Mulder. Many have speculated that, this too, was part of Mulder's dream. That this is how he sees Scully - driven to save him no matter what the cost and who she must trust for help. This could work, but for the sake of argument I'd like to propose that this is actual Scully working and separate from Mulder's dream and that everything that happens off of the 1939 ship is not a part of Mulder's subconscious (it fits in with the split-screen effect later when the two Scully's pass each other on board the ship since that seems to suggest two realities at work).

I agree that Mulder probably sees Scully driven in such a manner and people wonder why the "real" Scully would kiss Skinner in the elevator after he bails her out. Well, I'm tossing that aside as a personal little something from Chris Carter to all of us just for fun (remember this is TV and besides I'd hate to speculate on what would drive Mulder to dream about Scully kissing Skinner). Perhaps I shouldn't, but that's how I choose to view it.

Other than that, I think the Scully we see in the FBI is every bit the determined Scully we've come to see of late (especially in the movie). Perhaps her actions are somewhat broad, but they are nowhere near as broad as the Kung Fu Scully we saw in "Kill Switch," which was clearly Mulder's subconscious at work. Consider this: If the man she loved was lost at sea, wouldn't she hurriedly and doggedly try to help him in any way possible. That means trying all possible avenues and refusing to take rejection as an answer (witness her verbal assault on "rat bastard" Spender).

Yes, I will agree this could be viewed as Mulder's vision of how Scully reacts under crisis. But I think we've seen enough evidence to date to theorize that this is not just a vision of who she is, but who she is ultimately. So on that basis, I'm inclined to believe the real-time Scully actions at the FBI are not a product of Mulder's rather vivid subconscious.

Which brings us to the final scene. No matter what other parts of the show were a dream or not, this ending was clearly based in real time. Again, the "Oz" references seem to make that point rather convincingly. And given Mulder's state of apparent delirium (at least in the eyes of Scully, Skinner and The Lone Gunmen), Scully's response to his declaration is perfect since she doesn't think he's making any sense at the moment. I certainly don't think it could be viewed as dismissive given how close (literally) she is with him in that scene and how tenderly she treats him.

So how did he get the bruise? Well, he was face down in the ocean for awhile with debris scattered everywhere so it's more than possible he got banged around by parts of the ship he was on. That could account for any bruises or injuries he might have suffered. Then again, maybe he was in a parallel universe and none of it was a dream at all.

"DREAMLAND"

"Look, any of that information could've been gathered by anyone."

"Even that yogurt thing? That is so you. That is so Scully. It's good to know you haven't changed. It's somewhat comforting."

Is it a comedy? Is it a body-shifting, shape-shifting drama with a few laughs along the way? Is it all an enigma wrapped in a lizard caught in a rock? Does anyone have the slightest idea?

I'm not really sure what to make of "Dreamland." On a purely entertaining level, it was fun. I laughed at the jokes although some seem forced (yeah Mulder and Morris' mirror routine was cute, but was it really necessary?). I enjoyed Mulder's obvious unease at family life and his desire to retreat to a place where he feels safe (in his case, sprawled out in a recliner watching porn. Beautiful).

I'm not one of those fans who needs every episode to have dark undercurrents of seriousness and foreboding danger. I enjoyed "Triangle" immensely for its light air and I've enjoyed many of the more humorous shows in the past as well. But I have to admit as I watched "Dreamland" a part of me was hoping there would be some nasty episodes with aliens or even a confrontation or two with Spender in the weeks ahead.

That's not to say I turned my nose up at this episode. It was enjoyable and left me curious to see what will occur in its second act. Perhaps it will be the opposite of the two parter started in "Tunguska" which started out stronger than it finished. Guess we'll just have to wait and see.

But on to the things about this episode which jumped out at me.

First of all, I disagree with the idea Scully was dumbed down for this episode. Yes, I do believe she should have picked up sooner that something was amiss with Mulder. Considering all of his actions were polar opposite of the Mulder she knows should have tipped her off to something.

And then after confronting Morris and his claiming to actually be Mulder, she may not have believed what he had to say, but given all she has experienced it seems only logical she would have suspected something. Especially after getting a pat on the behind from Mulder. And her stunned look there was a pretty good sign that was a first for both of them.

Having said that, however, I did enjoy watching Scully try to come to grips with this new Mulder. Her slow burn at Fletcher's "panties on straight" comment was priceless and she clearly was not thrilled to see another woman exiting Mulder's apartment (by the way, THAT should have tipped her off that something was wrong. She's known Mulder for six years now and has she ever seen him have a date, much less have sex? C'mon Scully, wake up will ya?).

I believe we will discover that Morris was Mulder's contact and this was some sort of ruse set up for some purpose I have yet to ascertain. Was all of this a Consortium plot derived just to get Mulder out of the way? Not sure I'm buying that. I'm hoping for a better answer than that.

Certainly, Morris' rather blase reaction to suddenly being in Mulder's body leads me to believe he had some idea this was about to happen. That would explain his appearance out there in the middle of the night at the precise time Mulder arrived.

I also liked how the show continues to provide subtle (and sometimes not so subtle) development of the Mulder and Scully relationship. Scully's speech at the outset about her desire to have a normal life sure seems fueled by something, perhaps a near kiss in a hallway or a declaration of devotion in a hospital room?

It's nice to see everything that was set up in the movie hasn't been casually dismissed as some fans feared, nor has it been the focal point of every episode as others believed might be the case. But it is there and it is real and it is being addressed in a very thoughtful and well-handled manner in my opinion.

In short, my final judgment on "Dreamland" is that I enjoyed the entertainment value it presented. It was fun and I'm not one to begrudge anyone a little romp now and then. And if nothing else, David Duchovny sure looked like he had a good time. But I guess I'd just like to get hit with something that provides a little more bang for the buck.

"DREAMLAND II"

"You know what would really be fun?"

In the land of a thousand dreams, I've heard Scully say that over and over and over again. And each time, she was brandishing a pair of handcuffs, just as she was when she uttered those words in "Dreamland II."

Unfortunately for me, my dream always comes to an end before I find out what Scully had in mind (although the riding stick I saw out of the corner of my eye left me a tad bit concerned). Unfortunately for Morris Fletcher, those words mark the end of his dream as well.

For Morris, the jig is up. Scully knows he isn't really Mulder and something really weird is going on.

For the rest of us, Scully's discovery only meant there were still several agonizing minutes to go before Morris went back to being Morris and Mulder got back to being Mulder. Or was I the only one who felt as if "Dreamland II" lasted an eternity?

After a light-hearted, but somewhat-promising first part, "Dreamland II" went nowhere. Was it cute? At times it was. Mulder's awkward attempts to adapt to the role of husband and father were enjoyable to watch. And Scully certainly made it clear she's not easily seduced by such trifles as champagne, waterbeds and ceiling mirrors.

Then again, "Baby me and you'll be peeing through a catheter" could be Scully's way of letting everyone know she's a take-charge kinda gal in the bedroom.

The problem with "Dreamland II" is it never really went beyond cute. In "Dreamland," Scully is the one who wonders if Mulder ever considered getting out of the car and pursuing a normal life. Where "Dreamland I and II" falter is they never really touched on any of this in a meaningful way. It was all superficial.

Mulder is clearly a fish out of water in Fletcher's "normal" life. While that made for some amusing moments, it never really went any further. We never find out anything about why this life isn't the one Mulder would ever choose for himself.

There's a few jokes, some punch lines, but nothing of any real substance.

We're all supposed to laugh at how quickly Fletcher endears himself to Kersh and becomes his new "golden boy," as Scully calls him, even though it's completely ridiculous to think Kersh would have such an abrupt change of heart when it comes to his feelings about Mulder. And Fletcher's constant come-ons to Scully are meant to have us splitting our sides with laughter.

"I've still got my gun," Scully warns him after one advance. Oh how I wish she would've used it.

Even on a deeper level, Mulder's entrance to "Area 51" provides no real payoff either. General Wegman is revealed to be Mulder's source, but it doesn't go any further than that. For Mulder, "Area 51" could be viewed as an entrance to the Magic Kingdom given all its pertinent UFO information.

However, Mulder is so busy trying to get out of Fletcher's body he spends no time using his newfound access to possibly pursue matters more germane to his quest. Mulder is given the keys to the kingdom and promptly drops the ball.

And since time was snapped backward at the end of the episode, everyone conveniently forgot what had just happened. So Mulder could have no regrets about something he would never remember not doing in the first place. Got all that?

Hey, at least he got to toss off a couple of snappy one-liners, so the episode wasn't a total waste, right?

Other than a joke here or there (none better than the final scene of Mulder entering his apartment and obviously seeing the new designs done up by Fletcher in his absence), the only times the episode really moved came during two scenes.

The first occurred between Mulder and Scully near an abandoned desert building. With a gentle hand squeeze and a few shared sunflower seeds, Mulder and Scully communicate volumes to one another about the pain they're feeling as they confront the possibility of this situation.

The best scene in the episode, however, belonged to Fletcher. Seeing the pain his wife is feeling as she believes she has lost her husband forever, Fletcher (still in Mulder's body) draws her to him with recollections of events from their past. Ultimately, it's his description of the night their daughter was born that brings both of them back together.

In that moment (wonderfully played by Michael McKean), Morris Fletcher becomes a character instead of a caricature and the episode rises above its otherwise pedestrian level.

It's scenes such as those two which show what "Dreamland II" could have been. Instead, it feels strung out, as if there was a two-hour hole that needed to be filled, but not enough story to make it all work.

And at the end, Mulder and Scully are left with no memory of what transpired. Everything that occurred has been lost and none of it had any real significance for either one of them.

Their trip out to "Area 51" had proven to be nothing more than a waste of time. Just like "Dreamland" turned out to be.

The Mulder-Scully Dynamic

Initially, what drew me to "The X-Files" was the concept. A show that dealt with the paranormal, vampires, werewolves, UFOs and the like, shades of "Kolchak The Night Stalker," a show I grew up loving as a kid. But I soon found myself drawn further toward the relationship between the two lead characters and found their interaction to be the heart of the show. Obviously, I'm not alone here.

As I recall, many fans were concerned about the direction the show would take after the movie came out. There were concerns the show would follow the path of "Moonlighting" or "Northern Exposure," two shows that lost their creative edge when their lead characters became romantically entangled. Some believed Chris Carter painted himself into a corner with that near kiss in the hallway and were concerned "The X-Files" might turn into "Dana Loves Fox."

I think it's safe to say those concerns were unfounded.

I'm pleased with how Chris Carter and Co. have deftly handled the Mulder and Scully relationship thus far this season. They have taken that scene in the movie and built upon it without making it the centerpiece for every show each week. It remains the underlying strength of the show and it pushes each episode along.

However, it has not become the focal point each week as Mulder and Scully ponder their relationship and plan getaways or try to be co-workers and lovers or however else a television drama would try to keep the idea of two partners falling in love fresh. Instead, it has been handled intelligently and smoothly without forsaking the themes and ideas "The X-Files" have developed.

Certainly, there can be debate about the nature of their relationship. But the beauty of what Carter has done is keep that debate alive without giving us anything conclusive. That, in its very essence, is what "The X-Files" is about. So it only makes sense that this "love story" be developed in a similar manner.

In the movie, there was a near kiss and two people who clearly were about to succumb to feelings long pent up inside of them. How has Carter dealt with the aftereffects of that moment? He could have had an episode or two where they sit down and talk about the pros and cons of getting together and then we could've had a show just like virtually every other on TV. Instead, he stayed true to the heart of the show and kept the idea of Mulder's and Scully's quest for the truth and not their relationship as the impetus for what drives the show forward.

And yet, he did not sacrifice anything he developed in the movie. Instead, every episode has had moments of development for their relationship. But typically, those moments have been less explicit and defined more emotionally as opposed to endless verbal communication about the nature of their relationship.

Certainly, we see two characters who are clearly closer now than ever before (almost literally at the end of "Triangle"). Even in "Dreamland," we get this wonderful monologue by Scully as she wonders about having a "normal" life. Given the subtle body language used by David Duchovny and Gillian Anderson in this scene, it is pretty simple to see that these are two characters clearly in tune with one another and here it is Scully who is quietly pondering the future of their relationship (I don't think it's out of the question to assume she is factoring Mulder into this imagined future life).

Again, here is a moment spent dealing with their relationship and in a subtle way furthering it along without making it the focal point of the show. Therein lies what I believe to be the strength of the show this season in terms of Mulder and Scully's developing relationship. Quiet moments of character development without sacrificing the content of what has made the show great even though we all know that Dana Really Does Love Fox.

"HOW THE GHOSTS STOLE CHRISTMAS"

"Two lost souls"

Indeed they are. This time, these two lost souls are stuck in a haunted house on Christmas Eve. A frightening predicament, you wonder? Not really. Instead, what we have is another version of what is commonly being referred to lately as "X-Files Lite."

A trip to a haunted house where two lost souls are confronted by two ageless souls who deduce their innermost thoughts and motivations, hoping to drive them mad. All done with tongue planted firmly in cheek.

OK, I liked a lot of this episode. It had a sweet fantasy-based touch to it and I adored the final scene with Mulder and Scully together as we continue to watch their relationship deepen through the most subtle of interactions. The chemistry between David Duchovny and Gillian Anderson has been superb the entire season, but it really has been in overdrive the past two weeks (the goodbye scene in "Dreamland II" and the final scene in this episode in particular).

But while I've enjoyed the sheer entertainment value of the past three shows, I really am longing for something a bit sinister and darker.

I don't need my "X-Files" to be constantly foreboding with Cigarette Smoking Men filtering about and mysterious double agents and aliens lurking around the corner. But I miss that sense of danger and mystery when it goes away. And lately, the shows seem more cute than serious and I keep waiting for something sinister to show up on the horizon.

Now even in these instances, I still think "The X-Files" is better than just about anything else on TV these days. And I do not begrudge Chris Carter or anyone connected with the show for embarking upon a flight of fancy. Or two. Or three. Or four. But perhaps if they were spaced out throughout the year, they would flow better.

Instead, we're getting hit with them all at once, leaving me for one wanting something with a bit more bite to it. It all began with "Triangle" which I enjoyed immensely. But now it's been four such shows in a row, all fun to be sure, but none as good as "Triangle." It just seems to me to be time to step up to the plate and take the game a little more seriously.

I feel the same way about "How The Ghosts Stole Christmas" as I did with the two "Dreamlands" episodes. I liked a lot of what I was watching but I just kept wanting something more. A sense of angst perhaps. Or danger. Or tension.

It's not that I disliked any of them greatly or felt disappointed when they ended. But I just felt myself wanting something other than the tongue-in-cheek "X-Files" we've been seeing so much of lately. Again, I'm torn when I say that because I think taken individually these past three shows are satisfying, but strung together as they have been, it just seems to be too much smirk and not enough substance.

At least for me.

My biggest beef with "How The Ghosts Stole Christmas" was playing Scully like some frightened waif who just wandered in out of the cold. I haven't necessarily agreed with the idea that she has been dumbed down this season. But here, I felt like her shaking in her boots with fear behavior was done more for plot sake than actual character development. I just have a hard time believing that the Scully we've come to know would wilt so easily in such a situation.

Yeah, it was cute when she fainted. But realistic? I doubt it. This is a woman who had Leonard Betts' severed head wink at her, so I doubt a couple of possible ghosts and their respective bullet holes would knock her for too much of a loop.

Now, my two favorite scenes were the dead-on analysis done on our two heroes by their ghostly friends. Talk about holding a mirror up to one's soul, their entire lives and motivations summarized in mere minutes. Mulder the narcissistic loner whose only goal in life is to chase what is hidden from everyone else. And Scully, who truly does take pleasure in proving Mulder wrong if for no other reason than to validate her own belief system (but as she comes to realize at the end of the episode, there is another reason why she tags along).

This was wonderfully done and superbly acted by all involved. Duchovny especially shined showing a Mulder who feels as if he's being stripped bare emotionally and revealed for what he really is and yet somehow trying to convince his ghostly accusor that he is way off base.

"Paramasturbatory?" Indeed.

The other gem came at the end when Scully arrives at Mulder's apartment on Christmas Eve, bearing gift in hand for Mulder, who has one as well for her, showing that there truly is no place these two would rather be than with each other. Scully's mischevious grin as they raced over to the couch to open their presents was priceless. What were those gifts? Food for all of us to ponder.

Perhaps that is the lesson we are supposed to draw from this episode, and perhaps the lesson Mulder and Scully derive from their ordeal as well. That they are joined together, they are meant to be with one another and their quest is a combined one and whatever goals they search for must be found together.

Seems to me we knew that. But what the hell, I'll let Carter tell a ghost story to make the point again if he so desires.

Big scoop moment of the week: We do have Mulder saying quite clearly that he and Scully are not lovers. So that clears that up for now, doesn't it?

Symbolic touch of the week: Mulder and Scully essentially running in circles inside the house and constantly running into walls. That pretty much sums up their life's work to date rather nicely I dare say.

Anyway, like I said before, I don't begrudge anyone their flights of fancy and desire to have a little fun. But I do hope that we get something a little more serious in the very near future. "The X-Files" can work on a variety of levels: From drama, to suspense, to mystery and comedy. But it seems to me it works best when there is enough variety doled out to keep us all guessing as to what's coming next.

Lately, the shows have all ventured down a very similar path. While they have not been disappointing, they have left me wanting something with a little more punch.

"TERMS OF ENDEARMENT"

"Scully, this is a classic case of demon fetal harvest."

And this was more along the lines of a classic "X-Files" episode. At least the type of episode that drew me to the show in the first place. I know many others liked "How The Ghosts Stole Christmas" for all the fun it presented, but this was more along the lines of my idea of a fun episode with a nice dark presence encasing it.

I'll admit it, I'm a sucker for the supernatural. Place a devil in the plot and I'll follow you to see what you can cook up. And while "The X-Files" has followed a devilish route before (see "Die Hand Die Verietzl") I enjoyed this tale of a devil looking to be just a normal dad immensely.

I've mentioned in previous reviews my feelings about the numerous "X-Files" Lite episodes we were recently handed and while I enjoyed them on a base level, I was longing for something a little darker and less comedic. "Terms of Endearment" gave me what I was looking for.

And then some.

From the opening teaser (terrifyingly done) right until the end, this episode took me on a ride back to the days of the old X-Files. This wasn't an exploration of Mulder and Scully's relationship done either in dream-like form or in a guessing game of who's in who's body or with Screaming Scully's and curious plot developments. It was simply a standard X-File about a devil who ultimately meets his match.

I thoroughly enjoyed the way Mulder dove into the case with relish, literally piecing together the case from Spender's circular file. And his delight in antagonizing Wayne on the street and allowing the three boys to have a little fun in Wayne's car.

While I'm sure many fans will lament the relative lack of Mulder and Scully scenes together (I admit I miss them when they're apart as well), it was still a great deal of fun to watch the zeal with which Mulder latches onto this case and finds to his delight that all of the pieces are in place to prove his theory.

Special kudos to the casting of Bruce Campbell as Wayne. With all the "big stars" dropping in this season, this was easily the best casting coup thus far. I have been a fan of Campbell's since his "Evil Dead" days and he was superb here. A little on the hefty side, I might add, but this was the best use of "The X-Files" move to L.A. yet in terms of casting. Whereas Ed Asner and Lily Tomlin did little for me as ghosts, Bruce Campbell's devil did the trick.

Rather than playing it over the top as a devil incarnate, he played Wayne as a man with a dream. One that has driven him across the world to try and achieve it no matter what lengths he must go to in order to fulfill it.

Nicely done.

I loved many of the little touches here as well. I mentioned Mulder rooting through Spender's trash so he can escape the background check on the Jerry Garcia-wannabe he and Scully have been assigned to question. And Scully's bemused look at the one-time flower child as he denies having ever smoked marijuana or "consorted" with anyone who had was wonderful. As was her obvious delight at having this session interrupted by the call from Mulder.

OK, I admit the twist at the end with Betsy actually being a demon was not handled too delicately (there certainly were enough zoom-in close ups of her eyes to tip us off that something was amiss with her). But it was a nice twist all the same. And the modernized "Rosemary's Baby" like ending (to the tune of one of my favorite Garbage songs "I'm Only Happy When It Rains") worked for me as well.

While I mentioned before that this episode deviated away from the intense examination of the Mulder and Scully relationship we had seen in the previous several shows, it certainly can be argued that 1013 is doing its best to present alternative relationships that can be used as counterpoints to Mulder and Scully's relationship. Witness Wayne and his eternal quest for what he perceives to be a "normal" life and the parallels that can be drawn by what Scully has thought of in the past as what could be a "normal" life.

Wayne's desire merely to find a nice woman who will bear him a "normal" child sounds quite a bit like the standard American dream. Heck, Mrs. Britton (another potential victim?) even has a white picket fence. The lengths he will go to fulfill this desire are what makes him a figure of evil. But his simple desire is genuine and oh so human.

And in the end, Wayne proves his humanity by sacrificing his life to allow Laura to live. At that point, a devil clearly has become a man.

Yes, next week looks like another round of "X-Files" Lite with seemingly further light-hearted exploration of the Mulder and Scully relationship (although I dread seeing Victoria Jackson, never one of my favorite performers). But unlike how I felt after "Dreamland" and "How The Ghosts Stole Christmas," I eagerly await that new offering. For with "Terms of

Endearment" I have gotten my fill of something a little more devilish. And that is just what the doctor prescribed.

"THE RAIN KING"

"That cow had my name on it."

Once again, dear "X-Files" fans we pass down the road of light-hearted fun with comedic turns around nearly every corner and nary a sense of angst or darkness about. It's a path we have traveled quite often this season and one this traveler has not always found fulfilling.

But this time, I did.

"The Rain King" was cute. Very cute. Very, very cute. In fact, it practically dripped with cute. And yet I never found myself suffering from cuteness overload. In fact, I laughed and smiled the entire way through.

It's hard to resist an episode which gives us a flying cow, The Hues Corporation's "Rock The Boat," Mulder and Scully swaying in perfect harmony on a dance floor and ends with yet another "Wizard of Oz" reference. I enjoyed this episode from start to finish. And I say that despite the fact the very presence of Victoria Jackson makes me cringe.

Personally, I dreaded seeing her in an episode of my favorite show. Unfortunately, my worst fears were realized. Her whiny, unappealing presence almost ruined every scene she was in. But I bravely ignored her and focused on the story at hand.

And that is what kept me going.

There was a nice sleight of hand as we were given not one, but two red herrings as to who the real culprit behind the massive weather problems this little town was having. Problems Scully, quite naturally, was loathe to accept. Initially we thought it was Daryl Mootz, giving Mulder a chance to slip in a brief Elvis impression: "We're looking for the king." But, alas, Daryl was simply the fortunate victim of circumstance.

As it turned out, the source could not have been more identifiable (the local TV weather man) and his problem more understandable (unrequited love).

Into all of this step our two heroes, constantly mistaken for husband and wife or boyfriend and girlfriend, much to their apparent dismay. Scully is taken aback initially by this misidentification. But later it is Mulder who wants no part of the association as he is grilled by Holman and ends up telling him "I do not gaze at Agent Scully."

A certain interlude in a hallway would tell us differently, wouldn't it?

Holman, of course, has no idea how off base he is when he goes to Mulder for romantic advice. Scully, naturally, is stunned to hear such a development, pausing for a (very) long time before asking Mulder, "When was the last time you went on a date?" a response that Mulder does not find extremely endearing. Mulder tries to help, but his simplistic view of relationships ("Just tell her you love her and everything will be fine") naturally backfires since there is rarely anything simple about love. Especially the unrequited kind.

There is the inevitable mix-up that leads to Mulder playing the hero and receiving his first kiss in ages and some more confusion about who loves whom and what should be done now to stop the rain from coming down? And then comes the climax where true love eventually conquers all - not just for Holman and Sheila, but for Daryl (the original Rain King) and his secretary as well who utters the best line of the episode "I brought you a leg" as the two of them make up.

All around are couples in love, dancing together to the strains of Judy Garland's "Somewhere Over The Rainbow" (another "Oz" reference, the start of a trend?) while Mulder and Scully stand alone.

In the midst of numerous couples, they are the one couple that is not a couple. Observing as always. Detached from the events, yet completely involved in it as their relationship is seen in comparison to those they come into contact with and how those relationships in fact mirror their own.

Consider Scully's closing remarks to Sheila. They seem to reveal something deeper, something more personal. "One day you look at a person and you see something more than you did the night before, like a switch has been flipped somewhere and the person who was just a friend is suddenly the only person you can imagine yourself with." A touch of foreshadowing? Perhaps.

For anyone looking for something deep and dark and mysterious, this wasn't the show for you. On the cuteness meter, it shot through the roof and I have to admit I enjoyed it more than its cute contemporaries this season: "Dreamlands" and "How The Ghosts Stole Christmas." This was admittedly a heavy dose of "X-Files" Lite, but in the end, I still felt quite refreshed.

"TITHONUS"

If imitation is the highest form of flattery, what is a fascinating offshoot of a previous incarnation? I'd say it looks a lot like the latest entry into Season 6 of "The X-Files." The engaging "Tithonus."

Here was a well-told tale of an immortal man obsessed with looking into the eyes of death in order to confront the one moment immortality has taken away from him. The act of death itself. Under the guise of a crime scene photographer, he moves silently in the night, moving from death scene to death scene, unaffected by the loss of life all around him, seeking only "the shot" of death he craves.

Casting Geoffrey Lewis in the lead role of Alfred Fellig was an inspired choice given his background in B movies and history of playing off-beat and dangerous characters.

The obvious connection "Tithonus" will make in "X-Files" lore will be with "Clyde Bruckman's Finale Repose." And clearly, there are striking similarities between two men who can see death and are tormented by that ability. But instead of merely copying what CBFR did wonderfully before, I would venture to say that "Tithonus" instead takes that initial theme as a starting point and then travels to a different level.

Like CBFR, Scully was the one drawn most closely into the story's core. Here she bonds with Fellig in a manner similar to the closeness she shared with Clyde Bruckman. The relationship takes on added weight in this story given all Scully has gone through.

Having once been on her deathbed, she appreciates life more than ever before and the idea of dying before she has accomplished all she set out to frightens her. She insists her time has not come yet to pass on. She even wonders about love, possibly a reference to the one glaring thing missing in her life, and whether it is worth living eternally for.

Fellig insists it is not. His belief is that life is only precious for a short period of time and once that time has passed, there is no pleasure in living. Fellig finds no joy from living and therein lies the great irony with his final gesture to save Scully's life. It is not a selfless act, instead it is a completely selfish one. He allows Scully to live so he can escape what has become a never-ending punishment.

Life.

But what does this final gesture actually entail? Remember, Fellig attained immortality by choosing life over death. Perhaps his choice here of death over life in some way transfers this immortality on to Scully. As Mulder says at the end, her recovery has gone quicker than her doctor expected. Again, think back to CBFR when Scully asks Clyde Bruckman how she will die and he replies quietly, "You don't."

Were the continuity gods smiling down upon 1013 and is there a conscious message here? If so, it reinforces further the idea of Scully as savior that has filtered in and out of the show's themes in the past.

This is all interesting stuff and it is handled well. On a night when she is denied another Golden Globe award, Gillian Anderson, as usual, shines. Her quiet strength and fortitude have always been two of the strongest characteristics she has brought to the character of Scully and both are in full force here. Lewis is also strong in displaying his utter contempt for life itself and it is fascinating to see how Fellig and Scully play off one another.

It is not a stretch to view Fellig and Scully as mirror images of one another. He embraces the idea of death in the very manner Scully embraces the idea of life. That he sees death in cold, harsh black and white was also a nice visual touch and a perfect representation of Fellig's emotional state of mind. In addition to the "big" ideas, there were also some little moments I enjoyed.

First, the absolute boredom Mulder and Scully can barely disguise as they work on their non-X Files cases. It was also a nice twist to have Mulder using the role he has been frustratingly assigned to (background checker) come in handy as a way to aid Scully.

I also liked the way Anderson played her scene in Kersh's office. Clearly unnerved by being separated by Mulder, she cannot bring herself to look directly at Kersh as Agent Ritter is explaining the case. Her comfort zone is clearly affected and her distrust of Kersh is impossible to ignore as she tries to find her footing away from her favorite partner.

It was also cute the way Mulder continues to be "a pest" in his continuing effort to remain connected with The X-Files. First he's rooting through Spender's trash and now he's hacking into Kersh's e-mail. Nice work Agent Mulder. Another interesting twist is how Scully is thrust into an X-File as a means to "save" her career in the eyes of Kersh, whose motives remain unclear.

We know he cannot stand Mulder and seems to believe there is still hope for Scully. Beyond that, it is difficult to truly ascertain his motives for involving Scully in a case that is practically oozing as X-Files material.

And finally, I loved "Take no guff Scully." First, she slaps a punk after he has the nerve to call her "Red" and then she freezes pathetic Agent Ritter with an icy "Scully" after he calls her Dana for (I'm sure) the last time. OK, I get the hint, it's Scully. I won't ever forget it.

Trust me.

It takes a brave show to consciously look back upon one of its stronger efforts as a starting point of ideas for a new episode. Many shows would fall victim to constant repetition and produce an hour of television that fails to deliver. It is a credit to 1013's creative ability and daring that with "Tithonus," we were given something fresh and not a rehash of what came before.

"Scully's Immortality"

The idea that Scully may be immortal has always fascinated me. I don't find it ludicrous or insulting to her character. Quite the opposite in fact. I'm not saying I buy into it, but the idea that there is something "special" about Scully has been utilized to various degrees enough times that I think it's something we're meant to consider.

Now, do I believe she's immortal? No, I do not. I'm certainly not going to dispute the writers who claim the line in "Clyde Bruckman," for example, was a throwaway line. But my question is, what would be so bad if she was immortal?

I don't want to see her turned into a superhero (not that I even worry that would ever occur) and we don't even have to spend a minute addressing the issue with an episode or two. I'm just saying the "idea" that there is something special about Scully, something possibly different, is fascinating and one that adds an interesting dimension to her character. And I think it's been utilized enough times now that it's something we're at least meant to think about.

I agree what happened to Fellig was a curse he was trying to rid himself of. That is why I saw his final act with Scully completely selfish for it was his way to finally ease his pain. His existence had clearly driven him to feel nothing but disdain for anyone else with his only purpose in life being a relentless search to rid himself of this curse.

But that's how Fellig saw it. Would Scully feel the same way? Perhaps not.

Perhaps the opportunity to live forever would give her every opportunity to seek out everything she could possibly consider. I gathered from her conversation with Fellig that the idea of eternal life fascinated her. Clearly her religious faith has presented that possibility in at least some form and it's something she already may believe in. So what if she was given the reality of eternal life? How would she handle it?

Perhaps she would embrace every feeling, every experience, every moment of love (that seemed prominent in her mind during that discussion). Perhaps that is how Scully would live as opposed to viewing what she had been given as a wretched curse the way Fellig did. Personally, I don't see her becoming as embittered as he became.

But back to my original question: What is wrong with the idea Scully is immortal? My answer is nothing.

This is a show that deals with many otherworldly ideas, so the idea that one of the characters could possess such a quality is hardly out of the question. I'm not saying I endorse the idea that Scully is immortal or that I even believe it.

What I am saying is that one of the prevailing themes with her character is that she is special. We have seen the idea of Scully as savior enough times to believe that theme in particular is one Chris Carter wants us to at least ponder.

I think that may be the case with the idea of Scully's immortality as well. It may be completely outlandish and Carter may think we're all nuts for even considering it. But in "Tithonus," we are presented with a man who has been given some form of immortality (I know that description has been debated as well) and Scully is the one person who becomes closely linked to this man.

Ultimately, she ends up being his "savior" as well.

Just a coincidence? Perhaps. But personally, it's a coincidence, as well as the idea of immortality as a theme, I enjoy thinking about.

"S.R. 819"

A tale of intrigue with mysterious plots, suspicious figures, lurking menace and a nice surprise at the end, "SR 819" banishes the continuing episodes of "X-Files" Lites into the great beyond.

And nearly takes Walter Skinner with them.

From the opening moments of Skinner's "death" to the surprising appearance of Alex Krycek, "SR 819" was a tension-filled blend of mystery and intrigue.

"SR 819" also drew upon some film noir roots, harking back to the classic 1949 Edmond O'Brien film "DOA," which follows the final 24 hours in the life of a man who discovers he has been poisoned and attempts to find out the reason why and who is behind this destruction of his life.

In "SR 819," Skinner is the victim of a mysterious attack on his system and it is up to Mulder and Scully to find out who is responsible and if anything can be done to save Skinner's life before his 24 hours are up. Little do they know the man pulling the strings is someone very near and dear to both of them.

Their investigation leads to the re-appearance of another familiar face from the past, Senator Matheson, who this time is in no position to help Mulder and instead appears to be a pawn in the game Skinner has unwittingly joined.

What is this game? In classic X-Files fashion, that isn't spelled out too clearly. We know it has something to do with the development and exporting of microscopic technology revolving around atom-sized machines that apparently have some nasty side effects. Mulder believes it also has something to do with The X-Files, although the connection is never clearly spelled out.

Krycek's ultimate motives are sketchy as well. He is using Skinner as a pawn (that is made clear when he saves Skinner's life at the end), but is willing to kill anyone else who is involved, including the good doctor who apparently tried to warn Skinner of what is about to happen to him.

Got all that? Good. Figured out how it pertains to Skinner? Well, then you're one up on me.

But the lack of explanation over the hows and whys did not bother me in the least. In fact, I found it downright refreshing. And I did not feel cheated at the end when the explanation was left dangling with Krycek's ominous "All in good time" remark. One of the central reasons I gravitated toward "The X-Files" was its refusal to play by the rules and give us pat, standard, here's what happened and what it all means endings.

"The X-Files" dared to play against the rules. It dared to leave the audience guessing as to what had just occurred and why it had all happened. "SR 819" was standard "X-Files" fare in that regard. And I loved every minute of it.

I found this to be one of the season's strongest entries. The plot was kept hidden for the most part, but the tension kept building throughout (the use of the countdown toward Skinner's apparent doom was nicely done) while allowing only microscopic (to draw a parallel) information to be uncovered by Mulder and Scully.

What's more, we were treated to a Skinner, who continues to remain a murky figure despite all we know of him. His motivations remain unclear, but we do get glimpses into the man he wishes he could be. Fearing his demise approaching, he apologizes to Scully for not being a stronger ally, for not backing them unconditionally and, in his words, allowing them "to pull me in."

Here is a man who regrets playing it safe and by the rules. He realizes that by doing more, he could have possibly spared the turmoil that has been inflicted upon arguably the two closest people in the world to him: Mulder and Scully. The fact he confesses to Scully is a nice twist given how distrustful she was of him as recently as "Redux II."

After hearing his confession, Scully tries to convince him otherwise. But it is done in a somewhat half-hearted attempt. She seems to realize as well this was the one man who could have done more had he only been more forceful with his desire to help. Some old wounds take longer to heal apparently.

Then after being saved by Krycek, Skinner again adopts a more familiar path as he brushes aside Mulder's and Scully's desire to probe into the matter further. Instead, he is confronted by Krycek, who evades any attempt at explanation. Is Skinner working in Mulder's and Scully's best interests? Or has the matter become more personal and one Skinner intends to decipher for himself? Or is Skinner a part of something that has yet to be ascertained?

We shall see.

It was refreshing to see a good use of Skinner after keeping him in the background for most of this season. I have always enjoyed his grander moments and believe he is one of the most interesting characters in "The X-Files" universe. And again, we are given glimpses of his pysche but ultimately left to wonder for ourselves where exactly he stands in relationship to Mulder and Scully and what he is willing to do for their cause.

He implies their cause has become his own and yet at the end, he clearly has his own agenda. Is this his way of protecting them? We cannot say for certain. Again, more questions than answers.

And I loved it.

Krycek's appearance (and I'll admit that came as a very strong surprise to me) would seem to indicate whatever Skinner has become involved with will be dealt with again at some point. His character has too great a role in the conspiracy for that. And it clearly suggests that Mulder was right, that this somehow has to do with The X-Files since Krycek's role there has become pivotal. So it will be interesting to see what the seeds planted here sprout into later.

I realize I haven't mentioned the lead characters often. But this is a case where Mulder and Scully's relative lack of involvement in the core of the plot was not a detriment to the episode. Aside from the humorous touch of Mulder again wasting his time away tossing pencils into the ceiling, what we were given is Mulder and Scully using their strongest attributes to their advantage (Mulder's ability to piece together an abstract puzzle and Scully dogged determination through scientific means) in an attempt to save their friend's life.

It's pretty straightforward detective material, but it was pulled off nicely.

"SR 819" re-established some wonderful conspiracy overtones and perhaps set the stage for more interesting developments in the future. It touched base with the very roots "The X-Files" sprung out of and did so in strong fashion.

We were given few answers about what had just transpired. But instead of feeling cheated, I welcomed the mystery and anxiously await the next step in this continuing saga.

"Two FATHERS"

"The truth is out there."

It just depends on whose truth we're searching for.

The truth as we are told in "Two Fathers" is that this is a world on the brink of destruction. Alien forces threatening to have their plans of world domination foiled by another band of alien rebels who are out to expose those plans and the humans behind them. A woman who carries the essence of that plan as an alien-human hybrid. In the midst of it all is an FBI agent caught in a web of lies hoping to uncover the truth about this plan and his family's place in it.

That man's name is Jeffrey Spender.

Here lies the beauty of "Two Fathers," a gem of an episode written by Chris Carter and Frank Spotnitz. One of the interesting aspects regarding the evolution of "The X-Files" has been in the way it has broadened Mulder's search for the truth and transferred it to the show's many participants. Where it once began with Mulder and then Scully and later Skinner, the search for the truth has been conducted by many people and taken on various meanings for each of them.

With "Two Fathers," we are now given another figure thrust in the middle of the spider's web with just as much at stake as Mulder has had all along.

Agent Spender.

At its core, "Two Fathers" takes many of the mythology ideas offered up in "The Red and the Black" as well as "The Beginning" (nice quick line about aliens coming to "reclaim" this planet) about the warring aliens and their respective plans and uses it as a way to deepen the relationship between father and son. At the same time, it clarifies further some of the precise details of the mythology Chris Carter has constructed. But in typical "X-Files" fashion, it does so by also raising other questions as well.

The biggest twist here, however, is in putting Spender at the heart of the story. "Two Fathers" is ultimately a story about a father and his son and the son's slow uncovering of the facts behind his family's place in the scenario his father has helped orchestrate. As Spender's journey continues, he becomes a fully-realized character. Not some spineless agent out to show up Mulder or some flunky working for his father as a way to keep Mulder in line.

Instead, we see the humanity involved with a man who has become a pawn in a more elaborate game than he could have ever conceived. Ultimately, it is a game he does not understand until it becomes too late. While Krycek coming to his rescue to kill the alien rebel can be viewed as another sign of Spender's ineffectiveness, I view it as a subconscious way of showing his inability to take that next step (shades of Darth Vader and Luke Skywalker loom) and become "a great man" like his father.

He cannot bring himself to kill merely for the sake of his father's wishes to support a plan he does not understand and cannot comprehend. After his failure, Spender finally realizes what is at stake and what place his father plays in this massive chess game (to borrow from one of the CSM's favorite comparisons) and how his mother has been used as a means to facilitate this plan. It is then, in his father's words, his "betrayal" takes shape. And like Mulder before him, Spender walks away from the offer the CSM has laid in front of him.

This was the beauty of "Two Fathers." It gave us another avenue of exploring the themes and ideas we have been presented with for the past six years. Mulder's quest is truly no longer his own and in order to find the answers he seeks, there is no way of knowing who will next join in him in his crusade. Perhaps Spender's ultimate betrayal in will be to work side-by-side with a man he despises: Fox Mulder.

We shall see.

What "Two Fathers" did so wonderfully was offer us this fascinating character development as it unveiled many of the answers to the questions that have been dangling about for some time without using Mulder or Scully as conduits for many of these answers.

That's not to say Mulder and Scully are left out of the loop entirely. Together, they unearth the true identity of the CSM and Scully follows up that search to uncover further information about Mulder's father and his link to the master plan and the interesting little nugget that Cassandra Spender and Samantha Mulder were abducted on the same night.

And, of course, there is the juicy little piece of information thrown Mulder's way: The sister he met a year ago was another charade created by the CSM to deceive him. Instead, she is alive, "out there with the aliens" as Cassandra Spender tells him.

Given how much information was doled out in this episode, it is impressive how well-paced it was. Much of that, I believe, is a credit to the wonderful dialogue the CSM is given in his helpful narration of the events we are witnessing and their hidden meanings.

All the while, we are led to believe this aging warrior is confessing his soul, perhaps as a means to bargain himself into another position of authority with an unseen faction. Instead, we see his storytelling ability merely is a means to further an unholy alliance with Diana Fowley. The game goes on with different foot soldiers all serving the CSM's agenda.

Now for some little touches I enjoyed:

Gotta love Fox Mulder drawing upon David Duchovny's collegiate basketball background to show us that he's "got game." And Scully seemed genuinely bemused by Mulder's attempt to be a home boy.

You have to admire Dana Scully's dogged determination to track down the "true" identity of CGB Spender. Give that woman a couple of initials and watch her go to work. You go girl.

The CSM sure knows how to play dirty. After slapping his son silly, he offers Spender the ultimate putdown: "You pale next to Fox Mulder." Not surprisingly, old Jeffrey's ready and waiting for his dad's bidding the next time we see him.

Krycek seemed very much at ease anchoring the discussion with the Consortium. It would seem the hints we were given in "The End" that Krycek would be the WMM's successor have been realized.

What it all added up to was a delightful and powerful episode. One that clarified many things we had long suspected or had been hinted at, but also left open the possibility for other issues to be explored further. First and foremost, will Fox Mulder pull the trigger and put an end to Cassandra Spender's existence and who the hell is pounding on his door?

I found this to be a riveting first-part of what Chris Carter has promised is the ultimate revelation of the show's mythology. Whether that actually transpires or not remains to be seen next week. But this was an impressive and intoxicating step in the right direction.

"ONE SON"

"I wouldn't bet against him."

The power of relentless pursuit can sometimes be every bit as fragile as it is insistent. The intense desire to search for the truth only to be turned back at every corner can be a heavy burden to bear, one that can potentially leave the searcher exhausted and on the brink of lost hope.

In many ways, "One Son" provided the culmination and yet another starting point in Fox Mulder's continual search for the truth. In "One Son" we see a weary Mulder, broken by the continuous failures he has endured and the inability of the truths he learns to soothe him. So many wrong turns, so many unexplained mysteries. So willing to believe, but endlessly betrayed and lied to.

We see him even briefly doubting the one he trusts most, Scully, as she attempts to warn him of the potential danger that lies ahead in any alliance with Diana Fowley. Scully believes her words fall on deaf ears and storms off. But her words strike a chord as Mulder's desire for the truth leads him to Fowley's apartment in search of reasons to doubt her.

What he finds however, is one CGB Spender, willing to turn the knife further into Mulder's heart in a further attempt to weaken him. And he succeeds, telling Mulder about the great plan the syndicate made, men like Bill Mulder who were willing to sacrifice their own loved ones in an attempt to forestall the future and save their own asses in the process.

The CSM spins his tale so poetically and with such conviction that Mulder is convinced there is no point in trying to fight the inevitable outcome that looms ahead. At that point, he resembles his own father years before, weary of the struggle, unable to muster the will to fight, resigned to the inevitable consequences of the allegiance he has made with humans and aliens alike.

Mulder is saved from his choice of desperation by Scully, whose insistence to find the truth convinces him there may still be a chance to put an end to the dealings others made so long ago. It is at that point that Fox Mulder rises from the ashes of his despair. The search for truth consumes him again.

He pulls away from a possible alliance with Fowley that would result in his demise and returns to his rightful place alongside Scully in an attempt to stop the plans that could eventually lead to the destruction of all life on this planet.

They are unable to prevent the death of the syndicate by the alien rebels. But Mulder's strength to keep on searching has returned and may be rejuvenated by a return to The X-Files.

In this respect, "One Son" represents a significant turning point in the life of Fox Mulder. Not only have the plans of the syndicate been laid bare (not to mention the entire syndicate with the exception of one Cigarette Smoking Man), but the knowledge of what is to come may spur Mulder and Scully forward with even more intensity.

The knowledge of what will happen should they fail could serve as a powerful motivator to succeed. Mulder finally has the answers he has been seeking, now he has become invested with using that information for the betterment of a race destined for extinction.

Powerful stuff. And nicely done. "One Son" proved a worthy followup to "Two Fathers," giving us an episode rich in character development and fascinating twists. As was the case with "Two Fathers," "One Son" was more about the characters involved in this story and how each of them directly impact upon the plans made by the syndicate which now hover above all of them like a dark cloud of destruction.

Mulder: Riddled at times with uncertainty and feeling powerless to stop a chain of events set in motion by men such as his father. Unsure who to trust or what to believe. For the first time all of the answers he has sought for so long are right in his hands and yet he is uncertain what to do with information he has been given.

The CSM: Determined to paint himself as a man of conviction, a man willing to make the ultimate sacrifice in his mind for humanity, only to be revealed again as a coward, someone willing to barter the lives of those close to him in an effort to prolong his own existence. He tries to pass himself off as a victim, knowing full well the only victims are those he comes in contact with. People like his wife and Marita, who has been reduced to a living lab rat, scurrying about in the darkness, pleading for help.

Bill Mulder: A man of dignity who could see the future and wanted desperately to fight it. But ultimately a man whose alliances forced him to take part in a plan he did not believe in. Yet despite the decision he made to give up his own daughter, he continued to fight against the inevitable colonization plan by trying to concoct an antidote to the black oil.

Diana Fowley: More involved in the project than we had been led to believe. Her allegiance with the CSM dates back years and she is the one who is there for him when his ultimate betrayal leads to the deaths of people he once worked in compliance with.

Jeffrey Spender: Only too late did he realize the true scope of the plan his father had helped instigate and his mother's role in it. And at the moment when he became so much like the man he once despised (Fox Mulder), he paid the ultimate price for "betraying" his father with his very life.

Perhaps the one figure here who is given little impact on the story is Scully. We see her urging Mulder to be wary of Fowley and we see she is the one Spender turns to with information that could save his mother's life.

She also is there to save Mulder's life effectively after the CSM and Fowley had laid the trap to take him to where the alien rebels were waiting. Mulder had been broken to the point where he even tried to bring Scully along as well. But it is Scully's spirit and personal investment in the search (as evidenced by the scene with The Lone Gunmen) that saves them both. She is able to get through to Mulder and bring him back to the fight.

Ultimately, though, Scully is kept in the background as others play more crucial roles in this story.

The figures so closely aligned with this story are two fathers and their respective sons. At one point, the CSM and Bill Mulder shared a common path, but while the CSM was more interested in self-preservation, Bill Mulder, despite the anguish he felt over his actions, saw the greater good, a trait he passed onto his son. The battles they fought together and against one another are passed down to their sons who wage a similar battle years later only to be aligned together briefly as the plan their fathers made nears a fateful fruition.

The irony is that at the very moment Jeffrey Spender ceases to be his father's son and someone Fox Mulder could possibly trust, his life is taken away from him by his own father.

It's amazing how rich in character development and delivery this episode was. While Chris Carter insisted this two-part arc would bring the mytharc to a head what it really did was close some some doors and open several others in true "X-Files" fashion.

For example, we still know there is a still plan for colonization. Even though Cassandra Spender has been killed, others who were sacrificed (namely one Samantha Mulder) are still alive and so the possibility of another alien-human hybrid remains. That means there is still a battle with aliens yet to be fought.

And with the CSM and Fowley out and about, there is no telling what evil will be lurking around the next corner Mulder and Scully pursue. And what role does Alex Krycek play in all of this as someone who knows so much and yet whose own allegiances remain murkier than ever?

Now for some other thoughts.

I loved the shower scene. A hint of embarrassment from Scully as she turns away from Mulder's gaze (and, yeah, he was gazing big time), but a sense of comfort as well. Nice touch showing the totality of their relationship even if it is still somewhat undefined.

The way the CSM tore apart Mulder's inner resolve with his concise storytelling ability was brilliant. In front of him was his most fearsome adversary, prepared this time to literally pull the trigger, so what does the CSM do? He climbs into Mulder's head and uses the very knowledge Mulder seeks as a means to undermine his spirit, leaving him feeling that any attempt to "fight the future" (if you will) is futile.

Mulder is left broken and in his very hands the address for his ultimate demise as the CSM had obviously planned all along. Along comes Fowley to reel him in further. It is left for the sense of urgency in Scully's voice to pull Mulder away from the depths of despair he has fallen into.

So Spender has bitten the dust, just when he was getting interesting. He dies a tragic hero, unable to wage a war against his father at the very moment he has all of the necessary information to do so.

In summary, the "Two Fathers/One Son" arc was extremely powerful stuff. Tightly written, beautifully filmed and filled with more affirmations than revelations, but fascinating looks at the characters in the drama.

While a portion of the world Mulder and Scully has been closed off to them, there is obviously much more out there and if they are indeed back on The X-Files, they will not only have the knowledge to fight the plans the CSM and others like him have made, but the ammunition to do so as well.

"The CSM's Ultimate Betrayal"

After rewatching the hangar scene in "One Son," I again am left with the feeling that the CSM set up the members of the syndicate so they would be killed by the alien rebels.

I got that feeling after the CSM gave Mulder the location of the hangar (what better way to eliminate your most bitter rival than guarantee his demise?) and after watching what transpired in the hangar and the CSM and Fowley's reactions there, I believe they knew what was about to occur. Someone laid a trap for these people and strong evidence could point to CSM as the culprit.

Obviously, there was an alien rebel masquerading as a syndicate doctor who could have alerted the rebels to the location of the syndicate and their family members. But would he (or it I guess to be more accurate) have known precisely who was going to be there and for what purpose? Possibly, but maybe not, since all he was aware of was that Cassandra and the alien fetus were being taken somewhere.

The CSM, however, would know what was transpiring and it would not be out of character for him to eliminate as much of the evidence surrounding the syndicate's plan as possible in order for him to escape and carry on with whatever agenda he has constructed.

Remember, he has mentioned before (think "The End") that he has his own agenda separate from the syndicate. Throughout the scene at the hangar, he and Fowley were loitering behind the other members of the syndicate, making it easier for them to get away if need be. And think about it, even though they were attempting to flee, I have a feeling the rebels would have had little difficulty tracking them down quickly and adding their names to the massive body count.

Unless, of course, there was a reason for them to be spared. A deal perhaps? Another element to the CSM's agenda we don't know about yet?

I also think Fowley's mannerisms hint that there is something amiss. The look in her eyes as she's hugging Mulder in her apartment is not the look of a person who is about to save someone but instead set them up for their demise. There is the sense of betrayal in her actions with Mulder that lead me to think she knew what was about to happen at the hangar should Mulder go there as the CSM had given him the chance to do.

Also, as she got out of the car at the hangar, again she presented the impression of someone who knew what was coming, not someone who was going to be saved from annihilation. Her body language implies the knowledge of impending destruction, not potential survival, which is what the syndicate members believe. The CSM had that same body language tone as well.

I think, and keep in mind this is just my theory, the CSM and Fowley bartered the lives of the syndicate and their families (and Cassandra Spender, the key to the entire plan as we were told) in exchange for their own survival. It certainly adds another layer of deception to the CSM's character and makes Fowley's role with him more interesting as well.

"ARCADIA"

Is the true evaluation of a television episode its ability to move the viewer and leave him or her with something of substance? Or is simple entertainment enough? Sixty minutes or so of passing time that doesn't leave us starving, but not as nourished as we would hope to be?

I ask this only because after watching "Arcadia" I feel like I just had a couple of slices of pizza for dinner on Thanksgiving Day. Not bad, but hardly the feast I have come to expect. I feel like any thoughts or analysis I might even begin to explore will dissolve right in front of me the same way that lumbering monster did in front of Mulder at the episode's climax.

And I will then be left shaking my head just like Mulder, unable to make any real sense of what I had just witnessed.

The thing is, "Arcadia" had all the makings of a real fun ride. All season, "The X-Files" has been exploring the relationship between Mulder and Scully and contrasting their version of a couple with that of others they come into contact with.

Personally, I've enjoyed this sometimes subtle and often direct examination of their relationship and found it to be a perfect followup to the events in the movie. In my opinion, that's been one of the strengths of this season and it's given us a real sense of their place in one another's lives and how they have grown individually and together.

Well, here they are given a chance to be an undercover married couple and frankly, that is where the enjoyment of the episode resided for me.

Scully grimacing at the name "Laura Petrie." The two of them exchanging a "kiss" several feet apart. Mulder gasping at Scully's mud mask, making cute sexual overtures ("Let's get it on" as Scully is snapping on her rubber gloves) and the way he has some fun at Scully's expense by saying they met at a UFO convention and how she's the one who believes in every outlandish theory that comes down the pike.

That's all fun stuff although I could've done without Scully calling Mulder "poopyhead." That's her idea of a term of endearment? And to think this is the woman who cringed at the idea of Mulder doling out dating advice in "The Rain King."

Unfortunately, there was a monster on the loose as well in the midst of all this make believe coupling. And that's where the story turned to mush.

The idea of a community with an unyielding demand for perfection held promise. But the barely glimpsed monster looked more like something out of some bad '50s B movie and the explanation for its existence carried as much credibility.

OK, so Gene - the sinister Pier 9 Imports guy - summoned the monster to keep his little community pure and it did his bidding only to end up killing him in the end? Am I the only one who wonders why this might not have happened sooner if the monster was ultimately that uncontrollable? I'm sure there's a nice moral tale to be told here, but I'm not really all that interested in digging that deep into the ground to find it.

Pardon the pun.

Oh, and the monster wipes away couple after couple after couple with frightening ease, but Jerry from "ER" is able to escape and hide in the sewer? Then he later takes Scully's gun and refuses to give it back to her after she identifies herself as an FBI agent so he can push her into a closet and try to kill the monster himself?

Ummm, ok ...

At least we did get to hear Scully say "It" was in the room after Mulder found her, a direct reference to the monster on the loose. If anything, I like the fact we are seeing a less-rigid Scully who's more willing to believe in unscientific possibilities. I find that a logical development with her character and in an episode that left me feeling rather blase, that was at least something to enjoy I guess.

Unfortunately, it was the little moments in "Arcadia" that were worth savoring and not the episode as a whole. It's always fun to compare and contrast Mulder and Scully the couple with those around them.

It seems clear, based on all the other couples they have encountered, Mulder and Scully remain unique, an entity unto themselves who truly do not seem to fit in anywhere. Not in the over the rainbow world of "The Rain King" and certainly not in the unsullied environment of "Arcadia."

Maybe another episode down the road will give us an even deeper look at this relationship. And hopefully offer up a much more interesting X-File to go along with it than "Arcadia" provided.

"AGUA MALA"

"All the nuts roll down to Florida."

And a few of 'em are stuck in a condo with a rain-drenched Mulder and Scully as they, summoned to Florida by a familiar face (Arthur Dales), try to solve a series of murders commited by some form of water-based sea monster forced inland by the driving force of Hurricane Leroy.

Got all that?

As far as MOTW's go, "Agua Mala" was pretty standard fare. A little too substandard actually. We have the ready-to-believe-anything Mulder striding side-by-side with the all too disbelieving Scully. They disagree, Scully casts Mulder a questionable look or two, Scully wants to leave, they disagree some more, Mulder rattles off a theory, Scully looks at him like he's nuts before Scully finally kills said water-based monster in question mere moments after it has attacked Mulder and left him close to death.

Oh, and Scully gets to deliver a baby, too.

Am I sounding a tad sarcastic? I just feel after watching "Agua Mala" that I'm the one who got caught out in the rain.

OK, the monster was a form of water but only materialized in monster form when attacking? OK, I'll go along with that. But how does Scully come to the realization that pure water is the monster's form of kryptonite? She didn't seem to pay too much attention to the salt in the tub when the deputy's body vanished. So now, she's delivering the baby, the monster's about to strike, the monster strikes, the baby arrives, she looks at the bucket of water and WHAMMO, the way to kill the monster with pure water magically appears in her head?

Dales is right. If he had a partner like that, there's no telling how long he'd be on the job. I'm not even going to get started on how the cat saved Mulder by apparently talking to him.

There were a few nice touches along the way. TakeCharge Scully bossing around the militia man as she prepares to deliver the baby was nice and Mulder had his share of clever comebacks (my favorite being his response to the dense deputy's question of "Are you gonna shoot me?" "No, but I'd like to."). And the "Car 54, Where Are You?" reference was cute, too.

But ultimately, I didn't feel a sense of awe as I watched this episode unfold. In the end, "Agua Mala" had the feel of "been there, done that." Now given the fact this is "The X-Files," even the most formula of hours is an hour well spent in most cases. But even in a standard MOTW, there's usually some nice character touches, some moments where Mulder and Scully truly shine together or separately.

However, I didn't feel anything rich in that area here. Mulder and Scully were essentially cardboard cutouts of people they have outgrown. Their behavior actually felt very much like a first-season episode and that worked to the show's detriment.

Mulder was stereotypical first-season Mulder. Scully was stereotypical first-season Scully. Mulder was too quick to believe a sea monster was responsible. Scully was too quick to discount it. These are rigid actions these two characters have long since abandoned. It's one thing to have them on opposite ends of the spectrum. It's another to abandon all they've shared together and the knowledge they have accumulated merely so they can disagree with one another.

Mulder wants to believe in sea monsters. Scully tells him he's nuts. The creature in question likes to bury itself inside human hosts (think "Ice"). Bodies disappear (think "Darkness Falls"). One body even disappears practically in front of Mulder and Scully's eyes. Scully still thinks Mulder is nuts.

Like I said, "Been there, done that."

Even the fact they spent an entire episode together for a change couldn't really lift this episode above the ordinary. It was all standard fare. Too routine.

My biggest disappointment was with how little Darren McGavin was given to do once again in his second "X-Files" appearance. As an acknowledged inspiration for the show with his character of Carl Kolchak (a show I also loved as a kid), I would like to see him do more than recite history (as he did in "Travelers") or sit by and listen on the police scanner as Mulder and Scully solve the case.

That seems like a waste to me, especially given his link to Bill Mulder. Think of all the possibilities that could now occur given what Mulder has discovered about his father.

Instead, Dales gets to sit in his trailer, drink a lot and listen to his scanner. What a waste of a potentially interesting character.

The problem with "Agua Mala" was that it didn't really grab me. It wasn't wonderful. It wasn't a show I'll be thinking about for days on end. It just kind of came and went.

Of course, the cold, harsh reality of network TV is that even with the best shows, some stories work, some don't and some fall right in the middle. "Agua Mala" will just sort of sit there until something better comes along. Hopefully next week.

"MONDAY"

"Ever have one of those days you wish you could just rewind and start all over again from the beginning?"

Who hasn't? The idea that we can right wrongs or change the course of events is a very real, very human emotion. Who hasn't had a day when everything just went wrong and you wished you could do it all again? Or perhaps there was one small misstep in an otherwise perfect day that you wanted to have back. It's something most of us have experienced at one time or another.

In "Monday," this is something Fox Mulder and Dana Scully get to experience. Again and again and again and again ...

For Mulder, this particular "Monday" starts at 7:15 a.m. with a leaking waterbed (wonderful reference to the phony Mulder's behavior in "Dreamland II") which is flooding his bedroom and the apartment downstairs as well. With his alarm clock and cell phone shot and not enough money to pay for the damage, he's forced to head to the bank to deposit his paycheck. Only to die there with Scully at his side courtesy of a bank robber armed to the gills.

Again and again and again and again ...

This is the premise of "Monday" which takes Bill Murray's "Groundhog Day" and puts a perfect "X-Files" spin on it. Blessed with strong supporting performances by Carrie Hamilton (who looks more and more like her mother Carol Burnett all the time) and Darren Burrows (an alum of a great show from the past "Northern Exposure"), a tightly wound script, some terrific Mulder-Scully byplay, this is one of the strongest entries of Season 6.

And a wonderful entry after the disappointment that was "Agua Mala" a week ago.

Where Bill Murray's movie played the idea of a day repeating itself for laughs and romance, "Monday" uses it to discuss the concept of fate vs. free will, the question of whether a person can alter what is to come or whether they are predestined to live out their lives in a particular manner no matter what they try to do. Not surprisingly, Mulder and Scully are on different sides of this debate.

Mulder takes the free will approach. He shoots down Scully's idea of predestination, saying with every choice you change your fate. Scully, ever the pragmatist and scientist, believes character determines one's fate. Little do they know the ideas they express will play a large role in whether they live or die.

Mulder and Scully's fate in "Monday" is supposedly to die in the bank. No matter what they alter, no matter what little details are changed, that is always the final result. On one of the Mondays, Scully tries to intervene by taking Mulder's check and going to the bank herself. But Mulder still winds up in the bank, Bernard sets off the bomb and everyone dies.

Yet again.

As the day repeats itself, Mulder begins to feel a sense of deja vu. This is as it should be since Mulder is more open to unexplainable possibilities. So it is fitting he is the one who begins to get a sense he has experienced these events before. He notices Pam, he pauses after opening his check. It all strikes a familiar chord.

Scully initially uses science to debunk the idea of deja vu. But having been warned moments earlier by Pam about their impending deaths, she stops Mulder from going to the bank. Mulder needs little convincing to believe the unbelievable and decides to bypass the bank in favor of the ATM. Fate, though, remains against him as the ATM is closed. So he heads to the bank, Scully follows, Bernard sets off the bomb and everyone ends up dead.

Yet again.

A week ago, I pointed out the stereotypical dialogue and characterizations of Mulder and Scully in "Agua Mala" and how they didn't ring true because Scully has experienced too much to be as rigid as she was in that episode. One of the strengths of "Monday" is in showing us Scully's evolution and how her experiences with Mulder allow her to embrace, albeit reluctantly, ideas that are not grounded in science.

Witness her reaction to Pam's warning and the way her mental alarm clock goes off after Mulder tells her he is going to the bank. Clearly, she doesn't want to believe what Pam has said. Given her shabby appearance and cryptic message, Scully could easily write her off as a crackpot, another nut Mulder may have come across at one time or another.

But after Mulder says he's headed to the bank, she stops him, telling him what Pam has said. In essence, she is trying to prevent Mulder from tempting fate by going to the bank. Scully is not convinced Pam's warning holds any semblance of truth, but she has seen enough to know that everything in life cannot be readily explained by science.

So rather than disregard Pam's warning as gibbersh, she uses the information to try and keep Mulder out of harm's way. That is one key reason why "Monday" works so well and why "Agua Mala" failed. It understands who the characters are now and how they can no longer be easily categorized.

These are not the rigid stereotypes of "Agua Mala," disagreeing only to move the plot along. Here is a more evolved Scully, if you will, using the knowledge she has acquired to embrace the unthinkable in an attempt to keep her partner alive.

So where "Agua Mala" failed with its cardboard cutouts of Mulder and Scully, "Monday" succeeds by allowing the characters to use their past to affect their actions. By not dismissing what Pam has said, Scully tries to alter Mulder's fate with the knowledge she has been given, even if it holds no concrete basis in conventional reality.

How very unscientific of her.

The ease with which Mulder and Scully slip into their debates about fate and predestination is also wonderfully written. Unlike the scenes in "Agua Mala" which seemed stereotypical and forced, these scenes flowed beautifully and David Duchovny and Gillian Anderson were in top form. It is a treat watching how Mulder and Scully can go from discussing a leak in Mulder's waterbed to the idea of predestination and a human being's ability to alter their future. It is a joy to simply listen to these two people talk.

And listening to their debate in "Monday," I couldn't help but feel a sense of deja vu myself. Their dialogue, their defense of differing viewpoints felt very much like discussions Spock and McCoy used to have that were often at the heart of old "Star Trek" episodes. The humanist vs. the scientist. Passion vs. reason. I have a feeling Mulder and Scully would feel very comfortable thrust into one of those debates in the future.

Throughout the first 45 minutes, we are led to believe it is Mulder who holds the key to the endless repetition of this Monday. His leaking waterbed leads to the damage in the apartment below which causes him to be late for his meeting and forces him to the bank where Scully soon follows and Bernard is waiting.

But in the end, the key turns out to be Pam, a woman tortured by the knowledge that she is the only one who bears witness to this day's repetition. Her attempts to warn Mulder, Scully and Skinner go nowhere. It is only her death which brings this Monday to a close. Like a bad dream that she cannot wake up from, her ultimate release from the hell she has been thrust into is her own demise.

A sad fate indeed.

Now for some less foreboding moments worth savoring. Mulder's difficulty explaining to Scully when he got a waterbed. It reaches a point where he doesn't even try since he has no idea how it wound up in his apartment in the first place: "I think it was a gift."

I also enjoyed Scully's bemused "When do I not?" response after Mulder asks her to cover for him at the administration meeting. Also, the look on her face when Mulder tells him he woke up "soaking wet." And notice how Scully tenderly cradles the dying Mulder in her arms and then try and tell me she doesn't love this man.

Many years ago, The Boomtown Rats provided an anthem for those of us who usually have disdain for the second day of the week with "I Don't Like Mondays." Bob Geldof has a kindred spirit with me since I don't usually like Mondays either. But this "Monday" I not only liked, but thoroughly enjoyed.

And won't soon forget.

"Scully's Transformation"

Having rewatched "Drive," I was struck again by a theme that has emerged this season that seems to have been overlooked at times: Scully's evolution into a person more willing to embrace ideas that run contrary to the rigid laws of science.

"Drive" came on the heels of "The Beginning," where it appeared Scully had reverted back to previous form following the events of the film and wasn't willing to back up Mulder's claim of aliens. Instead, what we saw was her using that belief and the experience they shared together as a springboard to make an even more alarming discovery that was totally based in science (the idea that the real aliens on this planet are us).

This was a splendid use of one of Scully's strengths (her exact use of science as a means to uncover a mystery) and her willingness to open herself up to alternative possibilities (due, of course, to her relationship with Mulder). The latter, as it would turn out, would be explored further this season. And quite interestingly in my opinion.

Clearly, Scully is evolving not only personally, but professionally as well. For the first time, she is more willing to embrace some of the ideas Mulder clings tightly to. Moments that led her to discovering what really occurred between Mulder and Morris in "Dreamland" or her willingness to believe in an omen by a stranger in "Monday" that could save Mulder's life.

Yes, these are plot-driven moments, but they ring true because of where this particular character has come from and the emotional journey she has undertaken. It is one thing for a writer to have a character go from Point A to Point B. It gives that moment added dimension, however, when we understand how the effects of the past have enabled the character to make such a move.

For Scully, all of these actions may not have been possible before. But they are now occurring because she has seen too much to just dismiss anything, no matter how implausible or unscientific, without a second thought.

I think this, in some ways, could also account for some of the emotional responses we've seen from Scully this season. Many have theorized that she is grappling with her true feelings for Mulder and that has, at times, led to her distancing herself emotionally from him.

But her professional life is also in upheaval. Not only were both of them forced off The X-Files, but her scientific insights no longer supplied all the answers she seeks. In every sense of the word, Scully has been in a state of upheaval this season. And it has led to an evolution of her character that would not have been possible before.

For the first time, she has opened herself up to alternative possibilities. For someone grounded so completely in science and logic, this is not an easy transition to make.

We know how the events she has endured, starting with her abduction to battling cancer to Emily, has affected her emotionally. But I think we are also seeing the effect the altering of her belief system has had on her professionally. Couple that with a particular moment in a hallway or in a hospital room and it's easy to understand how this particular person might. at times, shut herself emotionally in order to get her bearings back in order.

Given her devotion to science and logic, I have always read Scully as a character who needs to feel comfortable in her own skin every second of the day and in control of everything going on around her. Given her emotional state of flux and coupled with everything she has been involved with, it's perfectly understandable she would be more willing to explore other avenues and other ideas to find whatever answers she seeks since in so many ways her belief system has often been turned upside down.

My take on Scully in the first season was that she was a highly competent agent who was somewhat smitten with her new partner but believed almost none of the ideas he explored or tried to expose. What kept her by his side was her strong respect for his skills and the passion he displayed in the pursuit of the answers he sought.

Along the way, Mulder's journey became Scully's and many of the answers they sought became vital to them both. But it wasn't until the events of the film that Scully became truly committed to some of the "truths" that were at the heart of Mulder's quest. Little by little this season, we have seen how these "truths" have altered Scully's approach and the ideas she is now willing to embrace.

In some respects, she is becoming more and more like Mulder every day. To coin a phrase, what a long, strange trip it's been for Dana Scully.

"ALPHA"

"I Want To Believe"

Four simple words. A mere sentence to some. A way of life for Fox Mulder. The desire to believe in all things unbelievable. To uncover the truth of the mysteries that permeate throughout his life. Each step of the way, those four words have guided him along the path he has chosen and all those who dared to join him.

"I Want To Believe."

It was embodied in a UFO poster that adorned Mulder's office wall until the devastating fire in "The End." And it remained at the heart of nearly every action he has taken during his long journey through The X-Files.

As I watched "Alpha," those four words ran through my head repeatedly. Four words which can often sum up a lifetime of hope for those whose lives seem without it. We have seen the lengths Mulder has been driven by that credo. In "Alpha," it enables him to connect with another person whose beliefs run contrary to the norm, another person who wants to believe in the unbelievable.

Karen Berquist.

I realize the plot here involved a modern-day werewolf on the loose. And that portion of the story entertained me. Hey, I'm a sucker for a good werewolf story dating back to the classic Lon Chaney Universal films to the wonderful Marvel Comics series "Werewolf By Night" in the '70s. Watching Mulder and Scully get to the bottom of this mystery was engrossing.

But what struck me most about this story was the connection between Mulder and Karen (or "The Wolf Woman" as Scully not so fondly calls her). A connection between two loners made possible in the most modern of ways: The Internet.

Through the wonders of cyberspace, Karen found Mulder, a man she found interesting, intellectually stimulating (perhaps physically as well, who knows what online chat rooms these two lost souls hooked up in although WolfWomanSeeksHandsomeUFOFanatic quickly comes to mind) and someone who allowed her to open up as much as she could with another human being.

The Karen Berquist I encountered wanted to believe there was someone out there she could embrace, perhaps not literally, but intellectually and emotionally. Fox Mulder was, in her eyes, that person. For Karen, Mulder was the embodiment of everything she had wanted to believe was out there for her. Perhaps she spent hours upon hours online, looking for that one person she could connect with.

She wanted to believe that badly. And when she found Mulder, she believed she had finally found what she had been looking for. In that respect, I viewed "Alpha" as not so much about a werewolf on the loose, but about the ramifications of four simple words.

"I Want To Believe."

Scully senses Karen's longing immediately. Female intuition? Perhaps. In any event, she quickly gets to the bottom of Karen's feelings about Mulder and what led her to bring him to San Pedro.

On the surface it was to disprove the idea that a dog, the only other thing in the world Karen can relate to, was responsible for the murders. Her real reason was to see the only human being she felt a connection with. She wanted desperately to meet this kindred spirit.

So she asked Mulder to come to San Pedro. Mulder, wanting badly to believe in the unbelievable, needed little persuasion to make the trip.

For me, this was the beauty of "Alpha." The way it intertwined these ideas about relationships and the separation people feel from one another and their desire to believe in something closer. It was, if you will, a bit of a love story with an X-Files twist.

We see the feelings in Karen, whose physical condition forces her to avoid the light and essentially avoid all human contact. Her only connection is with canines. She wants to connect with Mulder and yet is afraid of being honest enough to connect with him completely. Hers is simply unrequited love.

We see it in the interaction between Mulder and Scully. Their interaction in his office ("I am home"), the ease with which they banter ("He doesn't listen and he chews on the furniture."). They have a much more complex relationship. What Karen longs for, Mulder already has: That one person to believe in, who will believe in him no matter what.

But even their relationship gets tested. Scully's jealous side flashes briefly (her look when Mulder briefly touches Karen's hand is telling). Some might call her possessive, I call it concern. That leads her to confront Karen and tell her the gig is up and she will not be allowed to easily dupe the most important person in her life.

Scully takes this step, in part, due to some frustration at Mulder's willingness to believe whatever Karen is telling him. His desire "to believe" is an obstacle she must always hurdle and it is often physically, mentally and emotionally taxing.

Her frustration is evident in their final scene in the hospital. Upset at being drawn away from her stakeout, Scully's body language reveals all as they settle down on the couch (she takes the magazine out of his hands and sits with her back toward him). Even the strongest relationships can occasionally lead to separation.

Of course, there's is a bond too great to be broken and in the end, it is Scully doing her best to lift Mulder's spirits after Karen has died. Mulder, though, is well aware it was his desire to believe in Karen that led him away from her home and enabled Karen to lay the trap for the canine/Detweiler that leads both of them to plunge to their deaths.

In the end, Mulder is left with the knowledge that his desire to believe helped him solve this mystery and yet prevented him from saving the life of someone he felt a connection with. As he stands staring at the new version of the poster that has so summed up his life, he is forced to ponder the consequences of such a willingness to believe and what those four simple words can entail.

All of this, for me, made "Alpha" a very entertaining episode and a strong MOTW. As I said before, I love a good werewolf story and this one was nicely done. But it had a little something extra going for it than just a routine monster tale. It left me with more to ponder than just the whos, whats and whys behind a legendary Chinese canine capable of shapeshifting.

I read a complaint recently that the move to L.A. had robbed "The X-Files" of the use of darkness that so typified the episodes in Vancouver. Well, here was an episode that harked back to the days of yesteryear. Like Karen, reduced to living in darkness, "Alpha" made great use of the shadows.

From the opening shot of the canine's blazing red eyes to the final moments of Mulder and Scully exiting their car amidst the fog and darkness with only the headlights of their car to guide them, this was an episode that made great use of darkness and all of the perils that lie waiting out there among the shadows.

This was an episode that lived in the shadows.

It was also an episode that dared to be a little more than a typical MOTW. Perhaps I am alone in sensing the off-beat love story I found to be at the heart of "Alpha." But it reached out and grabbed me and I found it to be touching, interesting and worthy of analysis.

Much the same way we see Fox Mulder at the episode's end.

"TREVOR"

So how do you like your MOTWs? With intrigue and mystery or straightforward and to the point?

"The X-Files" is quite adept at serving either up with flair. With "Trevor," they gave us the latter and in the process, offered solid proof to those who thought otherwise that "The X-Files" can still deliver a powerful MOTW when the mood strikes.

I have not been among the camp who have lamented the MOTWs this season. A few did sink into the ground (in the case of "Arcadia" one could argue literally), but others such as "S.R. 819" and "Tithonus" were extremely well done. "Trevor" also offered up a direct MOTW with no frills attached. And boy did it pack a powerful punch.

Once again, the move to L.A. paid dividends with the casting of John Diehl (an alum of my favorite '80s show "Miami Vice") in the role of Pinker. Diehl projected the proper dash of evil, but also in the end displayed the accurate emotions of a man who finally realizes how terrifying he has become to those around him.

I liked the fact that this realization dawned on him suddenly and non-verbally. There was no need for dialogue to explain to us what was going through his mind and why he stepped back away from the phone booth.

The look on his face said it all. He had become horrified by his own horrific nature. Perhaps for the first time in his life, he saw himself through someone else's eyes.

And the image he saw terrified him.

It's a credit to the writers that they took this potentially one-note character and injected additional layers that humanized him rather than simply turning him into a stone-cold killer who could walk through walls and perform some really nasty facials. Pinker may have had a vicious streak to him (that story of him chasing down a fellow motorist 62 miles before bashing his head in offers serious proof of that). But in the end, we discovered a man who simply wanted a second chance to be a father to the son he had never known.

The intent was all too human. The delivery, however, was all too evil. And that was what made him a complex and interesting villain.

While I'm on the subject of deliveries, let's take a minute to note some terrific Mulder and Scully interaction. Not only were they working together in perfect harmony, but their banter and deliberations were right on the money. From Scully's "Shut up Mulder" (with only her beaming eyes to make the point behind a surgeon's mask) to her willingness to accept a non-scientific possibility (again one of my favorite themes this season) to Mulder's comeback later that he wasn't ruling out a scientific answer, this was Mulder and Scully at their best.

We weren't provided any clues as to how they came across this case, but they solved it TOGETHER, using their individual strengths and powers of investigation to get to the bottom of things.

It was nice to see them just working on a case together without dealing with any additional emotional or psychological baggage. Don't get me wrong, I enjoy the relationship twists and turns and I love to try and analyze their conscious and possible subconscious motivations. But it is nice every once in a while to just watch them solve a case together.

"Trevor" gave me that chance and for that I am grateful.

Along those same lines, I want to point out one of my favorite moments of this episode. I use it as an example of just how good this show truly is and how terrific the acting is.

Flash back to that moment where Scully and Trevor are on the run from Pinker only to see him coming toward them after Scully fumbles with her keys trying to open her car door. Note how Scully catches sight of the telephone booth, mentally replays her previous conversation with Mulder about Pinker's possible weakness and then reaches her hand out to Trevor (a nice reference to the idea of Scully as protector and savior) so they can make a mad dash to safety.

In just a matter of seconds, Gillian Anderson's wonderful acting ability allowed us to go inside her head as she deduced the moment at hand and came to the realization there was but one chance at safety. All of that done quickly and without a line of dialogue. Just intelligent acting, the kind that enables the viewer to be part of the moment and try to think their way out of that predicament along with the characters.

Nicely done.

As was the entire episode. From first-rate Mulder and Scully dialogue and teamwork to a sharply drawn villain and supporting characters to some wonderful special effects (the shot of Pinker entering the hotel room from the ceiling brought back visions of Bram Stoker's original novel of Dracula where the Count scales face first down his castle wall), there was plenty to like about "Trevor."

Personally, I have enjoyed this season quite a bit. There have been a few pitfalls along the way, but I've been impressed by the energy in nearly every episode and 1013's willingness to take chances and embark upon different directions. Some have worked for me. Others have not.

What "Trevor" did was remind me that despite all of the new avenues that remain open to this particular show, there remains room for a good, solid MOTW. "Trevor" was another reminder that "The X Files" continues to be the one show on television that can handle a wide variety of subject matter and genres with expert skill.

"MILAGRO"
"A Divine Heart"

The character of Dana Scully is a great many things. An intelligent, independent, caring woman, extremely efficient in the workplace who has endured countless tragedies during her involvement with The X-Files.

But the one side she has chosen to keep carefully locked away is her sexuality. Perhaps it frightens her. Perhaps the sheer power of those feelings overwhelm the keen scientific mind she possesses. Whatever the reason, Dana Scully as a sexual being has rarely been exposed for anyone to see. She has refused to allow that to occur.

Then along came Phillip Padget in "Milagro." Suddenly, Scully's sexuality became an open book. Quite literally.

Rarely have we seen such a powerful depiction of Scully's sexuality. We see it in terms of appearance (early on, the camera hovers above, lingering lovingly as it gazes down her top. Later we get a glimpse of her legs and ultimately a glimpse of her without her top) and in subconscious thought. The depiction grows stronger thanks to the story Padgett creates and the force with which he feels it.

His words paint the picture that we see unfold in front of our eyes. His words become actions. Is he forming some psychic connection that allows him to dictate the events of those around him? Can he really tap into Scully's mind and see what she has prevented prying eyes to ever view? Whatever the reason, the words he types, the ideas he conjures up become real.

They center around Dana Scully and her long-repressed sexuality and Padgett's desire to be the key that unlocks that closely guarded door.

As Padgett types away, his words take shape. We see a very sexual Scully being undressed and aching for the contact she has denied herself for so long. The words are Padgett's, but who does the fantasy belong to? Is it his own? Merely a visible realization of the words he is conjuring up? Or have his words merged with Scully's subconscious and what we see are her thoughts, her feelings, her desires? Are we seeing her unrepressed mind at work, dancing wildly with images and thoughts she would not normally allow herself to think?

Perhaps they are truly linked. Perhaps what Padgett desires, Scully suddenly feels. Clearly, his entrance into her life stirs something deep within the fabric of her being.

Her confusion over these feelings leads her to go to Padgett's apartment. Her awkwardness is apparent. Her unease dominates the room. So powerful it literally drowns out the light. She may have her gun, but her confidence shakes. Padgett is clearly in control and it must frighten Scully to sense this and wonder why she is in his room and why she cannot bring herself to leave.

Her conflicting feelings seem to overwhelm her. The intensity rises only to be interupted by Fox Mulder, the one person who symbolizes order in her life, the one constant that brings her back to the person she feels comfortable being.

Mulder uncovers the truth behind Padgett's novel. It is not only about a string of brutal murders that revolve around the removal of the human heart, it is also about Dana Scully and the feelings that exist within her. Feelings she dares not allow anyone to know or see, not even the person closest to her. Feelings she cannot yet bring herself to express. Feelings of love for Mulder, feelings Padgett senses by a mere touch of their hands and feelings he will no longer let Scully bury deep within her.

"Milagro" ends with Padgett confronting the killer he has conjured up in his mind. Again, it is all in his mind but the actions again becomes real. The killer attacks. Scully is seemingly left for dead when Mulder arrives. Only when the words are destroyed is Scully saved. Only then does Padgett's tale come to its end.

By taking his own life, by holding his own beating, bloody heart in his hand, Padgett saves the one thing he desperately craved.

"Milagro" was, in a word, brilliant. Brilliant in the way it examined one of its central players and stripped her of the walls she has locked herself behind. Brilliant in the way it examined the power of words, the power that lies deep inside a writer's mind that can conjure up any scenario for any character he or she may create and how those characters can become all too real to the creator.

In "Milagro" we are left to wonder if Scully's actions are her own. Or is she being manipulated by Padgett and thus locked into his will, his desires and unable to impose her own sense of direction? Can the writer hold such influence over his desired character? Or is this simply a case of obsession, a frightening example of how an unhinged mind can conjure up horrifyingly real scenarios that will play themselves out to the bitter end?

For everyone frustrated by how the writers have developed Scully this season, this was a brave attempt by 1013 to allow the curtain to fall and allow us to see them in as negative a light imaginable, as master puppeteers who exist merely to pull the strings and force the characters to perform to their liking. It is rare to see this creative process be examined, and criticized, so closely by those who make their very living in that environment.

I find myself sitting here at my own keyboard, hoping to conjure up the precise words that can paint the picture I am trying to tell about how I felt after watching this episode. Ideas that I can express that will allow you to understand how this episode moved me. How it pulled me in from the outset and offered so many ideas to ponder. From obsession, to sexual repression, to true love, to the blinding blur that is our subconscious mind and how it often tries to force its way to the surface, this episode tackled all of those ideas and more, and never once lost its firm grip.

It was a story about hearts and the most poignant being the one belonging to Dana Scully. The idea that a woman so devoted to logic and science could be at the emotional heart of this series has long been one of the most fascinating twists 1013 has created. But in "Milagro" that idea was placed in front of us in full view.

Dana Scully was, in essence, stripped bare by a writer whose own heart was filled by misguided love. He exposed the feelings she fights so hard to cling to as if their mere presence could somehow destroy the very fabric of her being. Padgett released all of that with his words. Through his desire for her. He sought her heart and conjured up a tale that would bring her heart to him. But his obsession created a killer who tried to literally rip the heart from her chest.

Ultimately, I realize "Milagro" for what it truly is: A love story. The kind of love only a writer can feel for his fondest character.

The kind of love Padgett felt for Scully, a real person he tried to manipulate as a character in his novel. The kind of love 1013 feels for the character they truly did create. By creating a writer who wanted so badly to open up Scully's heart, they opened up Dana Scully's very being. Not with her own words, but by allowing someone else to climb inside her head and reveal the private thoughts she cannot yet bring herself to say. The power of those revelations was stunning.

As was this episode.

"The Sexuality Of Dana Scully"

Upon further examination of "Milagro," something occurred to me regarding the character of Dana Scully. Does Scully view herself as sexually desirable?

Certainly, she has repressed her sexuality deep inside her. Prior to "Milagro," she barely allowed it to exist. She is so determined to function in a male-dominated work environment on legitimate terms that she refuses to let her physical beauty become an asset in her favor.

So he buries it, puts it away and rarely deals with it or even allows it to be acknowledged. So perhaps as she's done all that for so long, the idea that she could be capable of arousing someone is foreign to her.

Clearly, she has gotten Mulder's attention and in "Milagro" she realizes someone else has begun to lust after her. Padgett's overt obsession makes her uncomfortable, as it should. But I also believe that part of her discomfort, initially, is at being in a position where she is looked at in such a purely base sexual manner. In all the years she's known Mulder, has he ever said how pretty she looked or what a great dress she was wearing?

I joke, but only to a degree. I think Scully has become so efficient at her job and gained so much of Mulder's respect as a person, friend and confidante that she has forgotten she is also a beautiful woman capable of piquing men's sexual interest.

That is what fascinated me about "Milagro." The re-awakening of Scully's sexuality. She sees how Padgett views her and begins to subconsciously embrace the desire he feels for her.

That is not to suggest she longs to be with him or is remotely attracted to him. But I think the idea of feeling desirable is something she hasn't felt in ages and it intoxicates her. She welcomes it because it has been so long since she felt it.

It also confuses her because perhaps she has forgotten what it is like to be attractive, to be desired, to be wanted, to be made love to. That leads to her confusion as she becomes entangled in the words Padgett is creating as his mental images become intertwined, possibly, in her head.

As I said in my review, I believe much of what Padgett puts in his novel has been inside of Scully the entire time. It was there, lying dormant, waiting for someone or something to unleash it. Padgett's novel was merely the vessel which sparked that release.

In the process, Scully became reacquainted with the sexuality that had always been inside of her. It freed her from the restraints she binds herself in on a daily basis. For the first time in who knows how long, Dana Scully was a sexual being. Once again, she saw herself as a beautiful woman.

As viewers, many of us have seen this for some time. Undoubtedly Mulder does also. But I wonder if Scully had ever looked in the mirror and understood her sexual appeal.

It is entirely possible that she had forgotten that feeling and the effect her beauty could possibly have. But after encountering Phillip Padgett, I think it is unlikely she will soon forget the sexual power she possesses.

"THE UNNATURAL"

Perhaps there's a reason why it took almost four decades for someone to break Roger Maris' famed home run record. Perhaps it was a record no human could ever break. Perhaps it would take someone, or something, non-human to break that pristine achievement.

Mark McGwire an alien? Sammy Sosa a shapeshifter from another galaxy? Could that possibly be the truth? Just the kind of unearthly controversy you'd expect Fox Mulder to become embroiled in. And in a way, he did in "The Unnatural."

Or more precisely, David Duchovny did.

In his entertaining debut as an "X-Files" writer/director, Duchovny took us down a very familiar path this season: "X-Files" Lite Avenue. But unlike some previous navigators, Duchovny stayed on course, made sure we saw all of the spectacular landmarks along the way and when we reached our final destination, I found I thoroughly enjoyed the ride.

Duchovny clearly had some fun here and his wry sense of humor was evident everywhere in his story of a Negro league baseball player who blasted 61 home runs in 1947 and then disappeared from sight. In typical "X Files" fashion, there's much more to this story than meets the eye. The player in question is an alien. Mulder's informant is one Arthur Dales, but not THAT Arthur Dales, instead his brother who was a police officer in Roswell and assigned to protect Josh Exley from the Ku Klux Klan. Exley's team? The Roswell Grays.

Like I said, Duchovny's tongue was planted firmly in his cheek.

Baseball has long been referred to as "America's pastime." So what a nice twist that an unfeeling alien from another world would fall in love with the most human of games. The idea that game can humanize us all ("I saw the baseball game and the laughter just rose up out of me," Exley tells Dales after the latter discovers his secret) was also deftly handled.

And given how blacks were not allowed to play Major League Baseball at the time, there could be no better place in 1947 to make a big splash in the game without generating any attention than in the Negro Leagues.

Duchovny pulls the story off quite nicely. As a director, he shows a visual flair and a nice sense of style. His opening teaser is just that, a tease. It turns out to be the climax, when the Alien Bounty Hunter (a welcome return for Brian Thompson) comes to end Exley's life for violating the sanctified "project." He also seamlessly merges the timeline of the story, effortlessly moving from present day to 1947 and back again.

I especially liked the peek into Dales' TV that merges from a scene of Thompson as the bounty hunter from "Colony" (another Duchovny generated story) into the 1947 version of the bounty hunter waiting for Exley's bus to pull into town.

As a writer, Duchovny keeps the pace moving. He delicately tackles diverse subjects such as race and what makes each of us human (in the end, the alien truly becomes one of us, only to die because of his desire to be more human) as well as insights into life and love. He also tosses a few one-liners and visual jokes here and there. Some fall flat (Dales calling Mulder "Agent McGyver" felt a little cheesy), but most of the moments hit the mark such as Mulder's remark that he is "past ripe. I'm so ripe I'm rotten."

But while Duchovny does nicely with the light-hearted and X-Files moments of this episode, he clearly is a romantic. How else would you describe the sequences that frame this episode involving Mulder and Scully? Given his chance to express his feelings about these two characters, Duchovny proves to be a shipper at heart by creating two of the most romantic moments these two characters have ever shared.

And in those brief moments together, "The Unnatural" became magical.

For the first time, we get an up-close look at the Mulder and Scully relationship from the eyes of one of the participants. And what a scintillating view Duchovny provides us. As much as the shippers out there love this relationship and long to see Mulder and Scully together, they can't hold a candle to the feelings Duchovny has for these two characters.

Wouldn't you know it, he loves 'em as much as we do. And he clearly loves Scully.

Duchovny allowed Scully to loosen up and be playful as she teased Mulder about spending his time buried in his office on a beautiful Saturday afternoon. She even gets to be crass ("grabbing life by the testies") and (gasp) she even giggled.

Twice.

The fondness Duchovny feels for his character is perfectly understandable. So there's nothing surprising about the Mulder we see onscreen here although he is fun as always to watch. But the way Duchovny views Mulder and Scully together is nothing short of beautiful. While other writers this season have tip-toed around the aftereffects of that famous moment in the hallway, Duchovny clearly wants to build upon it.

Not only that, but he attacks it with passion.

I found it impossible to watch their interaction here without thinking about the longing Mulder felt for Scully in that hallway and how the desire pent up within him to kiss her. The actions he creates for Mulder clearly show the love he feels for Scully. And unlike previous episodes this season, Scully does not resist the flirting or the closeness Mulder initiates.

She embraces it. Willingly. Happily. It all added up to a fascinating look at the relationship from the most personal of perspectives.

As enjoyable as the first sequence was, it was the "birthday present" Mulder gave Scully at the end of the episode that will undoubtedly send shippers' hearts racing. From the flirtatious ("nice piece of ashe") to the romantic (Mulder's hands gently on Scully's hips guiding her swing. "Remember hips before hands") their moments together were both sexy and sweet.

One of the themes Duchovny presents is that baseball is the ideal metaphor for life. During one moment, Dales even suggests if Mulder understood the game better, all the questions to the mysteries he pursues would be answered. Typically, Mulder is baffled by such a simplistic suggestion to his convoluted quest.

But since that's a theme Duchovny wants to play with, allow me to use it to suggest that baseball is not only the ideal metaphor for life but in this instance, the ideal metaphor for Mulder and Scully's relationship.

Watch again that final scene between Mulder and Scully and see how it takes on a greater sense of feeling and depth coming on the heels of Scully's sexual rebirth in "Milagro." The way Scully allows Mulder to hold her, to guide her could be viewed as her taking that first step in allowing Mulder to lead her to the next phase of their relationship. As she opens up her hips, perhaps that is symbolic of her opening up her heart as well and allowing Mulder to guide her where she previously had been reluctant to go.

Baseball an ideal metaphor for life and love? In the case of Mulder and Scully's relationship, I'd say that's hitting the ball right out of the park. If nothing else, perhaps Duchovny should serve as a script supervisor the rest of the series just so Scully is allowed to loosen up once in a while.

She giggled. Did I mention that?

And I chuckled and laughed and enjoyed myself watching this fun-filled, witty and intellectually stimulating episode. I can only hope Duchovny gets another opportunity down the road to regail us once again with another flight of fantasy. It could prove quite interesting and who knows where Duchovny envisions Mulder and Scully going next.

"Why 'The Unnatural' Worked"

As a huge sports fan, I have often lamented the ridiculous attempts by Hollywood to pull off an interesting story about sports. The attempts have actually grown few and far between because the failure is at such an alarming number. Because of that, a good one comes out, I am stunned because I've seen so many missteps beforehand.

For every "North Dallas Forty," there is John Goodman as the Babe. For every "Field of Dreams," there is Anthony Perkins in "Fear Runs Out." If Hollywood was a pro baseball player, it would have been banished to the minors years ago.

The one reason why I believe Hollywood fails is because it doesn't understand the simple connection that sports makes with everyday life. Yes, the games are exciting, the players riveting. But it is what these moments say about us as people that fill often these sports with meaning. Hollywood, though, would have you believe it's all about who wins the big game.

Well, in the world of sports, that is correct. But as far as why we love the sports we do, that couldn't be further from the truth. It's about people and the stories they have to share with all of us.

Think about it, the greatest sports movies are the ones which do not focus on "The Big Game," but rather the participants involved and the stories they tell. Does anybody even remember that in the first "Rocky" movie, Rocky Balboa LOST the title fight? The point is, the outcome didn't matter.

As Apollo Creed's victory was pushed into the background, what we discovered was that what was really important wasn't the outcome of the fight, but the journey this fighter took to get there. That's what made "Rocky" unique. The fighter actually lost, but became a winner because of it.

What a novel concept. And that is why that movie worked.

That is precisely why David Duchovny's excursion into sports with "The Unnatural" also worked so well. While the theme of baseball was prominently on display, the wins and losses and home runs being hit by Josh Exley were periphery figures to the greater story Duchovny wanted to tell. It was the story of two men and how their mutual love of this game united them and enabled them to hurdle the gigantic obstacles in front of them in 1947 (namely the fact one of the men was white and the other black, and oh, did I mention one of them was also an alien?).

When Dales discovers Exley is an alien, that obviously shocks him, but there is no permanent damage. Why? Because there already has been a bond forged between them that cannot be so easily tossed away. It is the mutual respect these two men now share which allows their relationship to persevere.

Yes, it all stems from the game of baseball, but the game itself has taken on less significance now as they now have become friends. They share a common bond that unites them in the face of tremendous adversity. The bond is so powerful that even years later after Exley's death, the older Arthur Dales still sobs uncontrollably at the thought of the passing of his friend.

These are the types of things that make sports stories work. Relationships, watching the evolution of people who are brought together through the power of a game. We see it with Dales and Exley and we also see it with Mulder and Scully, as Mulder's love affair with baseball allows him to inch closer to the woman he loves. Again, the game is the impetus for these actions, but it quickly becomes a secondary figure to the story being told and the moments being shared.

This is all powerful stuff and so much more interesting than "The Big Game." As I watched the baseball moments in "The Unnatural," I couldn't help but be reminded of "Field of Dreams," another great movie which is about so much more than baseball. It is about a son's abandonment of his father and the emptiness that has filled his soul because of it.

Kevin Costner's character is released of this burden at the end of that film when his father magically reappears on the baseball diamond he has built. Perhaps Dales, through the tears he sheds and the story he tells Mulder, feels something similar.

For the first time, he can express the true power behind the relationship he briefly shared with Josh Exley. And rather than simply tell others what a great player Exley was (which is something Josh asks him to do when he's gone), he finally has found the one person (Mulder) with whom he can share the totality of that relationship.

Only Mulder will believe the events as they were told to him. And Dales understands that only Mulder will then comprehend their true meaning. The fact that we next see Mulder using a trip to the batting cage as a means to welcome Scully into his arms clearly suggest the message got through loud and clear. He has finally gotten to "the heart of the matter" by embracing the "matters of the heart."

It's a tribute to David Duchovny that he understood all this and used the games themselves not as the catalyst for the story, but as the underlying element which are bringing people closer together. He knows what makes a great sports story and it isn't who wins "The Big Game."

It's the men and women who make the journey and the stories they have to tell.

"THREE OF A KIND"

Whenever I see The Lone Gunmen, I am reminded of the William Shatner skit on "Saturday Night Live" a few years back where he stands in front of a group of Trekkies at a "Star Trek" convention and chastises them for not having lives beyond their fierce obsession with a television show.

"You," Shatner cries out, pointing to one sorry-looking Trekkie adorned in Vulcan ears. "I bet you've never even kissed a girl."

The answer, of course, is no. And therein lies the joke.

The Lone Gunmen are the Trekkies of "The X-Files" universe. Three outcasts united by a singular obsession. The punch line with The Lone Gunmen is that their obsession while rooted in paranoia, is also shoulder-deep in reality. They may appear to be as odd as one of those Klingons at a "Star Trek" convention, but they have every right to feel as if the Federation has tapped into their tricorders.

It's the truth and they know it, even if no one wants to believe them. And like those Trekkies, there's some real heart beneath the obsession.

What that enables "The X-Files" to do is utilize them as comic relief and yet continue to further the paranoia that permeates throughout the series. "Three of a Kind" took that premise and ran with it, offering up a quasi-entertaining effort that indulges The Lone Gunmen's paranoia, banishes Mulder from sight and offers up a very flirtatious Dana Scully.

It was all cute and harmless. Kinda like The Lone Gunmen themselves.

The plot, for those interested, revolved around the mysterious Suzanne Modeski, whose provocative presence originally brought TLG together 10 years ago in Baltimore, a meeting which also paved the way for their first encounter with Fox Mulder. Since seeing her kidnapped in front of him at the end of "Unusual Suspects," Byers has been unable to forget this woman.

She has literally become the woman of his dreams. Fittingly the straight-laced Byers' dream world is right out of a '50s drama. A house with a white picket fence, two cute kids, one devoted dog and the beautiful wife waiting to greet him when he comes home from work.

The beautiful wife, of course, is Suzanne. And ever since their initial meeting, Byers has been desperate to find her again. Ten years later in Las Vegas, he finally gets his chance.

When he sees her again, Byers finds that Suzanne is again embroiled in a government conspiracy that involves brainwashing. Oh yeah, there's also alleged suicides, one costly poker hand, a convenient double-cross and one phony death. But none of that is really important. It's all a setup for Byers to rescue his dream woman and give us, the viewer, an out of her wits Scully.

The latter moments are the most endearing in the episode. And Gillian Anderson is in priceless form. She giggles (two episodes in a row now) and flirts with a group of men at the bar (including one very interested man in black, Morris Fletcher, who gets a taste of his own lecherous medicine from Scully, a nice, albeit brief, reprise from Michael McKean), pats nearly every man she sees on the ass (including Frohike, who appears flustered by an aggressive Scully) and mocks the seriousness of her situation as Suzanne explains it to TLG in their hotel room.

All of which led to the single-funniest line of the episode: "Why does the government wanna turn Scully into a bimbo?"

Well, if the answer was to give me something to smile about, then I'm happy they did it. Scully, though, may want to get in touch with Mulder and warn him about spending too much time alone with TLG. Every time one of them does, they end up drugged, naked or both. Hardly the ideal position for an FBI agent to find him or herself.

But this wasn't about Scully the "party girl" driving men wild at the bar with her feminine wiles. It was about Byers getting a chance to realize the most significant portion of his dream.

Byers nearly gets what he longs for. He saves Suzanne and gives her the gift of anonymity as a means to escape the men who continue to use her and her knowledge for their own well-being. She, in turn, asks Byers to come with her, giving him the opportunity to allow his dream to finally materialize to the best of its ability in these paranoid times.

But he turns her down, instead choosing the path he has carved out for himself with his two friends instead of the life he possibly can no longer embrace. Yeah, he's an idiot. But he's a good-hearted one and that's gotta count for something.

In some ways, he is seen here as the antithesis of Mulder. Like Mulder, the woman he longs for is right in front of him, but Byers chooses what he believes is the greater good instead of his own personal reward. Mulder, unlike Byers, gets to have it all with Scully. He gets to have his cake and eat it too, while Byers is left to play the slots with the only two people in the world who will even attempt to understand him.

In The Lone Gunmen's universe, it would seem that some noble gestures are done without a just reward.

What this all added up to was 60 minutes of fluff that won't go down as one of the more esteemed "X-Files" moments ever, but was entertaining enough for those who needed a Lone Gunmen Fix. In the end, it was cute, clever and ultimately harmless.

Just like The Lone Gunmen themselves.

"FIELD TRIP"

"It's a rare day when the two of you sign off on the same report."

Amazing what a potent drug can do to Agents Mulder and Scully, isn't it?

Throughout this season, "The X-Files" has deftly explored the furthering connection between Mulder and Scully. Their relationship and its ongoing development has been one of the central themes. What we see in "Field Trip," however, is their connection goes far beyond love, respect or friendship and transcends even the touch of their hands which symbolizes their ultimate union at the end.

Their connection is so strong, so powerful they even share the same narcotic-induced hallucinations. Soul mates indeed.

"Field Trip" shows us the lengths that connection can go to in order to keep both of them alive. But there was a lot more going on here than a simple "trip" in the woods for Mulder and Scully. So much more.

In many ways, "Field Trip" dealt with the concepts of perception vs. reality. As an audience we were forced to ponder that question repeatedly. What was real and what was fantasy? We knew Mulder wasn't really dead, but what exactly was going on and what was the cause? Where had the line between reality and our perception of reality been crossed?

We were not alone in that search. Mulder and Scully went through it as well. Every step of the way after their entrance into the woods was a juggling act of perception and reality. Drop one and watch the reality melt away. Drop another and their perception of what was occurring disappeared. It went so far as to affect what lies at the heart of their subconscious. We were given a look at their partnership and how they view one another and themselves in their union.

All courtesy of some really nasty mushrooms.

The mushroom tip-off was obvious and made clear the direction this episode was heading. But that did not detract from the journey in any way, shape or form.

What I found especially interesting was the peek inside of Mulder's psyche and how it pertains to Scully. Witness the hallucinatory dream he has in his apartment where Scully becomes a believer after seeing the alien Mulder has abducted. It seems to set Mulder up for everything he could possibly want. His endless pursuit of the truth has finally been realized with one of the grays right there in his bedroom. There it is, conclusive proof of all he has believed and he can show it to the one person whose belief in him matters the most.

And yet, there's something not quite right about having it all from Mulder's perspective. There's something about having such total confirmation of his beliefs which clearly nags at him. Total acceptance, even from Scully, causes him great concern.

Scully apologizes for being wrong for all these years and yet Mulder rejects the apology and Scully's "conversion." Interesting how that plays against their opening scene when Mulder, apparently tired of the same old song and dance he and Scully do on opposite sides of the equation, asks Scully for "the benefit of the doubt" with his beliefs.

His argument that he is almost always right generates no comeback from Scully because she seems to realize he is correct, even if his statistics may be heavily weighted in his favor. On one level, Mulder is willing to go so far as to demand some acceptance from Scully about what he holds so dear. But when he finally gets it in his hallucination, when he finally has the one moment he would cherish, Scully converted to his beliefs, it causes him to question her.

He rejects her conversion and her apology as being unScully-like. As much as Mulder protests Scully's aversion to his beliefs, he clearly needs her disagreements and opposition. It strengthens him and as he made so abundantly clear once before, she makes him whole.

The reversal is also true, as we see in Scully's "dream."

There, we see her easily slide into the Mulderesque role of believing the unbelievable while everyone around her from Skinner to The Lone Gunmen buy into "the party line" (or what could be termed the "Scully" approach) that Mulder was murdered by some crazed killer. Interesting again, how Scully is frightened by the idea that these four people are so willing to buy into the logical approach and yet are all too willing to express their intense desire to find the killer and subject him to their own form of justice.

That could be an episode to itself: Scully's real opinions of Skinner and TLG. But I digress.

What we really see here, though, is another example of how open Scully has become to believing the unbelievable, another theme of Season 6. She even begins to deny her own sense of self as every logical comment Skinner makes regarding her report regarding Mulder's death seems to wound her as she struggles against what she normally would cling to.

Clearly, the reliance on science to find her answers is not as powerful as it once was and even she has begun to question it. It's become somewhat of a stereotypical response.

Mulder notices that in their first scene together. "Every time I bring you a new case, we go through this perfunctory dance," he says. It is clear from Scully's hallucination that, at least subconsciously, she agrees the Mulder-Scully two-step has become routine.

The one difference now, though, is that Scully is more willing to accept what she steadfastly avoided in the past and though it may take some prodding, she is more determined to fight for that belief. Her belief system has been altered dramatically.

When she believes Mulder has died, Scully is desperate to find another possibility to the scientific and logical answer everyone around her clings to. It is her newfound openness to alternative possibilities which ultimately allows the door to their hallucinations to be opened. That moment occurs once Mulder returns to his apartment, but only after knocking on his own door (symbolizing his entrance into her hallucination). At that point, they begin to share the same dream.

Clearly, their connection is so strong it unites them even in their subconscious.

Once he has returned, Scully puts the pieces of this drug-induced puzzle together. By doing so, she influences Mulder's hallucination to the point where he is able to rise above it later and save them both.

Mulder may not be right "98.9 percent of the time" when it comes to his theories. He's clearly wrong here as his belief that aliens are at the heart of the matter is disproven. But his ability to find alternative solutions to the situations they find themselves in has rubbed off on Scully. And here, her ability to open herself up to such beliefs saves their lives.

Dipping into Mulder and Scully's unconscious minds has been another theme throughout this season. Once again, we are allowed access to some of their innermost beliefs and conflicts they have with one another, and with themselves. Though the hallucinations were false, the reactions were all too true. It made this episode shine and again furthered the exploration of their unshakable connection.

Mulder and Scully tuned in and tripped out in "Field Trip." As an audience, we shared that trip and it was so memorable I don't feel like coming down from it anytime soon.

"BIOGENESIS"

For Fox Mulder, his quest forward in life has always been linked directly to his past. Every step forward he has taken has been tied into his past. Tied into the one moment in his life that continues to haunt him.

The abduction of his sister Samantha.

What Mulder has also come to realize during his lengthy journey is that his quest to solve the biggest riddle of his past has opened the door to something even bigger: The mysteries of this planet's past. Mysteries he believes are linked to the answers he seeks. Solve his most personal riddle and the biggest puzzle surrounding all mankind will be solved as well.

Where did we come from? Who put us here? And why?

"Biogenesis" attempts to answer some of those questions. But in typical "X-Files" fashion, it creates other questions in the process, more riddles for Mulder and Scully to solve. Assuming Mulder isn't driven mad in the process.

We see him locked away in a hospital at the end, screaming at the unseen forces in his head which terrorize him. Wailing against the walls that confine him, screaming out the name of the one person who can comfort him in this time of insanity. The one person he can sense is there.

But not even Scully can begin to ascertain what is wrong, what has led Mulder to the breaking point. She only knows that while he may be a danger to others, he is not, and never will be, a danger to her.

While Scully and others are puzzled at the cause of Mulder's behavior, for us, the implication seems clear. The infamous "God module" that has been referenced before has been inside Mulder all along. The ancient Indian artifact uncovered at the beginning of this episode in Africa is the key to opening that part of Mulder he never knew existed.

And as that door to his being is opened, we see another portion of the Consortium's plan possibly unveiled as well. For the first time, we finally have a real understanding why the Consortium has been loathe to kill Mulder in the past. The martyr idea was nonsense. The reason is much more significant, much more meaningful to their "plan." He is the one who holds the key to everything that is in The X-Files. And the key is in himself.

How's that for irony?

Of all the questions that were raised here, that is one of the few that seems to have a genuine answer at this point in time. So many others remain hanging in mid-air, suspended by the unknown, awaiting answers that will not soon be forthcoming.

Krycek returns, holding Skinner's life in his hands and forcing the assistant director to do his bidding at Mulder and Scully's expense. Beyond that, he remains a shadowy figure who knows the rules of the game, but seems intent on bending them for his own benefit.

Skinner's motives also remain unclear. We know the power Krycek wields over him (in a nice continuity reference to "S.R. 819"), but what we are left to wonder is if he is simply biding his time until the proper moment arrives when he can again ally himself with Mulder and Scully. The pain on his face when Scully calls him a liar hints at a man who wants to do the right thing, but is powerless at this time to do so.

Diana Fowley also returns, arriving by Mulder's bedside although possibly in league with Krycek (the cut from Mulder writhing in pain at the university with Krycek above him to next being in bed with Fowley at his side suggests as much). Her purpose (other than to disrobe and reveal one seriously disturbing Cross Your Heart bra) remains murky as well, but alas, nowhere near as interesting as Krycek's.

And then there is the CSM, sitting quietly in another board room, perhaps having formed another Consortium. Perhaps he is the only one who truly knows what is at stake and what will happen from this point forward.

Questions everywhere. Answers so few and far between. And I'm not complaining one bit.

What "Biogenesis" did so well was return "The X-Files" to its roots and use that step as a springboard to further revelations. Consider the moment when Scully tells Mulder he has foiled the Consortium's plans and so she wonders what more is left for him to pursue. His answer is simple.

"My sister."

No matter what Mulder may have accomplished to this point, the genesis of his quest remains unsolved. Until that moment comes, he will remain driven to find the answer to the biggest question which haunts him.

Amidst his search, however, is danger, intrigue and paranoia, staples of "The X-Files." The phrase "Trust No One" has never been more meaningful than here in "Biogenesis." Duplicity abounds everywhere and with everyone.

Mulder senses quickly he can no longer trust Skinner, telepathy being one of the gifts of the God module. Scully isn't as blessed, but she later recognizes Skinner's shift in loyalty as well. She obviously has no interest in trusting Fowley and makes that point abundantly clear. Even the CSM must wonder whom he can trust as we see Fowely and Krycek possibly united in a cause that remains unexplained.

The only ones Mulder and Scully can trust, of course, are one another. And although Scully refuses to believe the possibility that alien life begat life here on this planet, she refuses to walk away without solving the puzzle presented to them. With her partner incapacitated, she assumes his quest. She will find the answers he seeks, even if she is unwilling to believe the truths she may find.

Little does she realize that, in a moment that harks back to Charlton Heston at the end of "Planet of the Apes," the answers lie right beneath her feet. The symbolism there seems clear. Scully has always been unable to see the big picture right in front of her. For all the steps she has taken this season, this was the greatest step of all.

Chris Carter and Frank Spotnitz did not hold back in "Biogenesis" and I'm glad they did not. They infused the mytharc here with a sense of passion, a wondrous sense of discovery and alluring twists and turns with only one misstep (the continuing lack of explanation of the Fowley character) along the way. The questions continue to outnumber the answers by leaps and bounds, but they remain so tantalizing, my anticipation is heightened by the mystery that abounds.

"Biogenesis" gave us a Mulder gone mad, duplicitous allies and enemies, a rising body count and Scully on the brink of an amazing discovery. It was pure "X-Files" and a terrific conclusion to a standout sixth season.

"The Waste of Diana Fowley"

As another season of "The X-Files" comes to an end, I'm left with a feeling of sadness that there will not be any new episodes for several months, but also feeling utter joy for what I believe to be one of the strongest seasons in the series' run. Alas, I am also left with one nagging question that continues to haunt me ...

What the hell is Diana Fowley doing here?

Fowley continues to be the least inspired character Chris Carter has created for his series. And it really is a waste of a golden opportunity. I welcomed her initial appearance in "The End" because I believed the sudden arrival of someone from Mulder or Scully's past would prompt very real feelings of jealousy and very natural questions about where Mulder and Scully stood in one another's lives. And I thought it was handled extremely well and segued beautifully into the movie, where Scully questions her place alongside Mulder and Mulder finally tells Scully how much she means to him.

All of that was wonderful and it could be argued that it came on the heels of Fowley's entrance into the scenario.

But since that time, Fowley has popped up time and again but served no useful purpose. The jealousy angle doesn't ring true any longer because we've seen how close Mulder and Scully have gotten and to suggest someone else could step between them now is ludicrous. We know Fowley is aligned with the CSM, but even that has gone nowhere.

Again, that held some promise based on what could only be described as a genuinely frightening alliance (the implications they were "together" in more ways than one sends shivers up and down my spine). But in "Biogenesis" we weren't given any additional insight into where that situation may be at right now.

However, the biggest problem is how she continues to pop up alongside Mulder and why Mulder never seems to question her sudden appearance.

As much as I enjoyed "Biogenesis," Fowley's arrival at Mulder's bedside was a big problem with the episode. Perhaps there was a scene cut explaining her appearance, but it never should have been cut because her arrival was awkward and out of place. Not to mention the problem with having Mulder, granted, not entirely himself but coherent enough to strike a debate with Scully, easily allow Fowley into his apartment after seeing the CSM in her apartment back in "One Son."

Mulder is not an idiot, but he continually is drawn that way whenever Fowley is around. Depicting him in such a way is not only insulting to the character, but to the audience as well.

All of this could be blamed on a lack of continuity or Carter's attempts to tease us and leave us with more questions than answers. As far as the latter is concerned, I don't have a problem with that, as long as the questions he poses are ones I'm interested in answering.

The problem here is I have no interest any longer in learning what Fowley's place in all of this is. That time has long since passed.

I blame that on Carter and his utter refusal to give us any insight into her character and, more importantly, why Mulder refuses to openly question her despite all he has learned about her. This isn't ambiguity and mystery, this is sloppy writing. We don't need all the answers, but we need some if we're going to continue to invest our interest in a character.

Compare Fowley with Krycek, for example. Krycek is another character completely shrouded in mystery, who appears out of thin air constantly and without explanation. He is very much what Fowley wants to be in terms of a supporting character. We don't really have a firm understanding as to what his role in the plan is either or what he knows or who is truly aligned with. All of that could be viewed as issues similar to what we're seeing with Fowley.

The difference, though, is we have been given nuggets (some very small to be certain) of info about Krycek and what he may or may not be doing. By opening the door slightly to his character, the viewer is sucked in and wants to barge in even further. So each time Krycek appears, we wonder what he will do next based on the actions we have seen before and knowing where he has stood in relation to the principles in the past.

We want to see what he will do because we know what he has done before. And we also have seen some of his motivations so we feel as if we're clued in (as much as we can be with this show) to what his agenda may be.

But we don't get that with Fowley. Yes, we know she's dirty, but we need more than that simple explanation if she's going to continue to play a pivotal role. And clearly Carter wants her to play a huge role otherwise he wouldn't keep trotting her out each time the mytharc swings into full force.

He wants to have her create some form of wedge between Mulder and Scully. That much is obvious. I wouldn't be opposed to such an idea if the single most important question here wasn't being avoided at all costs: Why doesn't Mulder confront her given all he has uncovered about her?

Each time we see them, there is a hint of some kind of bond that has yet to even be remotely explained. I don't have a problem believing such a bond exists between them, but to continue to mask it all in darkness is a case of cheating by Carter. Because of that, a potentially interesting character has been wasted and offers nothing to the proceedings than creating questions that no one seems interested in answering any longer.

The Fowley debate is sure to spark tons of discussion during the hiatus, which I'm sure is part of Carter's master plan. What he fails to realize, however, is that he truly had the opportunity to create some interesting dialogue with this character and how she fits into the grand scheme of things.

Instead, he has given us nothing but frustration with the character and seems to be blowing a chance to make things interesting as far as she's concerned.

"Mulder's Search For Samantha"

Two simple words. Two simple words that lie at the heart of what drives Fox Mulder in his ongoing quest to uncover the mysteries that have surrounded him for years. Two simple words that sum up his philosophy, the reasons behind his continued efforts to press forward despite all of the tragedy he has encountered.

Two simple words that Mulder utters when asked what more there is for him to discover.

"My sister."

A throwaway line in "Biogenesis" designed to enrage fans or remind them Samantha Mulder has not been forgotten by her brother or the series' creator? A cynic may think that is the case. But I do not. I think it was an important moment, a vital reminder that despite all Mulder has learned, the biggest answer he seeks remains tantalizingly out of reach.

Where is his sister?

Some fans have become bored by the Samanthas we have seen thus far and the realization they have been mere pawns in the game Mulder is caught up in.

72

The adult Samanthas we have seen, in fact, have been red herrings, designed to manipulate Mulder in one way or the other. Each time Mulder believes he has gotten closer to finding his sister, the rug has been pulled out from underneath him.

And each time, Mulder is left unfulfilled, painfully aware the key to his quest remains a mystery he has yet to solve.

For some fans, this has become an annoyance. They have grown weary of the constant appearances by one Samantha or another, only to be told she is not Mulder's sister and we, along with him, have been duped yet again. Because of that, some have suggested it would not bother them at all if Samantha Mulder never made an appearance of any kind in the series' final season and if her name was never uttered again.

I am not among that group. I believe that not only should Mulder find Samantha in Season 7, he needs to. In order for the journey to be complete, it must at some point come full circle. And that means Mulder must uncover the truth about where his sister is and what actually happened to her.

When the series began, Samantha was Mulder's Holy Grail. She represented the missing piece in his life and her disappearance was the driving force behind everything he did. Since he watched her being taken away those many years ago, it was if a piece of his own self had been removed that night as well. He needed to find her to become whole. He needed to find her to repair the damage that had been done.

The lengths he went in that quest led to him becoming an outcast to his colleagues and even, in "Demons," forcing him to undergo a painful series of experiments in an attempt to recapture the memories he had long since buried deep inside his mind. The fact he was willing to put his sanity on the line to recover those lost memories was a powerful indication of how badly he needed to find that missing piece of himself.

Since that time, Mulder has come to realize he no longer needs Samantha to fill that empty part of his being. Scully now has taken on that role. She is the one who now makes him whole. Her presence has repaired much of the damage Samantha's disappearance initially caused and much of the emptiness he has felt for so long since that fateful night.

The ongoing quest to find his sister no longer consumes him the way that it once did. But it remains a vital piece of his existence. It remains important for Mulder to find her. And I believe it remains important for the show to never lose sight of that fact.

The anguish he displayed during his coffee shop meeting with one of the false Samanthas in "Redux II" was a powerful reminder of how badly Mulder still needs to solve this puzzle. Watching that scene again, coupled with Mulder's comment in "Biogenesis," reminded me that no matter how far Mulder may go, no matter how much he may discover, the mystery of his sister's disappearance remains a conundrum he needs to solve.

That scene in "Redux II" resonates stronger, for me, than the moments Mulder shared with another of the false Samanthas in "Colony/End Game." Perhaps it did so because it coincided with Scully on her deathbed and ended with Mulder left alone, as if all of his answers were so close and yet so far away at the same time. Even though we later learned that was yet another false Samantha designed to dupe Mulder, I believe that is a moment we should not forget when we consider the path Mulder has been on.

It also provided possible insight into how the real Samantha may act should Mulder ever find her. Taken away from her home at the age of 8, possibly robbed of her identity, there is no way of knowing what Samantha Mulder has evolved into. Does she even remember her brother? Is she aware of the master plan she has become embroiled in and is it possible she understands her brother's pivotal role in the plans men and aliens have conspired to create?

All of these, in my opinion, are important questions for Mulder to unearth. What's more, I believe they are essential questions for the series to ponder in its final season.

Every journey has a destination. For Mulder, I believe his path needs to coincide with the reappearance of his sister. The reappearance could cause him great joy or great pain, that is left to the show's creators to decide. But no matter how it unfolds, it is a meeting I believe must take place in order for Mulder's journey to be complete.

Fox Mulder needs it. And we need it too.

"Scully's Awakening"

The last time we saw her, she was standing on the precipice of an amazing discovery, one that would not only change her life, but the lives of everyone on this planet. A gigantic ship from another world was beneath her feet and Dana Scully was about to come face-to-face with something she has spent the better part of the last six years denying could even be possible.

The existence of extraterrestrial life.

Her potential acceptance of this fact may symbolically parallel another piece of information she will have to soon confront as well, her true feelings for Fox Mulder. Season 7 of "The X-Files" may be about the doors Scully is willing to enter. Ones she has denied herself entrance to in the past but now can no longer avoid.

On the one hand, there is a tremendous discovery to be made of a majestic nature, an earthly nature. On the other, is one of a more personal nature but one that also carries a tremendous amount of importance. Both will change her and affect the belief system she has carried with her to this point in her life.

In many ways, Season 7 could be dubbed "Scully's Awakening."

Scully has always had eyes, but she did not always see. Much of that was due to the way her character was drawn. In order to continue the debate between the two leads, Mulder and Scully typically remained on opposite ends of the belief spectrum. What Mulder believed, Scully questioned. What Scully grudgingly accepted, Mulder often wondered about.

Dramatic tension it is called. But dramatic tension can only work so far when someone has been exposed to so much.

With a spaceship beneath her feet, the idea that Scully can deny the existence of extraterrestrial life is no longer possible. This cannot be explained away any longer in an attempt to continue her role as the resident skeptic. So the issue to be addressed in Season 7 will not only be how this realization affects Scully, but how she uses the belief system she has in place to process this information.

In "The Beginning," the idea was introduced that we were not the first inhabitants of this planet. Human beings, in fact, were the alien race. That idea remains at the heart of the mytharc, as evidenced by what Scully uncovered in "Biogenesis." Scientifically, that is a discovery of mammoth proportions. Scully used her science to uncover this amazing discovery. How she uses her science now will play a key role in how she processes the information that threatens to change everything she has believed in up until now.

As a scientist, Scully could not accept the idea of extraterrestrial life because it went against the very fiber of her belief system. Logically, she knew little green men were the stuff of fairy tales. There could be no belief because there had been no tangible proof. For Scully, proof is everything. She cannot believe until she can see.

But over time, given all she saw, she had to begin to believe in the possibility. The virus that crept inside her was a literal metaphor for the beliefs that had entered her being as well. Beliefs she could not explain rationally but ones she knew, somewhere in the fiber of her being, existed.

Emotionally, though, she was unwilling to take that step. She could not bring herself to alter everything that had fueled her. As Gibson said to her in "The Beginning," she knew, but did not want to believe. It was too much of a leap for her to take.

But now there can be no denying that leap. Another door has been opened to her. Now it's time for her to bury her fears and walk through it.

The same could be said for her feelings for Mulder. It is my contention that she loves this man as much as he loves her. For Mulder, someone prone to impulsive decision-making, the realization and admission of such feelings was not difficult. For Scully, logical, practical Scully, such feelings are not as easily addressed.

Or spoken of.

So in Season 6, Scully distanced herself emotionally at times as she tried to process the feelings she had for the man she loves. As any good scientist would, she tried to make sense of this situation logically. She weighed the pros and cons of the evolution of friendship into love (her speech about friendship blossoming into something deeper in "The Rain King" could be seen as an unconscious admission of what she was addressing within herself) The only problem is that love is rarely logical. It is spontaneous and passionate. And these are feelings Scully seems to have long since buried within her.

Only on occasion have they risen to the surface. We saw one indication in "Milagro," an episode I believe played upon the idea of Scully's acceptance that there remains within her, a vibrant sexual woman capable of desire.

Was it just a coincidence that not long after that we saw a moment with Mulder in "The Unnatural" unlike most others we had ever seen? I said at the time her acceptance of Mulder's obvious attempts to flirt with her was her way of allowing Mulder access to that part of herself, a part she had kept hidden for so long.

But of course, there remains a declaration of her feelings. Mulder has expressed himself and has patiently waited for Scully to do likewise. It is a door Scully has kept closed for the better part of six years, only to begin gently turning the key as Season 6 came to a close.

Only time will tell when she finally summons up the courage to walk through that door. Perhaps her greatest fear is how that entrance will change her. Like the spaceship beneath her feet, everything that she believed in until now will change under the weight of that discovery, of that admission.

Both doors Scully must walk through this season will be filled with trepidation and excitement. Both have been closed to her for so long because she was unwilling to open them. But finally, the time will come and it will be very interesting to watch her make this journey of self-discovery and self-realization.

"The Issue Of Trust"

As the dog days of summer roll on and Scully's hair likely grows more frizzy with each passing day, I think to myself that not only is this a wonderful world, but is there a more important theme on "The X-Files" than the issue of trust?

Strip away every fiber of this show, every peripheral theme and idea and what do you end up with? The issue of trust. The concept of trusting in our superiors, our government, our family and everyone closest to us. It's right there, the pre-eminent theme of "The X-Files" in my opinion.

Trust.

Are you willing to trust your own ideas, your own faith, your own beliefs as well as the ideas of those closest to you? These are the issues Mulder and Scully grapple with constantly, together and individually. They all lie at the heart of this series.

The concept of the show revolves around the inability to trust anyone in power. Mulder feeds off his own lack of trust and it inspires him to carry on his improbable quest. I find Mulder's views on trust to be the most fascinating. Here's a guy who knows he cannot trust anyone and yet is so eager to believe "someone" that he often swings back and forth on the pendulum that is his search.

As he learns more about the nature of his sister's abduction and his father's role in that plan, the issue of trust becomes paramount. He finds he can no longer trust the memories of his parents and the life he once lived. So much of it was a lie, hiding a deep, dark secret about what his father had done and the secret no one could reveal.

And yet as Mulder learns more and more about the lies that have filled his every movement, he finds it impossible to ignore them. He continues to pursue them endlessly with the hope that within the spider web of deception lies a kernel of truth from which he can draw some hope of salvation.

I think that's why he's been such an easy mark for The Consortium all these years. They knew that no matter how many red herrings they tossed Mulder's way, he'd chase each of them down in order to find the truth. In order to find that truth he sought, he had to trust someone, anyone who could shed some light on the mystery that engulfed his life. It didn't matter who that person was or how unscrupulous they may seem, Mulder was willing to believe if the lies were told convincingly enough.

So he trusted Deep Throat and X and Marita, Kritschgau and even the CSM, anyone who could open the door to the room which he hoped held all the secrets he so desperately wanted to find. He wanted to believe so badly he was willing to believe anyone. And in the process, he has often violated the one code of conduct he has lived his life by.

Trust No One.

That was one reason why I so enjoyed the Mulder/CSM confrontation in "One Son." How much of what the CSM was saying was the truth? Perhaps all. Perhaps none. Perhaps bits and pieces. We are left to decide that for ourselves. But he spun his tale so convincingly, Mulder grasped onto it entirely as the truth.

Within a matter of minutes, the CSM's truth became Mulder's truth.

The CSM had said it was his desire to break Mulder and that seems to be his moment of ultimate triumph. Mulder is broken by the time Diana returns. My personal view on that scene all along has been it was the CSM's way of setting Mulder up for a demise at the hands of the rebels.

But what I also see is a Mulder who had his desire to trust turned back on him so many times in the past, he is defeated spiritually and emotionally when he finds out that the truths he had clung to for so long once again appeared to be lies.

That really was a terrific scene.

Of course, the one person he can trust implicitly is Scully. One of the key reasons why I enjoy their relationship so much is because it is based on an essential value in my own life: Trust.

One of the greatest joys of "Field Trip" was how the idea of trust was played out. Specifically I'm referring to their shared "trip" near the end of the episode and how Mulder is shaken out of his delirium by what Scully has to say. He's so far gone in his belief that he'd been abducted it's possible no one could have shaken him out of that mental state. But Scully is able to.

Why? Simple. He trusts completely in the logic of her argument. And it is that trust in Scully that snaps Mulder out of his drug-enduced haze.

His intense trust in her ability to uncover the truth of the situation they're in penetrates his haze and shakes him back to reality. Once that occurs, their separate hallucinations become one. It could be argued the strength of that trust which underscores the power of their connection is what enables Mulder to shove his hand through the dirt where Skinner and the others are able to spot them and rescue them both.

It all begins with trust.

Of course, the very ending of that episode plays with that theme even stronger. Semi-conscious and still in a state of delirium in the back of an ambulance, Mulder looks over at Scully and reaches out for her hand. Without looking, Scully responds and their hands become one. An indication of their connection to be certain, but also another example of how Scully trusts enough in Mulder to know his hand is there. She can feel it without even looking. She just knows.

Her trust in him is that strong. That powerful.

The issue of trust remains at the heart of this series and it is one question Mulder and Scully ask themselves repeatedly. Who can they trust? Who can they believe? What truth is out there for both of them to find?

Ultimately, of course, they can only trust one another. And it is through that trust they share that supplies the strength they need to keep looking for the answers they seek.

"The Mytharc: A Giant McGuffin?"

What if, and I stress the word "if" here, the mytharc was nothing more than a giant McGuffin?

For those who may not know, a McGuffin is a cinematic term used to describe something that plays a central role in the story and yet is never completely defined or revealed. Hitchcock used McGuffins frequently and more updated examples include the black box in "Pulp Fiction" and the silver case in "Ronin."

So what if that's all the mytharc turned out to be? A McGuffin everyone in the story was embroiled in, but something none of them, or us, ever adequately figured out?

Certainly, we've learned more about the mytharc than we ever did about what that black case was in "Pulp Fiction," but what do we really know? As so many characters have said at various times, we know bits and pieces but not the whole.

We can blame some of that on the fact the show has yet to come to an end, a lack of continuity and Chris Carter's habit of leading us down one path only to create a new path in the middle of nowhere without a single reference to the road we've just traveled down.

But what if we were never meant to know the complete picture? What if this was all a means by which we were meant to examine the characters in the story and nothing more? Would that be so bad?

As someone who appreciates the show for its character examinations and the relationship between Mulder and Scully, I wonder if it would bother me a great deal. Now don't get me wrong, I want some answers (dammit), but I also love the ambiguity this show basks in. I always have. I love the idea that mysteries are constantly being created for me to try and decipher with no solutions immediately in sight.

But what if these mysteries are never meant to be completely solved? What if they were created merely to allow us to follow the path Mulder and Scully are on and watch how they grow individually and together as their quest continues? I wonder if that would be such a bad thing.

Of course, the quest itself is one that demands some sort of resolution. Doesn't it? So the idea of the mytharc as one gigantic McGuffin may be best served in theory only. But I also know that Carter is not one who is prone to "total disclosure" no matter how badly he wants to convince us otherwise. With that in mind, I wonder if he ever truly intends to reveal the answers to all our questions.

If not, perhaps that is what the mytharc will eventually turn out to be, a giant McGuffin used to propel the story of Fox Mulder and Dana Scully forward, a means by which they have been brought together to tell their story.

I admit, I am not entirely enamored with this idea. But I also know the mytharc mysteries in which Mulder and Scully have become embroiled provide more clues than actual answers. So I do not discount the possibility that the mytharc is merely a means to an end and not the end itself.

SEASON 7

The seventh season began with Mulder locked away in a asylum, the victim of one massive alien-induced migraine, while Scully trekked to Africa to find a cure to save his "beautiful mind." Behind-the-scenes, those associated with the series were preparing as if it would be the show's final season.

Neither Carter nor Duchovny had contracts beyond the season. And with Duchovny and Anderson both beginning to tire of playing Mulder and Scully, the time was seen as ideal for the ground-breaking series to come to an end.

"We're preparing as if this is the last year and we want to send these characters off right," Spotnitz told me in an interview prior to the start of the season. "It's a little sad to think the show might be coming to an end. But we're excited too because we think we have some very interesting stories to tell this season.

"We're going to do a lot of different things this season. We're approaching episode No. 150 and we've exhausted so many paranormal stories it's difficult to come up with something new. But there are a number of shows we're doing this year that we've always wanted to do.

"The first two episodes will explore Mulder's character in a way we haven't done before. The second episode was written by David and Chris and I think it will give fans greater insight into Mulder's character. The cliffhanger had Scully face-to-face with a spaceship, something we had avoided for six years. So she will confront some things that are completely different than what she's dealt with in the past."

The cast and crew were forced to confront something completely different as well. Before the season, Duchovny filed a multimillion-dollar lawsuit against 20th Century Fox Film Corp. It accused the company (a subsidiary of Rupert Murdoch's News Corp., which produces "The X-Files" for corporate sibling the Fox network) of intentionally underselling the show's rights to its own affiliates, thereby allegedly bilking Duchovny out of millions.

While reports said he was entitled to an estimated 5 percent of all profits, he contended in the lawsuit he'd seen only a fraction of that. The lawsuit didn't name Carter as a defendant, but it put a strain on the friendship between the show's creator and its top-billed star. Although the two collaborated to write "Amor Fati," sources said they rarely spoke directly to one another about the script, instead communicating via fax.

"The whole lawsuit thing revealed that Carter knew (Duchovny) was getting screwed and didn't warn him," one source said. "Carter proved where his loyalties lay with his actions."

The lawsuit hung like a dark cloud over the series throughout the season. Despite that, Fox wasn't prepared to cut the ties with its successful Sunday night drama. Negotiations continued with Carter and Duchovny, as Fox attempted to entice both men to return for an eighth season.

On the eve of the season finale, Carter signed on for one more season. Duchovny also agreed to return for an eighth season, but in a limited capacity. He also settled his lawsuit against Fox's syndication unit and though financial terms of the settlement weren't disclosed, industry sources estimated the total package was worth more than $20 million.

Duchovny decided to return to the series even though from an acting perspective, he had lamented what he called the show's lack of "accumulation of experience." In his mind, Mulder and Scully's progression since the film had become flawed. A near kiss in the movie would be followed by episodes of ambiguity or Scully would confront something of significance in one mytharc episode only to forget about it the following week.

Some of the decision makers at Fox reportedly agreed with Duchovny's complaints. But with the series still doing well in the ratings and generating revenue for the network, Carter was allowed to maintain the status quo, something that didn't always sit well with the show's passionate fan base.

"If only 1013 had a show bible," said Carol McConnell-Hallenbecht, a Canadian viewer since Season 1. "If they had recognized the need for steady character development and story continuity. Carter sold the sizzle, but where's the steak? All these wonderful characters, images, plots and it all goes nowhere."

Duchovny, meanwhile, was able to flex his creative muscles by writing and directing another episode in Season 7. "Hollywood A.D." was an often satirical look at the series and in many ways reflected Duchovny's love for "The X-Files" and his concerns about the show becoming a parody of itself.

Not only did he cast his friend Garry Shandling and wife Tea Leoni in the episode, he and Leoni were part of the dancing zombies that concluded the episode. He also cast several family members and friends of the crew in that scene. That helped some people get their Screen Actor's Guild cards and allowed other SAG members to qualify for a health insurance plan.

Anderson followed her co-star's lead by writing and directing an episode of her own. "all things" was a fascinating look at Scully coming to a crossroads in her life and making a crucial decision about the path she was on, one that included a stop in Mulder's bedroom.

Not to be outdone, William B. Davis (who played the show's resident embodiment of evil, the Cigarette Smoking Man) wrote an episode of his own. "En Ami" focused on the CSM's warped sense of humanity and his sudden affection for Dana Scully.

Each of these actors not only brought their own personal viewpoints to the show and their respective characters, but each episode cast a fascinating look at the Mulder-Scully relationship as well.

"I really liked the progression of the MSR (in Season 7) and the contributions made to it by David and Gillian behind the camera," said Linda Goldberg, a

Boston fan who started watching the show in Season 2. "And even Bill Davis' contribution in 'En Ami.' The scene of an angry Mulder, who can't even look at an almost tearful Scully, spoke volumes about the progressing intensity of their relationship."

Season 7 also saw the first on-screen kiss between Mulder and Scully (a New Year's Eve buss in "Millennium"), while arguably the most talked-about episode of the season was "Closure," which marked the final act of Mulder's search for his long-lost sister. Although numerous episodes had stated that Samantha was still alive, in "Closure," Carter and Spotnitz reversed field and threw something completely into the mix.

In "Closure," Mulder learned that after undergoing numerous tests following her abduction, Samantha had been removed from this world at the age of 14 by spiritual beings known as "Walk-ins." They escorted her to the after-life (referred to as "starlight"), where she would be free from the pain this world had inflicted upon her.

For seven seasons, Mulder's search for Samantha had provided the emotional pulse of the series. It not only spawned Mulder's belief in aliens, but also the alien conspiracy which had become the foundation of the show's mytharc. So it was not surprising that some fans bristled when Carter and Spotnitz brought in a heretofore unmentioned invention to explain Samantha's ultimate fate.

"It just seemed so out of left field to me," said Philadelphia fan Sean Mulloy. "While we didn't know exactly what had happened (to Samantha), we had some clues. Samantha was taken as part of The Project. It just seemed kind of out of the blue to come up with this idea that 'Oh yeah, she's been dead the whole time.'

"Not that I thought that Mulder would get her back alive, but I expected her fate to be due to some otherworldly factor. I guess I wanted a more 'alien' type resolution."

Brian Shea, a fan since the pilot from Massachusetts, had a similar, though more blunt, reaction.

"It completely blew up the show," he said. "I've never felt the same about the show since. It's a combination of contradicting every single episode before it, and leaving us with such a lame and cop-out resolution made me want to vomit. This is by far the single biggest mistake made on the show."

Other fans praised "Closure" for the emotional resonance it provided for Mulder's character. They also considered the episode, and the entire season, to be a worthy chapter to the show's overall story.

"Season 7 was my favorite (of the last four)," said Sam Skevas, a fan from Charlotte, N.C., who began watching in the sixth season. "The mytharc hadn't gone to hell in a hand basket, Mulder and Scully's relationship seemed to be coming to fruition, great MOTW's and a great cliffhanger to the end of the season."

"Compared to past seasons, many of the episodes (in Season 7) were character-centric as opposed to plot-centric," said Meredith Berrett from New York, who began watching the series at the very beginning. "Putting the evolving MSR aside, we really did get nice peeks behind the Wizard's curtain."

When the seventh season began, I was prepared to count down the days until the series came to an end. As much as I loved this show, I believed the time was right for it to ride off into the sunset while it still could bask in the glow of greatness.

Many of the episodes that season (such as "Amor Fati," X-Cops," "all things," "Je Souhaite" and "Requiem") were wonderful examples of the dramatic strength and emotional potency this series still was able to produce. There were even moments while watching those episodes when I believed the show should go on for another season.

But when the news came the series would return for an eighth season, I wasn't exactly bouncing up and down with glee - especially since Duchovny was only going to appear in half of the episodes. As far as I was concerned, if one of the stars was removed from the equation, the series would cease to exist or become something I wasn't interested in watching.

A season that began with such hope ended with a sense of sorrow given the end result of the season-long backstage wheeling and dealing. Not even the magnificent season finale ("Requiem," which ended with Mulder being abducted by aliens and Scully telling Skinner she was pregnant) could erase the nagging doubts I had that a series that had been so amazing for so long would soon embark upon a new course wrought with pitfalls and turmoil.

"THE SIXTH EXTINCTION"

The beliefs we have, the truths we hold dear lie at the core of our very beings. They sustain us, empower us to go forward along whatever path comprises our destiny.

So imagine if those belief systems were suddenly shattered. If what we once held close to us, what once comforted us in the sanctity of its truthfulness was suddenly turned on its ear. Imagine how we would react. Imagine how our lives would change.

Imagine how our concept of the truth would be forever affected.

"The X-Files" has always been, at its heart, about the truths that we cling to and how the perception of those truths can be tantalizingly altered by even the slightest hint of a lie. In last season's finale, "Biogenesis," the truths Fox Mulder and Dana Scully clung to were turned upside down.

Scully was forced to confront the existence of extraterrestrial life and Mulder was locked away in a padded cell, perhaps realizing for the first time how futile his quest for the truth had been. How he had pursued and pursued one false lead after another when all along, the truth to what he had sought for so was inside of him.

The seventh season premiere, "The Sixth Extinction," takes those ideas and runs with them. It offers precious few answers that we didn't already know or hadn't suspected. Instead, it forces us to consider what may now be the truth and what the consequences may be of that knowledge.

I speculated in an essay earlier this summer that Season 7 could be viewed as "Scully's Awakening." We see the first signs of that here. She is clearly a different woman than the one we last saw standing on the beach, a spaceship beneath her feet (and I'm not just talking about how handy she looks with a machete, her desire to pack plenty of push-up bras for her trip to Africa or her carefree 'do). Her monologues are filled with the conflicting beliefs of what once held her and the knowledge that those long-held beliefs no longer can nurture her.

The science that made her strong can no longer be the sole source of her survival. The spaceship she has found and the mysteries that coincide with its appearance (real Old Testament, wrath of God stuff, too: A plague of locusts, a sea of blood, not to mention a bizarre figure in the darkness) have forced her to consider, and confront, other possibilities.

The spaceship she finds seemingly holds answers to every question anyone could conjure up. As the crazed Dr. Barnes puts it, it is THE answer to everything (My two questions for it then would be: Why didn't Scully pack a gun for her trip instead of wandering around with a machete and is she always that nonchalant after being attacked by locusts?). Passages from the Bible, the Koran, a detailed map of the human anatomy. This is quite a little find indeed.

Not only that, but it also apparently can raise the dead before conveniently vanishing into thin air. Neat trick.

This is the artifact Scully has uncovered and its power frightens her. In her mind, she reaches out to the one man who could hopefully make sense of all she has now seen, of all that she must now accept. She even considers it unfair that she is the one to make this momentous discovery. A twinge of guilt overcomes her as she realizes that everything Mulder has fought to learn is suddenly right beneath her feat and not his.

Perhaps it is that guilt that manifests itself in the form of that mysterious figure who, before tapping Scully on the forehead, instructs her that "Some truths are not meant for you." If not her, then who? Mulder perhaps?

Alas, he remains locked away in an asylum, slowly beginning to comprehend what is happening to him. The power that is locked inside of him that has been waiting for who knows how long to emerge.

He fights through his mental state of confusion to slip Skinner a plea for help after a well-timed scuffle. For reasons never made crystal clear, Mulder knows that a name from the past, Michael Kritschgau, can help him make sense of what is transpiring within him.

Mulder's form of ESP stems, he believes, from an extraterrestrial source. He is filled with a power he could never imagine and one his body is fighting to control. This is the truth Mulder now clings to. Although his motives are (not surprisingly) sketchy, Kritschgau reluctantly begins to help only to have Fowley intervene.

Ahhh Fowley. Her actions betray. Her presence annoys. Her characterization confuses. But here's a little secret for you. I found her interesting here for the first time in ages.

For the first time, she's on the up and up with Mulder (and by way of doing that, Chris Carter for the first time shows an inkling of playing fair with us). Knowing he can read her mind leaves her little choice, so she professes her love and her hope that they "now can be together." She leaves bolstered by what she believes is the truth.

But as Mulder's eyes follow her out the hospital door, we sense the truth Fowley now clings to is anything but the reality she will soon face. Not even the duplicitous Fowley is immune from the idea of proceeding under a falsehood.

"The Sixth Extinction" is all about truth and our perception of it. Skinner: Friend or foe? Fowley: Betrayer or lover? The spaceship from another world: The genesis of mankind itself? The CSM: Mulder's father or not?

Oh wait, that's next week's show.

The one truth we know for certain is the bond between Mulder and Scully has never been stronger. Even though they spend most of the episode apart, their connection remains powerful. Everything Scully does in Africa she does with one resolution in mind, to save Mulder.

She speaks of him lovingly, sadly referring to the disease that has struck his "beautiful mind." She aches for him to be with her as she is on the verge of this amazing discovery. Her words betray the emptiness she feels with him no longer at her side. Her feelings are manifested later when, at Mulder's bedside, she tearfully pleads with him to find the strength to hold on.

It is only fitting then that after being momentarily brought back to consciousness, the first name Mulder speaks aloud is Scully. And at the end, as he hears her voice, he cannot summon the strength to respond, but is clearly comforted by her presence.

Somewhere in that vacant gaze we sense a power that he is finally beginning to comprehend. A truth he is finally beginning to comprehend. It is left for Scully to make the declaration for him that "He is more alive than he has ever been."

After watching "The Sixth Extinction," the same could be said for "The X-Files."

"AMOR FATI"

Absolution for our sins. A life without guilt. It is a concept all of us would eagerly welcome. The idea that in some way, all of the wrongs we have committed could somehow be wiped away is tantalizing to us all.

Fox Mulder is no exception. For Mulder, the burden of guilt is heavy. The losses he has sustained on his quest have taken their toll over the years. He perseveres, but deep within himself he seeks refuge from the pain he believes he has inflicted upon others and upon himself.

He is given such an opportunity in "Amor Fati." Inside his jumbled head, as the CSM performs tests upon him, Mulder is given a chance to see what his life would be like if he were provided what he desires.

Absolution.

So the CSM rescues his "son" and plays the part of a chain-smoking sinister tour guide of what could be. He takes Mulder to a cozy little house in the suburbs, shows him long-lost friends from the past (the supposedly dead Deep Throat), tosses a woman his way eager to bed him (the treacherous Fowley just back from a trip to the lingerie shop) and literally points him in the direction of his sister. Everything a traumatized boy infected with alien black oil could ask for.

All with no guilt attached.

But what we quickly learn is Mulder doesn't really seek a quiet little life in the burbs where Fowley brightens his morning by bringing him coffee after a late-night roll in the hay and the CSM plays dad and lives right down the street. What he craves most is for the burden to be lifted.

Through various characters in his subconscious, Mulder examines what he perceives to be the consequences of his quest. His own personal suffering is exposed when the CSM tells him he's no Christ-like figure and he'll only die on account of his misguided heroism. Fowley calls his journey childish, saying he's avoided the real responsibility that men must choose (findin' a good woman and makin' babies). Deep Throat tells him he has been manipulated into believing what others wanted him to believe.

Mulder's worst fears about everything he has committed himself to are laid out in front of him. The only escape is escape, the CSM suggests. A new life, one devoid of responsibility and worry, one where Mulder can be the man he never could allow himself to be.

Take this new life, the CSM says, and all your worries will be washed away. This is the apple the CSM promises will leave Mulder in Eden forever. So, subconsciously, he bites into it, believing it is the only food he will ever need to nourish him.

He marries Fowley, raises a family, only to watch everyone around him die. At the end, he is alone, the world dying outside his home as aliens attack with only the devil incarnate immune from the coming apocalypse. Perhaps the only thing more frightening than the invasion was the realization that in Mulder's dream world, the CSM is just like Dick Clark.

He never ages.

But even as he chooses to stay in his subconscious Eden, Mulder realizes that is not where his place should be. The quest that sustained him for so long is never far from his thoughts (represented by the little boy on the beach in his dream within a dream). The boy endlessly building a spaceship that will continually get washed away in the sand represents the purity and the determination of Mulder's quest.

The boy serves as a reminder of who Mulder really is and what he ultimately stands for. But that is just one part of Mulder's truth. The rest is defined by Scully.

Scully is rarely mentioned in Mulder's dream. She is almost an afterthought, which to me suggests in his subconscious mind Mulder cannot bring himself to think of her because he knows if he does, she will expose his version of Eden for what it really is. A sham.

That is precisely what she tells him when she is finally allowed entrance into his dream (coinciding with her actual entrance into the facility where Mulder is being worked on by the CSM's doctors). She calls him a traitor and demands that he open his eyes and see the reality of his deal with the devil.

For Mulder, Scully is the key to unlocking his truth. She is his "constant" and it is through her that Mulder summons the strength to return to the land of the living and to carry on his quest.

The reality Mulder accepts is that there is no perfect absolution for our sins. We cannot escape what we have done, but only carry on ("fight the fight" as Scully says) along whatever path we have chosen for ourselves. That is the truth. Anything else is to lie to one's self.

Interesting ideas and enough to make "Amor Fati" one of the most fascinating episodes in the series' run.

One of the joys of "The X-Files" has always been its willingness to be daring. We see that clearly in "Amor Fati." Spiritual questions run hand in hand with the return of the alien invasion subplot. This was an episode that's hard to label because it aimed high.

Sometimes by reaching for so much, some small things were a bit puzzling. For example, now that the CSM has plugged Mulder's alien-hybrid genes into himself, does this mean CSM is now the key to "The X-Files?" And whose idea was it to turn Fowley into a heroic figure who died after helping Scully save Mulder's life? Can we have a show of hands from anyone out there who bought that load of crap?

Anyone?

Oh well, at least she's dead.

The lyrical poetry of this episode more than made up for a slight misstep here or there. There was enough intrigue (Krycek returning to put the plam on Skinner and adding another murder to his personal body count) to keep those juices flowing. But at its heart, this episode (as was "The Sixth Extinction") was about our perception of the truth and what the paths we have chosen for ourselves.

We see Mulder tempted with the "good life," but ultimately rejecting it. We see Scully agonizing over everything she has now seen and how it conflicts with everything she once believed. It was also a nice touch to have the more spiritual Scully be the one receptive to visions from the dead Albert Hosteen.

Ultimately, the only thing Mulder and Scully know for certain is that they can draw upon each other for survival. They represent the truth for each other. That is what they must cling to. Everything else is secondary. And Mulder being revived by one of Scully's tears had a fairy tale quality that was poignant and breathtaking in its beauty.

It was magical and at the same time, strongly represented the power of their connection.

So at the end, they stood together, sharing their truth with one another, drawing their strength from it and from one another. As they do so, they realize once again their bond is their most conscious reality.

Everything else is just the stuff of dreams.

"The Dream"

Leave it to Chris Carter and David Duchovny to give us an episode that undoubtedly will have us all talking for months to come. "The dream," in my opinion, was inspired television no matter what source material Duchovny may have drawn from. But it clearly left itself open to numerous interpretations, which I think is only fitting.

After all, it was a dream.

Dreams are abstract. They are filled with symbols. They may represent certain longings or desires. Or they merely be images that we connect with that have no basis in reality. The dream in "Amor Fati" has all of that working in its favor, which is why it was so intoxicating.

Much discussion has centered around the hows and whys of Mulder's dream. How did it occur (was it influenced by the CSM's drugs?) and why did certain things appear (Fowley as the doting spouse) and not others (no Scully-Mulder love scene?).

But a lot of that, I think, is window dressing. For me, the key is what is it supposed to represent and what does it say about Fox Mulder?

Are we supposed to believe that somewhere in the recesses of his mind Mulder longs for a life in the 'burbs with a wife and kids and the CSM as good old dad? I don't think so and I think to focus on that aspect is to lose sight of the bigger picture. I know much of what Duchovny wanted to do was based on the idea of the "road not traveled." But at the risk of over analyzing what he intended, I honestly think there was more to it than that.

First off, let me say I believe this was HIS dream. I like the idea that the CSM was perhaps controling things (it certainly facilitates the idea of the CSM as the master puppeteer). But I think that detracts from the character issues we were clearly meant to examine with Mulder in this scenario.

To make this examination really work, we must assume it is Mulder's subconscious directing this tale for him. We have to see these as HIS choices and HIS subconscious at work rather than some landscape the CSM was laying out for him.

So if we start with that assumption, the next question we have to ask is what does everything represent? The life in the 'burbs doesn't necessarily equate to some longing Mulder has for such an existence. Rather, by placing himself in that atmosphere, he is as far removed from the anxieties of the X-Files as he can be with all his guilt removed.

And that is the key to this dream in my opinion.

The guilt aspect is crucial. By removing it, Mulder's subconscious gives him an option to be free. *That* is the temptation for Mulder here. A life without guilt, where none of his previous decisions had the dark consequences he previously believed. *that* is the road less traveled, one where aliens and abductions and cancer are figments of his imagination, not the real horrors we know he has endured.

Which brings us to Fowley.

Why pick Fowley to be his betrothed? To answer that question is to remember that Fowley does not have to represent a physical longing on Mulder's behalf. So to question why Fowley shows up and winds up in Mulder's bed instead of Scully is to miss the point. Just because she's there doesn't necessarily mean she was the one Mulder wanted physically or romantically. Instead, she was a representation of the "wife" in the scenario his subconscious had created for him.

I believe Mulder's subconscious chose her for that role was an effort to demonstrate how invalid the entire scenario was. It further reinforced the untruth, the lie that was being created in order to appease the loss of will that Mulder was being tempted to accept. His subconscious could not pick Scully in that role because it would have shattered the entire "world" that was being created. A world where the key was a lack of responsibility and a removal of guilt.

Scully represents responsibility. She represents the determination to fight. Mulder, at that point, was resigning himself to a life with no struggle, one devoid of responsibilities beyond his own household. Scully did not, and could not, fit into that type of atmosphere and Mulder's subconscious knew that. So she was ruled out and Fowley was allowed in.

The key thing to make it work though is Mulder's acceptance of this scenario. The ultimate clincher comes when he finally sees his sister. With his guilt removed and his sister close to him again, Mulder finds what he believes is a peace he has lacked for so long. It is at that point when the acceptance of this "life" and this temptation clicks in for good.

At that point, Mulder makes the choice to stay, which in essence is his way of making a choice to die.

That parallel can be drawn given the experiments the CSM is running on him. The life literally seems to be taken from him at the very time he finds his sister in his dream. I don't think it's far-fetched to say that even in his drugged-up state, Mulder is somehow aware that something is amiss. So it is left for his subconscious to make the choice to stay or fight.

The appearance of his sister is the ultimate incentive. The ultimate temptation this scenario creates.

Which brings us to Scully. We are keenly aware of her absence in Mulder's dream. She is barely mentioned and when she is, it often is not is not by name ("your partner"). The reason why seems obvious: Somewhere in Mulder's subconscious he is still aware she represents the truth to him.. Had she been allowed entrance earlier, it would have exposed the dream for the untruth it was.

So giving himself an easy way out (the CSM's line that Scully will be harmed if Mulder makes contact with her), Mulder's subconscious mind allows him the chance to take the easy way out without Scully's "truth" to steer him back to the light. It makes his choice to resign himself to this fate easier because she is not there to shine a light on the reality of the choice he is making.

But his true feelings for her are revealed on his "deathbed." None of the deaths the CSM tells him about, from Fowley to Deep Throat or Samantha, touch him greatly until he hears Scully's name. At that point, he is overcome with emotion. That is a very telling response. She is the one loss he has suffered which moves him most and it is at that point when the door to Mulder's true self begins to open since his feelings for Scully are the only real part of this imagined scenario.

Not Fowley as his wife or the CSM as his neighbor, Sam alive and kicking and Deep Throat hanging around for a Sunday cookout. All of that was imagery, possibilities either real or imagined. His feelings for Scully are a "true" representation of his real self.

It is at that point when Scully is allowed entrance to his dream (in a parallel to her entrance to the lab where the real Mulder has been left for dead presumably). Scully, of course, orders Mulder to fight, first by insulting him in his dream and then by pressing her own emotions as close to him as possible, literally symbolized by the teardrop which snaps him back to reality.

She is his savior. She is the one who makes him whole again. She is his truth and her strength gives him the strength to fight. This is a nice parallel to "One Breath" when Scully tells Mulder she had the strength of his beliefs. Here, the reverse is true and through Scully, Mulder finds the will to shatter the untruths of his dream and reclaim what matters most to him.

In the end, the dream was a choice. The temptation was in the reality of what that existence meant, no guilt, no deaths to hang over him, no abducted sisters to anxiously search for.

But the dream also represented an untruth, a lie. And what Mulder has always craved, first and foremost, was "the truth." Although he came dangerously close to embracing a lie, Scully's "truth" guided him back to the path he was destined to be on and the continued search for the truth Mulder knows is still "out there."

"HUNGRY"

There's this little movie called "Return of the Living Dead." Typical zombies come back to life stuff. There's a graveyard just out back. Zombies get a whiff of some toxic fumes. They rise from the dead. They start to stumble about. Screaming over-sexed teenagers run amok as over-sexed teens are prone to do when being chased by zombies. You know the drill.

But here's the kicker. The zombies only ate human brains. Cute, huh? Well, I thought so. But don't mind me.

Now here's another kicker. The zombies in "Return of the Living Dead" were far more interesting than Rob the Lucky Boy fast food worker who feeds on human brains in "Hungry."

Given the powerful emotional resonance of "Amor Fati," it would have been incredibly difficult for a typical MOTW to follow in a similar vein. But would it be too much to ask for a MOTW that at least had a little bite to it? OK this one had some bite. But that's not what I meant.

Don't get me wrong, "Hungry" wasn't a horrible episode. There were no killer kitties and at no point did Scully start birthin' babies while Mulder was sprawled outside hacking and wheezing to death.

But there was little here of genuine interest. Nothing that really grabbed hold of me and demanded my attention. So the killer liked to eat brains and he had problems keeping his ear attached. Were we ever given a reason why he had such a dietary habit? Nope. Were we given any idea how he came to develop such a sweet tooth? Nope. Were we ever told where he kept finding substitute ears? Nope.

Do I really care to know the answers to these questions? Nope. Can't say I do. Well, OK, maybe the ear one. But that's it. Therein lies the problem. I just didn't care.

Maybe it's because I felt like I was watching another television show that just happened to have Mulder and Scully wandering through it. And make no mistake, that's where they were doing. Wandering through.

During their infrequent moments on camera, Mulder and Scully were given precious little to do. And what they did often strained credibility. The CSM must have forgot to check for table scraps of alien matter when he cleaned out Mulder's cranium because Mulder sure knew what was what with poor Rob from the get go. Apparently, all Mulder needs to figure out who the killer is to be introduced to him.

I think that's how Jack Lord used to do it on "Hawaii Five-O."

Then again, since Rob was the only one sneaking around in broad daylight to spy on Mulder and Scully, it couldn't be too hard to figure out he was up to no good. Or maybe it was the music which screamed "HERE'S THE KILLER" from the outset of the episode.

So much for the big mystery.

A bigger mystery is whether Gillian Anderson was paid by the word for this episode. I hope not for her sake because she barely uttered a line of dialogue. I think she may have squinted once or twice but that's about it. I guess it was decided this week that all she needed to do was walk around with a low-cut top, have the camera pan down from up high and that's enough to satisfy our Scully cravings for one week.

OK, some of my cravings were satisfied, but a little more ooomph wouldn't have hurt anybody. OK, the low-cut top had some ooomph but you know what I mean. Sadly, Anderson got to do little except be "the good cop" to Mulder's "insane cop" (All right, that was a great line). I doubt this will be among the episodes that get sent in for Anderson's Emmy consideration next year.

That's not to say the entire episode was without merit. Rob's obsession with curing his robust appetite through self-help videotapes and a 12-step overeaters anonymous program were nicely done. The special effects weren't bad either. I loved the scene in the shrink's office when Rob's ear fell off. And there was definitely something a bit unsettling about the way the shrink gravitated toward the deformed creature at the end that begged further discussion.

But all of that could not make up for the blasé reaction I felt throughout. Vince Gilligan has written some tremendous episodes. Some of the most exciting and scintillating the series has ever produced.

Sadly, "Hungry" will not be one of them. It was more like one of those low-fat frozen dinners you buy in the frozen foods section. You hope it'll help you drop a few pounds while eating right, but while it carries plenty of promise of quality cuisine there ultimately isn't enough nourishment to get you through the night.

"MILLENNIUM"

"The world didn't end."

No it didn't. Not from a quartet of zombies raised from the dead to facilitate Armageddon. And not from a liplock Mulder and Scully have been denying themselves for far too long.

But more on that later.

Chris Carter's diametrically opposed worlds of "The X-Files" and "Millennium" slammed straight into one another in the highly entertaining "Millennium," proof positive that last week's dismal "Hungry" was not an accurate representation of what we can expect from our seventh season MOTWs. Instead, "Millennium" was cause for celebration. It offered up two angst-ridden FBI agents, zombies rising from the dead and a kiss that was not hot and heavy, but worked beautifully because it wasn't.

But more on that later.

Despite their differing worlds, "The X-Files" and "Millennium" are clearly cut from the same cloth. Frank Black could be viewed as an older and more weary version of Fox Mulder. The similarities are so obvious Scully sees a kindred spirit when Mulder gives his brief description of the man they will soon meet.

As Scully quickly realizes, Black and Mulder are two men united by a quest for the truth. And both have suffered huge losses along the way.

When we first see Frank Black, he is in a psychiatric ward, having apparently abandoned his battle with the Millennium group. A battle that cost him the life of his wife and the presence of his daughter. Seeing Black here is eerily similar to the Mulder we saw in "Amor Fati," a man so wounded by the consequences of his fight he was prepared to give it all up and abandon his true character.

While Mulder sought absolution, Black merely wanted to regain custody of his daughter. A practical reason to be certain, but one which ignored his most basic instinct.

Like Mulder, Black is a fighter at heart. So while he claims disinterest in the case Mulder and Scully bring him, he still provides a clue about the true nature of the necromaniac who is raising four former FBI agents from the dead. Armageddon is at hand and Black quickly becomes aware that, as Mulder did in "Amor Fati," he cannot ignore his true nature.

To do so would be a lie.

In "Amor Fati," Scully was the source of Mulder's strength to continue fighting. Here Mulder provides the same inner lift for Frank Black. Mulder's intuitive nature, perfectly in character here after his Jessica Fletcher-like leaps of deduction in "Hungry," light a fire under the somber Black that forces him to confront his destiny.

And save Mulder's life in the process. Save him for a start to the new century he will not soon forget.

But more on that later.

Of course, Mulder's life wasn't the only one on the line here. The Millennium's plan to have the dawn of the new century result in Armageddon would have wiped us all off the face of the earth. Again, we see the link between Mulder and Black as both men have been forced to weigh the grave nature of the battles they are waging.

It goes beyond personal sacrifices. It involves the sacrifices of millions. Given that, it's easy to see why Mulder was willing to give it all up for a dreamscape home in the 'burbs and Black just wants to sit in front of the tube watching college football.

Scully, meanwhile, is tested as well. Religious symbolism was everywhere here and Scully's shaky faith was evident in her question to Black about who will ultimately prevail, good or evil. That simple question provided a deeper look at the inner turmoil she has been battling since unearthing a ship from another world in "Biogenesis."

It was a question Scully probably would never have considered before, given her roots in Catholicism. But given how dramatically her belief system has been altered, it is only natural that she question this most personal aspect of her being now. For Scully, nothing is sacred anymore.

Especially after you've been attacked by an undead state trooper with a nasty overbite.

Given the fact I never saw an episode of "Millennium," I wasn't sure what to expect here. While the exposition of Black's history and the Millennium's beliefs may have run long for fans of that departed show, I found it was integrated seamlessly into this episode. We were given enough insight to follow things along on this dark journey toward the possible end of man.

The mood of that show melded perfectly with the tone of "The X-Files." Rarely has "The X-Files" treaded in such somber territory, but one of the show's strengths is that it often lives in the shadows. Entire episodes often permeate with the idea that something dangerous lies in the darkness just around the corner.

"Millennium" draws its life force from that idea. Mulder's descent into the basement was a dimly lit descent into hell where four undead FBI agents were waiting to emerge from the ground and possibly feast upon his very soul.

Ultimately, Scully comes to the rescue and saves both of our idealized heroes with a well-placed bullet in the brain (in a nice nod to George Romero, the zombies are impervious to everything except gunshots to the head). The world is safe. Armageddon is avoided. Black is reunited with his daughter and Dick Clark begins his countdown to the dawn of a new century.

5

4

3

2

1 ...

All of which gives Mulder an idea.

An idea he has clearly been pondering for some time. Ever since a moment in his hallway and a bedside declaration from a hospital bed not long ago.

So as the year 2000 commences, he gazes (yes, gazes) at Scully who is watching intently as lovers embrace on television to celebrate the dawn of a new year. Sensing Mulder's gaze she turns and Mulder leans in for their first kiss. The attempt is bold, but his execution is done lightly, gently.

Like a nervous boy making the first move on a date with his beloved, Mulder is uncertain what will result from this first meeting of the lips. He even verbalizes his uncertainty after pulling away.

"The world didn't end."

No it didn't and Mulder is clearly relieved. The world did not come to an end. It might have if Scully had rejected the advance, if she had pushed Mulder away without any hint of reciprocation. But she did not. She returned his tender kiss and did so in a similar manner, lightly, with perhaps a question on her lips as well about the bold step they both were making.

This wasn't a steamy, rip your clothes off and get after it type of kiss. And that's the reason why it worked so well.

A first kiss between these two people would not have been filled with such unbridled lust. It would be uncertain, perhaps even trembling as both seek to move down a path they had been studying for some time but were uncertain how quickly the journey should take. Or begin.

That is why the kiss worked so well. The beauty lied in its simplicity, in the quiet way it expressed so much.

It was the first step on a new path in an episode filled with new beginnings. For Frank Black, that meant averting Armageddon and being reunited with his daughter. For the world, it meant the start a new millennium. And for Mulder and Scully, it meant a tender kiss that emphasized the bond they share rather than the lust they may feel.

"RUSH"

Teen angst is a bitch. Then again, so is growing old. At least for some people.

Something tells me Fox Mulder is feeling the effects of age. The knowledge that some of the joys and passions of youth are in his past with no hope of reclaiming them. For some folks, that's a painful reality to deal with. And I have a feeling Mulder is one of those people.

He's just not the spry young FBI agent he used to be.

We get that sense in "Rush," a rather enjoyable episode that rises above its premise (teens find mysterious "whateveritis" that gives them the power to move faster than light and eliminate all those who try to put them down) because of the wonderful character insights we are afforded.

The teen angst angle is supplied by a trio of high schoolers, Max, Chastity and Tony. Max is the first to stumble upon a cave (in typical X-Files fashion, the forest is a mysterious place where danger lies) which gives him the power to move faster than light, pack a Ruthian-sized wallop and wipe out a nosy deputy and a no-nonsense teacher. He lures the wide-eyed Tony to the dark side as well although Tony is more interested in blonde bombshell Chastity.

Of course, the power comes at great cost. Since Max's body is unprepared to handle the newfound speed, it will ultimately give out if he continues to feed on his new drug (the "Just Say No" angle is hard to miss here).

Ultimately, Tony stops Max from killing his father, Chastity kills Max and sacrifices herself (in a terrific special effects scene), perhaps sensing the drug was about to wear off on her as well and she could not bear a return to normalcy. She dies in Tony's arms and at the end, his "speed" is also gone as he stares longingly at a clock on a hospital wall, possibly lamenting the fact he too cannot go back to what he once briefly had.

All that was fine, but it was the nuts and bolts of the episode. That wasn't what hooked me. I'm a character junkie and we were given loads of it here.

We see it with writer David Amann's nice look at youth vs. ummm ...... let's call it "experience." Almost every time Mulder and Scully turn around, they're reminded how old and out of touch they are, no matter how fresh Mulder's pop culture references seem to be.

First of all, they spend an entire episode hanging around a high school and that's gotta be tough. All that youth, all those memories of yesteryear when the bodies were tight and the future limitless. I know what it's like for me to go into some nightclubs and see college kids whoopin' it up and having the kind of fun I used to have "back in the day."

It ain't always easy, let me tell you.

And it ain't easy being Mulder and Scully. Even though they're out of touch with the kids at Adams High, they are at perfect ease with one another.

The first "post kiss" episode sees them interacting in a winning and intimate way. They spent the episode together (always a plus) and there was a closeness and ease with which they worked together, discussing possibilities that was enjoyable to watch.

I especially liked the Scully we saw here, giving Mulder an unspoken "Don't do that again mister" after he gives Chastity a onceover in the police station (more Alpha behavior?), her flirtatious way of asking Mulder to let them please go interview some humans instead of calling 1-800-Ghostbusters and her little pout after Mulder's "Maybe we're too old" comment.

All of that suggested a bond of intimacy between these two without resorting to the type of over the top sentimentalism some people seem to believe will be the consequences of a Mulder-Scully coupling.

And we get to see my favorite theme of Season 6 enhanced greatly in Season 7, Scully's newfound willingness to bend her belief system. She doesn't buy into Mulder's poltergeist theory right away, but by the end, she's not turning a blind eye to his ideas, even suggesting his theory is "worth checking out." Of course, somebody puts a stop to that by filling that little cave in the woods with concrete, but it's nice to know Scully's willing to give it a shot just for him.

These are all nice touches and a way to lift an episode higher in my estimation.

A few other little touches I enjoyed:

Max telling Scully she must've been a "Betty back in the day" only to have Scully wonder what a Betty is. The look on Scully's face when Chuck talks about SCAG (one can only assume what she thought THAT must mean). Nice reference to the pilot with Mulder talking about the vortex in Oregon. And I especially liked the moment when the sheriff is checking out his son's room and looks under a pillow as if the solution to the mystery would be found there.

I know when I was a kid, that's where I always hid stuff I didn't want my parents to see.

A little can often go a long way. And in "Rush," we had a lot of little moments that enabled the episode to rise above its satisfactory premise.

"Rush" was sufficiently creepy and had some wonderful character interaction between Mulder and Scully. And that helped make it a very enjoyable entry into what is quickly becoming a very enjoyable season.

"THE GOLDBERG VARIATION"

Cute was not something "The X-Files" did all that well last season in my opinion. I think about the "Dreamlands" episodes or the Screaming Scully of "How The Ghosts Stole Christmas," moments that continue to make me cringe.

One notable cheery exception, though, was the marvelous "The Rain King." With its swaying Mulder and Scully, its fairytale-like ending and tremendous Mulder and Scully subtext, Jeff Bell's "The Rain King" was quite simply one of the joys of season six.

So it hardly came as a surprise to me that I enjoyed Bell's "The Goldberg Variation" entry for Season 7. It was cute, light-hearted, a little kooky with a happy ending to boot. Given how dark and ominous "The X-Files" can be, a little cheerfulness can go an awful long way.

Nearly everything about this episode practically screamed light-hearted. Yes, there were some serious moments to be certain (Weems being tossed from the high-rise was no laughing matter nor was young Richie's grave condition). But under the surface everything was very clear cut and we were made to feel as if everything would turn out all right in the end.

Henry was just a regular guy who believed he was cursed to have the good fortune of having everything go his way. He may have been a bit of a schmoe (is anybody really that naïve about how to conduct themselves during a card game with a room full of mobsters?). But he had a big heart as evidenced by his desire to save Richie, his young neighbor who was in desperate need of a liver transplant.

In order to do that, he runs afoul of a nasty Chicago gangster who sends hitmen to Henry's apartment to try and even the score after Henry survived his free fall. But these guys have worse luck than the red shirts on "Star Trek." Each time one of them shows up, he meets his demise thanks to Henry's uncanny ability to survive any potential catastrophe.

Mulder and Scully stumble into this situation thanks to Mulder's inquiring mind about how a man could survive the nasty fall Henry is subjected to in the teaser. And isn't it interesting that Scully's remark "Maybe he was lucky" proves to actually be the solution to the mystery? She says it in jest only to discover later that she was right on the mark.

Then again, perhaps it was no coincidence that they are the ones to investigate the matter further. Everything around Henry happens for a reason so perhaps Mulder and Scully were *meant* to find Henry's missing eye, track him down and become a part of Weems' luck-infested life.

Like every piece in one of Henry's gadgets, everything has a cause and effect. So perhaps Mulder and Scully are the cause for Henry's good luck to have the effect of finally rubbing off on someone else. In this case Richie, who gets the transplant he needs thanks to the very gangster who was trying to off Henry.

Not only that, but they were invested in this situation. Mulder clearly was fascinated by Henry and Scully's maternal instincts were brought out in a nice subtle manner during her bedside talk with Richie. Given how we've seen her respond to other children in peril, it's hardly surprising that she stayed by Richie's bedside in the hospital when Mulder tested his own luck by trying to track down Henry at the end.

This was hardly a perfect episode. Gangster Joe's omnipotent knowledge that he could get to Henry by kidnapping Maggie was a plot hole large enough to drive a semi through.

But running throughout the episode was this sense of …….. let's call it "feel good." Everything was kept in a very black-and-white basis (the good guys were good, the bad guys were bad and we even had a dying little boy). The fact everything was spelled out rather clearly, however, worked in this episode's favor, not against it.

We knew the good guys would win, the bad guys would die and the little boy would be saved because dammit, that's what happens to good guys and bad guys and dying little boys. It wasn't so much the resolution that mattered here, but the journey we took to get there.

And this journey was an enjoyable one.

Among the finer points was the continuing evolution of the Mulder/Scully dynamic. Mulder had some fun moments. His inability to master the finer art of plumbing and his flinching when Henry popped his eye back in were priceless as was his attempt at a Bruce Lee impression during his run-through with Scully about how "The Animal" may have met his demise.

The looser Scully was in evidence too. As was the case with "Rush," I think we can attribute this to her post-kiss state of mind. Not only does she have a bit of a carefree attitude with Mulder early on (I not only liked her attempt to suppress a giggle during Mulder's plumbing mishap, but also the way she playfully shines the flashlight in his face when he discusses his theory about Henry). But most of all, I really enjoyed her four-word aside to Richie: "I like baseball too."

Hmmm, I wonder when her newfound interest in that sport started?

It's all contributing to an evolution of this relationship that has been dead-on since the start of the season. By not trying to do too much, 1013 is doing it perfectly. Quite often, it's the little things that go a long way and we continue to see that here with Mulder and Scully.

A joke, a shared smile, a tuck of a tie, they all define a relationship that has progressed greatly in Season 7. "The Goldberg Variation" was obviously not about the Mulder/Scully dynamic, but by adding a few subtle touches, we continue to see the evolution of their relationship in conjunction with the case at hand.

Nicely done.

As was "The Goldberg Variation." More proof that season seven is off to a very good start and that "The X-Files" needn't always be about gloom and doom to get the job done.

"ORISON"

In the world of "The X-Files," pure evil has been best represented by one Donnie Pfaster. But in typical "X-Files" fashion, the evil we see is not easily defined.

Is Pfaster a twisted man driven by a murderous impulse? Or is he a demon in human form whose purpose is to bring terror and inflict pain on the women he preys upon?

We were left to ponder that during his first appearance five years ago in "Irresistible." Those questions affected Dana Scully most of all after she was abducted by Pfaster and came perilously close to death. Those are questions she must confront again when Pfaster escapes from prison and returns to find her in the disturbing and terrific "Orison."

When it comes to the paranormal, Mulder and Scully share equal roles trying to unearth the bizarre cases they are assigned. But when it comes to religion, that is almost exclusively the domain of Dana Scully. Her ongoing struggle to balance her religious views with her scientific approach has been one of the most fascinating subplots of her character throughout the series' run.

In "Orison," she again must confront her beliefs in God and the demons that may be sent to earth to defile all He has put into motion.

Having been raised a Catholic, I was taught that our lives, the decisions we make and the world we live in are generally broken down into black-and-white dimensions. Good is good and evil is evil. There is no middle ground.

Life, of course, is not that simple. There is more than black-and-white extremes. There is the muddling color of gray which permeates throughout our lives and makes the decisions we strive to make often that much more difficult to formulate.

"Orison" could have taken the basic Catholic belief and gone with it. Pfaster is evil. Scully and Mulder are good and thus good must somehow vanquish evil. But this episode dared to play in that muddling area of gray where all of us reside.

We see an apparent man of God, a figure of good. But appearances are deceiving as this man of God has a warped sense of what the Lord is asking him to do as he helps convicts escape only to bury them alive under the guise of religious judgment. Most importantly, we see Scully, another figure of good in our eyes, questioning the evil she carries within her.

The one constant is Pfaster. He is, as Scully mentions early on, "pure evil." We saw that in "Irresistible" and we see it again here.

One of my favorite scenes in "Irresistible" comes at the end. Scully is imprisoned in Pfaster's closet and when he opens the door, he morphs into other faces, including one of demon form. Is he a demon? Or was the terror Scully was feeling projecting itself into that moment?

We were left to ponder that for ourselves.

In "Orison," the evidence seems to suggest the demon Scully saw during that horrifying encounter may in fact be the true evil that is Donnie Pfaster. There are other signs as well.

A breeze awakens Scully with the camera settling on her Bible. Moments later, she glances at her clock to see the time registering the satanic 6:66. The clock strikes that demonic number again, both times coinciding with Pfaster's presence (first to signal his escape from prison and lastly his arrival into Scully's apartment).

In addition, we see Pfaster reveal what may be his true form to the reverend. A demon in front of him who ultimately kills the reverend and buries him alive in a grave that was meant for Pfaster. Is this the real Donnie Pfaster or again is it a terrifying hallucination, an attempt by an insane man to come to terms with someone he cannot even begin to comprehend fully?

Again, we are left to ponder that question for ourselves.

Given the religious overtones, it is only fitting that we are provided a final confrontation between good and evil. A violent struggle between Pfaster and Scully that leads to Scully again being imprisoned and forced to rely on her wits to escape. On the surface, this is the climactic battle between good and evil with good eventually triumphing when Scully disposes of Pfaster after Mulder has arrived to give help.

If only it were that simple. Once again, we have that muddling color of gray. The reality that there is no such thing as pure good no matter how much pure evil we see around us.

Scully, a figure of good, essentially commits murder. She steps in front of Pfaster and simply pulls the trigger. Could her action be viewed as justified? Perhaps since Pfaster was ignoring Mulder's demand to surrender though he was not attacking either of them. There's also the fact that Pfaster was planning to kill Scully and would have, as Mulder points out, killed again.

So a case could be made that she acted in self-defense.

The underlying question throughout, however, is whether Scully was acting as a messenger of God, an instrument of His will to dispose of an evil presence that was poisoning the world He created. We have seen this before with Scully, subtle signs that she has a greater purpose, a higher calling perhaps.

We see it again here as she wonders whether the coincidences she comes into contact with are something more. Perhaps signs from above that she has somehow been chosen for a task she has yet to understand. It could very well be her task was to put an end to Pfaster's depraved life.

Still, there is no escaping the muddling color of gray, the question that perhaps she was not chosen to do His bidding. And if that were not the case, what had she just done? Killed a man in cold blood? No matter how vile a creature he was, there is no ignoring what she had done.

If she was able to commit such an action, what does that say about the evil that may reside somewhere within her? Fascinating questions. Fascinating character study. Incredible episode.

"The X-Files" has always thrived in the darkness, in the shadows where evil lurks around the corner waiting to pounce. That was literally the case in "Orison" as Pfaster waits in Scully's closet, watching her every move. And that is one reason why this episode worked so well.

Unlike the disappointing "Pusher" sequel, "Kitsunegari," this wasn't so much a sequel as a continuation of the horror we first witnessed in "Irresistible." There was a chill in the air from the outset until the sensational climax, done almost entirely without dialogue and ultimately in slow motion, where Pfaster attacks Scully before perishing at her hands.

Quite simply, that was one of the finest moments in "X-Files" history. From a visual and dramatic standpoint, it was superb and horrific.

"The X-Files" works best when we are afforded the opportunity to peak inside the character's minds, to try and understand their inner conflicts and the journeys they are engaged in. Scully went on a terrifying journey in "Orison" that left her questioning the essence of her being.

It was a journey filled with horror, mystery and self-analysis. It was also one of the most exhilarating journeys the seventh season has produced thus far.

"Scully's Decision"

In an attempt to continue exploring the question of "Would Dana kill?" and how should 1013 respond, I want to take viewers back a few seasons to "Pusher."

If you'll recall, at the end of that episode, Mulder was locked in a deadly psychological game with Modell. A game where his life, and Scully's, was hanging by a thread. The "game" comes to an end when Scully sees the fire alarm, races to pull it, snapping Mulder out of his "connection" with Modell and he fires point blank into Modell's head. Modell, it must be observed, was unarmed at the time of the shooting.

Now, how did everyone respond to Mulder's actions at the time? What did Scully say in her report? Do we know? Do we know how this apparent "cold-blooded" shooting affected Mulder? Well, the next episode was "Teso Dos Bichos" (gasp!) and three episodes later "Jose Chung" arrived. So we never did see any meaningful follow-up.

In retrospect, I think there are numerous parallels between what Mulder did in "Pusher" and what Scully does in "Orison."

Modell, like Donnie, was unarmed. Mulder, like Scully, was clearly pushed beyond his normal state of mind. That much is evident by how he keeps pulling the trigger over and over and over again before Scully removes the gun from his hand. Like Scully in "Orison," Mulder is no longer acting in accordance to his normal set of values.

But because he has been pushed beyond the brink, he acts in a very primal action, just as Scully does during her showdown with Donnie. I'm aware he had been kidnapped (in front of law enforcement witnesses), but he is the one with the gun at the end and so he could be viewed as being in charge (although those of us aware of Modell's ability know otherwise).

I think there is a strong parallel here. And if there is a parallel, we must assume that somehow Scully's report vindicated Mulder for his actions just as Mulder was willing to do for Scully at the end of "Orison." We must assume that because we never saw an instance where Mulder was reprimanded, placed on leave, etc ...

Since this is "The X-Files," both situations run beyond the legal norm. Modell's ability had already been refuted by one judge, so it is possible no court of law would believe Mulder was being "pushed" by Modell or accept that as even a remote possibility. Scully, though, would know it and would do everything in her power to make certain her report reflected Mulder's condition in order to alleviate his guilt.

In "Orison," we are given the possibility that Donnie is a demon (something I'm pretty sure wouldn't hold up very far in court) which is something Scully may or may not have believed at the time. She clearly seemed to be wondering whether she was working under the guidance of God. Aware of those feelings and her previous encounter with Donnie, Mulder would clearly want to go out of his way to make certain his report paints Scully in a favorable light and alleviate her guilt.

I'm not saying this makes what either of them did acceptable (Modell did not die, but was left seemingly at that time in an irreversible condition). But I do think it goes to show the depth of the Mulder and Scully relationship in times of stress and what one of them might do for the other.

The point being, there has been a tremendous uproar over Scully's action in "Orison." And yet, this show has tread such a path before with Mulder in "Pusher." I don't believe we saw an immediate about-face with how Mulder behaved after that episode and I don't believe the series suffered in any way because of such a potential omission.

So it is possible that even if Scully's actions are not revisited (although personally I hope it will be touched on again), the show could continue to finish out what may be its final season in fine fashion.

"Scully Kills"

Since "Orison" was such a provocative episode and made such a strong impact on so many people, myself included, I wanted to add a few additional thoughts about the climactic scene and how it pertains to the character of Dana Scully.

The point in question is Scully's action at the end of the episode and the death of Donnie Pfaster. Many people were outraged by what they believe was a totally out of character act. My contention is that her decision to pull the trigger and end Donnie's life was well within the boundaries of the character of Dana Scully.

And here's why. It was a completely human thing to do.

Scully has always represented the moral center of "The X-Files." No matter where Mulder and Scully tread, we could always depend on Scully to represent a strong moral code. She was the light that often shone through the haze Mulder had to fight through in his search for the truth.

She had virtue and that virtue strengthened her character and her resolve. Ultimately it strengthened both of them.

But, and this is important, she's also seen as a human being. One prone to frustration, anger and pain. I believe what we saw at the end of "Orison" was a human being pushed beyond the breaking point by a man (or demon depending on how literal you want to take the two demonic versions of Donnie we saw) hell bent on killing her. She reacted, in my opinion, not with rage but almost as if she was outside of herself, disconnected and acting with a sort of primal response to all she had been subjected to.

I found that to be very human and very real and that's what made the ending so powerful. We understood clearly the momentary breakdown, that split-second loss of control when she ceased to be the person she has fought so hard to be.

It doesn't make what she did right, but it certainly wasn't a difficult thing to understand. It was easy to comprehend because it was a very human reaction to an infinitely powerful moment of stress.

It could be argued that Donnie got what was coming to him (the stance Mulder seems to take) and it could even be argued that Scully was possibly possessed by another force which led her to commit such an act. As far as the former, there can be no question although that does not vindicate such an action. The latter is interesting and well within the scope of this show, although we were given precious little evidence to support such a theory so I'm not sure I gravitate toward that idea.

Both of those arguments essentially absolve Scully from responsibility. However, that does not fit in with the anguish we saw on her face at the end of the episode and the moral question she poses, which is why I believe her action was hers and hers alone.

Perhaps it wasn't so much a conscious decision as one that resulted from the pain (emotional and physical) that she had just endured. But I do believe the decision to pull the trigger rested with Scully. To think otherwise, I believe, is to lessen the self-realization about what she had just done.

Those feelings are essential in how that moment should be viewed. This is an action Scully will have to live with her entire life and she knows it. Many people have said they want to see this action revisited at some point as would I. But I would argue that in those final moments in her bedroom we were given every indication Scully has been altered and she will never forget what she had just done, even if we are not given a moment in the future in which she discusses it or refers to it.

The anguish is written all over her face and embodies her every movement at the end. Nothing Mulder says can soothe her or release her from the pain she feels. It is also clear that no punishment that could be given to her will ever equal the punishment she will bestow upon herself and the guilt she will feel for knowing that she violated everything she had previously stood for.

That, of course, seems to be what alienated so many people. Her decision seemingly runs contrary to the person she had been before. But I would disagree. I believe the virtuous Scully is still there and her moral code remains strong.

But it's important to remember that her character is human, a person prone to failure. And in that instant, with that decision she failed herself. She was human and the result was something she will have to live with for the rest of her life.

In that moment, she became aware of the evil that resided within her. We all carry such evil around within us, but most of us are able to bury it and maintain control. But when pushed far enough who's to say each of us wouldn't have reacted in precisely the same way?

That's what made that moment work so powerfully for me. It didn't betray Scully's character, it enhanced it by showing she isn't perfect, she's merely human. And the fact she was forced to confront that part of herself unsettled her and left her with questions she may have difficulty answering.

But they were very human questions and ones none of us are exempt from potentially asking someday.

The wonderful thing about "Orison" was that it showed how flawed our perception of "good" can be. We saw a flawed messenger of God. And we saw a flawed Dana Scully.

But there is absolutely nothing wrong with that. The beauty of "The X-Files" has always been that its two lead characters are far from perfect. They make mistakes, they fail, they cause pain to one another, to themselves and to those they come into contact with.

It isn't always easy to watch but it has always made them human and that has made it easy for all of us to connect with them. They haven't been portrayed as superheroes, but rather two very real people caught up in events greater than they are.

So while it is difficult to condone the actions of Dana Scully at the end of "Orison," it is easy to understand them. I dare say everyone sitting in front of their television sets watching that powerful and disturbing moment in this fascinating episode could understand the feelings that led to her pulling the trigger. The reason why seems clear.

They were perfectly human and perfectly in character. It's why the moment worked and why "Orison" was such an unforgettable episode.

"THE AMAZING MALEENI"

A thought struck me midway through "The Amazing Maleeni." After the intense debate and discussion that "Orison" generated, what would happen if "The X-Files" aired an episode that was so fundamentally escapist, it defied intense analysis?

More importantly, would that be so wrong?

I ask this question because "The Amazing Maleeni" was the purist form of entertainment imaginable. Good, clean, escapist fun. It wasn't weighed down in symbolism or overcome with psychological and moral questions. It merely wanted to entertain. And you know what? There's absolutely nothing wrong with that.

OK, at times, "The Amazing Maleeni" felt a little too much like an episode of "Murder, She Wrote." The ending, complete with flashbacks, left me wondering if I closed my eyes I'd suddenly hear Angela Lansbury explaining the big mystery instead of David Duchovny and Gillian Anderson.

By the way, is it me or is Mulder on the fast track to becoming the new millennium's version of Jessica Fletcher? He sure is figuring things out quickly these days, although it was fun to see the look in his eyes when he appeared to be wrong after Maleeni's brother revealed he had no legs.

"Oy" indeed.

Also, some of the sleight of hand was telegraphed a mile away. I'm no magician and I can't pull a rabbit out of my top hat (or anyone else's), but the opening look between Billy and Maleeni was a not so subtle clue that something was up with the two of them. That rather important plot point could have used more misdirection.

But on the whole, the episode held my interest and, hey, magic is fun to watch even if David Copperfield isn't. On that basis, "The Amazing Maleeni" did what it set out to do. It entertained me.

For my money, you can't beat an opening that has a man's head spinning around 360 degrees. Not to mention a head bouncing like a rubber ball off the ground after toppling out of a truck. And I have to admit, I liked how we kept seeing close-ups of the gory head and shoulders although I twinged when Scully stuck her fingers into the goo to examine the spirit gum that had attached the head to the shoulders.

But I'm a little nutty that way.

Will this be an episode I'll always remember and cherish in the years to come? Probably not. Then again, I'm not sure how much of a criticism that should really be of any episode.

Let me put it this way. "Citizen Kane" and "Animal House" are two completely different movies. Yet both films accomplished on their own terms everything they set out to do. So you could make an argument that "Animal

House" deserves as much praise for fulfilling its promise as "Citizen Kane" receives for fulfilling its own. Taken on their own terms, both are great films.

Ultimately, I believe that's the only way we can judge the entertainment we gravitate toward. Did it work within the limits it created for itself? Did it accomplish all it set out to do? Looking at "The Amazing Maleeni" from that perspective, I say the answer is yes.

Coming on the heels of the superb "Orison," the lighter tone of "The Amazing Maleeni" was a little jarring. Although the Mulder-Scully byplay was playful and fun to watch (Scully's bemused expression during Billy's parlor tricks and her final "trick" for Mulder were highlights), one can only hope we will be provided an episode at some point that refers to the events at the end of "Orison" and how they affected Dana Scully.

But I digress.

"The Amazing Maleeni" wasn't interested in heavy theological or moral issues or questions that ran to the heart of the two lead characters. It was one big magic trick designed to keep us guessing until the very end. The important question then was did I care?

Well, yeah, I did.

My heart wasn't racing and I wasn't sitting on the edge of my seat as Mulder and Scully unmasked our two magicians and their rather elementary plot (nothing magical about revenge now is there?). But it was fun to put the clues together to see what it all added up to.

And what was that? A light-hearted episode that won't make anyone forget "Momento Mori" anytime soon. Then again, that's not what it was trying to do, now was it?

"SIGNS AND WONDERS"

I have always been the type of person who admires the creative attempt, even if the attempt isn't a complete success. I think I'm the only person on the face of the earth who admired the attempt Prince made with "Under the Cherry Moon."

OK, I admit I have no idea what the hell he was attempting, but I'm pretty sure he was trying something. For that (and the song "Kiss") I'm grateful.

That is precisely the mindset I'm feeling after watching "Signs and Wonders." I admire the attempt to spook me, to offer up conflicting views of religion and righteousness, even if I'm not completely sure what the point of it all was.

I will not punish 1013 for failing, only failing to try.

There was a lot to like about this episode. Mulder's quip about some Catholic girls he knew being adept "snake handlers" made me chuckle, the juxtaposition of the two "God vomiting" scenes and the religious ideas behind them was nicely done. The snake attacks were unsettling (I especially liked the staple remover turning into a snake) although they were nothing compared to Gracie's "delivery."

That was possibly the most disturbing moment this show has produced since Sheriff Taylor was eliminated by the Peacock boys in "Home." And of course, there was the final shot where Mackey has a little "snack" after setting up shop in a new town. I got a kick out of that even if it owed quite a bit to "V" and "Sanguinarium" (where the killer doctor got away only to emerge elsewhere).

But what were we to make of it all? Were we supposed to believe that Mackey was the devil incarnate? Or was he just another demon in the seemingly growing line of "X-Files" demons? Was he just responsible for the murders or did he have a devilish say in Mulder's casual attire as well?

Maybe it's me, but Mulder looked like one of the guys from those Dockers ads. "For the FBI agent on the go who has to investigate some nasty snake killings before stopping for brunch at the club ......" At least Scully wore her trenchcoat.

And finally, were we supposed to read into O'Connor's ordering Scully to repent as an indication she is still dealing with her actions in "Orison?" Or would that be taking liberties with the story? I have to admit, I don't know.

I do know this. I spotted Mackey as the bad guy right away. The problem with an episode that has only three guest stars is that the first suspect we see is almost always a red herring. So even though Reverend O'Connor and his snake act sure looked like a good place to pin the blame for the two murders, that was too easy.

Guest star No. 2 was Gracie and there was no way she did it. She's the fragile waif who had no reason to kill her boyfriend and the old school marm with the really frightening hairdo. That eliminated her as a suspect.

That left Mackey as the snake handler of death. So even though I'm no Fox Mulder, I had a pretty good idea he was the bad guy rather early on in the episode.

I did think I might have been wrong about Mackey when he talked Gracie into trying to save O'Connor's life by having the doctors inject him with anti-snake venom. I'm a little confused as to why Mackey would try to save him. Doesn't make any sense to me.

The one moment I'm sure will be discussed heavily was Scully's confrontation with O'Connor's snakes. As I said before, I wonder if it's reading too much into the story to believe this was a subtle moment of continuity and a continuing exploration of how Scully's shooting of Donnie Pfaster has affected her.

There are some signs, however, that could have been the case.

Earlier, she grimaced a bit when Mackey mentioned how Jarred had walked away from the belief system in which he had been raised. It's possible the seed was planted there to suggest to us that Scully is continuing to question everything about herself after that moment with Pfaster in her apartment.

The scene where O'Connor tries to get her to repent at the hands of his snakes could be seen as a more obvious indication of this. So is O'Connor's suggestion to Mulder during the interrogation that Scully "could've learned something about herself" if Mulder hadn't intervened.

To be honest, I'd like to believe this was Jeffrey Bell's desire to briefly touch on the significant character moment Scully underwent at the end of "Orison." I'm hoping it was his attempt to play upon the most interesting theme of Season 7: Scully's lack of confidence in her belief system.

But even if that were true, again I ask, what were we supposed to make of it all?

I wanted to like this episode more than I ultimately did. I liked many of the pieces I was given but when it was over, I found that as enticing as many of them were, they didn't add up to a terrific episode. A decent one but wasn't quite as good as it could have been.

Again, though, I feel as if I cannot truly punish 1013 because I honestly feel there was an attempt to try something with "Signs and Wonders." The outcome wasn't as satisfying as I would have liked, but at least the effort was there.

For me anyway, that's something.

"SEIN UND ZEIT"

The essence of Fox Mulder is comprised of loss. It began with the loss of his innocence, stolen from him when his sister was abducted when he was a boy. His all-consuming quest to regain that missing piece of himself briefly cost him the person who had grown closest to him, led to the death of his father, the death of Scully's sister and Scully's brushes with death.

In "Sein Und Zeit," yet one more piece of Mulder is lost. His mother. The foremost theme of "Sein Und Zeit," is loss. The episode begins with a family losing their young daughter. Mulder insists he be given a chance to solve the disappearance of Amber Lynn LaPierre only to find that as he immerses himself into the case, he is drawn deeper into the sense of loss that was brought on by the abduction of his sister.

Teena Mulder sees the events on television and tries to reach out to her son, her sense of loss symbolized by a picture of her young children taken before Samantha was abducted. Failing to do that, she burns every last picture of her daughter, removing any trace of the loss she has lived with for so long.

And then she takes her own life.

Clinically, Teena Mulder's suicide is thought to be in response to an incurable disease she had been afflicted with. It is her response to the loss of who she perceives herself to be. But in reality, it appears to have been spurred forward by the disappearance of Amber Lynn.

Somehow, a connection is formed between Samantha's abduction, Amber Lynn's disappearance and the disappearance of another young child more than 10 years ago. Are the three linked? Is there a connection between Samantha, the two young children and the mysterious Santa Claus man who, like the killer in Thomas Harris' "Red Dragon," films each of his victims before abducting them?

Teena Mulder seems to have some answers, but takes her knowledge to the grave. Her suicide prompts Mulder to question his own sense of loss.

Throughout his life, he has been defined by one moment above all others: The night his sister was abducted. Were aliens the culprit or does the answer lie in a more earthbound reality? Mulder traveled this dark road once before in "Paper Hearts," and now he wanders down this path of uncertainty again.

Somehow, he believes that by uncovering the disappearance of Amber Lynn, he can regain that missing piece of himself. Instead, he begins to lose himself in the loss that has consumed him for so long.

"Sein Und Zeit" does an excellent job of portraying the psychological damage that loss provokes. We see it in the eyes of the three mothers who have lost children, including Teena Mulder whose response to the loss of her daughter has been to shut herself off emotionally from her son.

And we see it most clearly with Fox Mulder.

Rarely has Mulder been "spookier." His speech is faint, his entire manner lacks energy. The further he pushes himself with the LaPierre abduction, the wearier he becomes. It's almost as if the constant sense of loss he has operated under for so long has drained the life force from him. Instead of answers, there are only more riddles.

This has always been one of "The X-Files" greatest strengths. Its ability to create a multi-textered layer of riddles, stacked one upon each other with the truth nowhere to be found. There are no ready answers. The only truth is untruth.

The strength of this episode lies in its subtlety. It works more on a psychological level than a physical one, which is perfect since that is where the heaviest damage of loss is felt.

Nearly everyone in "Sein Und Zeit" is suffering in some way psychologically. As the episode progresses, their inner turmoil is exposed in painful detail. It culminates with an exhausted Mulder breaking down in Scully's arms, the pain of his loss too great for him to momentarily bear.

"Sein Und Zeit" has an almost lyrical quality, with one scene flowing to the next in a hypnotic fashion. As more layers to the story are peeled away, others are discovered. It's like a dream that moves effortlessly toward a nightmarish conclusion that could only be guessed upon.

Perhaps this is a physical manifestation of Fox Mulder's continuing dream, one from which he can never be awaken and one in which he knows nothing but torment. Where everything is symbolized by loss, rather than prosperity.

For those bemoaning the lack of quality turned out by "The X-Files" lately, this episode serves as a tremendous argument against that position. "Sein Und Zeit" played upon the most fundamental themes of this series but did so in a mature way that could only occur after seven years of character examination.

The effects of "The X-Files" being in its final season were most keenly felt with the demise of Teena Mulder. Fittingly, she leaves the same way she existed in the series, with more questions than answers.

The dignified way she carried herself was evident right until the end. She never allowed anyone insight into what prompted her actions. Even though she hoped her son would come to understand her final action, she offered no concrete reasons for what she had done, or what she had done to him before. She was detached right until the very end.

How very Teena of her.

And how perfectly in character this episode was. "Sein Und Zeit" not only served as a reminder of Fox Mulder's ongoing pain, it provided yet another clue that although its journey is nearing completion, "The X-Files" still knows how to make the ride an enjoyable one.

"CLOSURE"

A moment in time.

Much of Fox Mulder's life has been spent revolving around two moments in time. The first being the memory of when his sister, Samantha, was abducted 27 years ago. The second being the hopeful reunion with her that had driven him to unearth the mystery surrounding her disappearance.

Both moments haunted Mulder in entirely different ways. He was haunted by the knowledge of what had been taken from him coupled with the uncertainty of whether he could accept what had become of his sister. In "Closure," Mulder confronts both realities and finally receives that second moment in time he had hungered after for so long.

A final moment in time with his sister.

"Closure" was certainly that in terms of Samantha Mulder. The mystery was finally solved. We learned how Samantha lived with the CSM while someone (alien colonists or Consortium doctors) performed tests on her after her abduction, only to escape at the age of 14 before being teleported to some faraway land of dead souls when the CSM sought to reclaim what he believed rightfully belonged to him.

The truth was indeed out there. And the truth was Samantha had been dead for years. Long before her brother began his all-consuming quest to find her.

It was up to Mulder to finally accept that fact, confront that "end of the road" and escape the personal hell he had created for himself.

Those were the facts that were presented to us. But facts alone were not what drove Mulder in his quest. And facts alone did not distinguish "Closure" and the moment in time Mulder finally shared with his sister.

Instead, this episode was driven by love. The love Mulder had for his sister. The love Scully has for Mulder as she tries to protect him from sinking deeper into self-obsessed oblivion. And the love a sister had for a brother she could barely remember, but could never completely forget.

It was all there in "Closure," an episode that almost floated from start to finish. Like a dream that Mulder can finally wake up from and be at peace with.

Before I go any further, however, I must say one word about Mulder's hair during the videotaped hypnosis scene from 1989:

AHHHHHHHHHHHHHHHHHHHHHHHHHHHHHHHHHHHHHHHHHHHHHHHHH!

For Scully to watch that moment without cringing is as strong a sign of true love as anything I can think of. Now where was I?

Oh yes …

From a story-telling aspect, this episode worked best if some of the previous Samantha-related clues were forgotten. The moment in "End Game" when the Alien Bounty Hunter tells Mulder Sam is still alive or in "Two Fathers" when Cassandra Spender tells a similar tale run contrary to the information we are given here.

Some other moments also felt a bit flat. The CSM's scene with Scully served no purpose other than to allow William Davis and Gillian Anderson to finally act together (although I did like the CSM's line, "I had an operation" referencing the events of "Amor Fati"). And given the fact Samantha was under the CSM's care after her abduction, I'm not sure what the big clue Teena Mulder wanted to give her son or was giving him when she appeared as an apparition while he slept (a scene that also served no purpose since it was never referenced again).

Such moments do not endear us to 1013. But it is made easier to look past them because "Closure" provided the only logical conclusion of Samantha Mulder's fate. It was only right that Samantha be dead since Mulder's life had always been defined by what he has lost, not what he has found. I believe his ultimate peace lies with Scully, but for him to truly move on, he needed to accept the reality that his sister would never be returned to him.

With two simple words, he showed he is prepared to live for the future and no longer be embroiled in the past.

"I'm free."

The words came from Mulder's lips with an almost poetic quality to them. That was fitting because this episode was like a perfectly written poem. A dedication to the purity of unconditional love and a belief and acceptance of the truth no matter how painful that truth may be.

"I'm free."

Indeed he is. Free from the torment. Free from the pain of not knowing. All that was wiped away by one embrace with a sister who also received her one wish. A chance to look into the eyes of a brother she had never entirely forgotten.

Mulder wanted to believe in his truth for so long it had threatened to blind him from the actual truth that had always been around him. As the CSM observes, Mulder was ignorant to the truth because he could not bring himself to accept it. But finally given a chance to see the truth, he accepted it and is prepared to move on, free of the burden he had been dragging around with him for so long.

He was free of the pain because he knew Samantha was free from it as well.

The best episodes this season have been spent examining the issues of trust and belief in one's self and one another. Mulder was tested in "Amor Fati" only to be saved by his trust in Scully and his belief in her. Scully was tested in "Orison," shaken to the core as her belief system was turned upside down.

Here, Mulder is put to the test. But unlike Taylor at the end of "Planet of the Apes," Mulder is not driven mad by the reality of his existence when he arrives at the end of his road. Instead, he exits his own torment and moves beyond it. He no longer allows it to define him. It is merely a part of him now.

As I said, this was not a perfect episode. But its plusses greatly outweighed any missteps along the way and the ethereal quality of the final few moments lifted this episode up and made it one of the season's most memorable.

Mulder is indeed free and it will be very interesting to see how his newfound freedom affects him from here on out.

"X-COPS"

"With all due respect, what the **** are you talking about?"

I seriously doubt that's the first time Fox Mulder has been asked that question. But without a doubt, it's the first time he's been asked such a question in front of a television camera on an episode of "Cops."

For its 150th episode, "The X-Files" crossed paths with another Fox hit, "Cops," to produce one of the most entertaining episodes of the season. The two worlds merged together in an episode that was as rich as a Vulcan mind-meld and was, quite simply, 60 minutes of pure fun.

It's episodes like this that make me wince at the thought of this series coming to an end. The creativity that was on display made me realize how little there is in network television today and how blessed I am that a show such as this gives me a chance to thoroughly enjoy an hour of my life each week.

This isn't Hank Aaron or Willie Mays fading away toward the tail end of their illustrious careers. This is John Elway still going strong while grappling with the decision of whether to retire while he's still on top or come back for one more glorious season.

It was a tour de force "X-Files" style with a whole lotta "Cops" thrown in for fun. And boy was it ever fun.

All the usual "Cops" trademarks were on display in living videotaped color. From the viewer discretion opening to the hand-held cameras, to the earnest discussions between the cops and the camera to the blotted out faces, it was all there. Not to mention the bleeped out expletives which prompted one of the best lines of the episode from Mulder ("I don't think it's live, she just said f**k.")

Wonderful.

Even more wonderful was our introduction to Mulder and Scully. They are mistaken for prowlers after a deputy has his car overturned by some thing after he's been called to investigate a prowler. In the gritty world of downtown L.A., it's obvious from the get go these two don't quite fit in.

That much is obvious after Mulder explains his theory about how a werewolf is on the loose. We discover, however, that what Mulder initially believes is a werewolf is actually an entity which feeds on human fear to kill its victims.

It can be anything and anyone, from a werewolf to a Wasp Man, to Freddie Krueger, a murderous pimp or even the Hanta Virus (nice throwback to the film there). Whatever frightens you will be your undoing.

In typical "X-Files" fashion (and with a nod thrown in the direction of "The Blair Witch Project"), we never see the creature nor is a resolution to the mystery provided at the end. But the hows and whys are really secondary to the main elements here: How Mulder and Scully fit into the world of "Cops." That is where the true energy and beauty of this episode resided.

Mulder gravitates toward the camera immediately. The chance to have videotaped documentation of a paranormal encounter is too rich for him to pass up. He is so relaxed he is soon talking to the camera, explaining his thought process as they try to find the murderous creature of the night (which prompts Scully to ask at one point, "Are you talking to me?"). Mulder is in heaven as he gets a chance to explain his theories and the reasons behind them to a non-judgmental audience.

Scully, more endearingly, wants no part of being on TV. From hiding behind the door of a police van to avoid the camera to eventually slamming the door on a pair of frightened cameramen at the end ("I hate you guys"), she has no desire to have her every move videotaped although she does mug beautifully during the autopsy scene to serve a reminder that "The FBI has nothing to hide."

This is all perfect stuff. Mulder, never once afraid of how wild his ideas appear, just goes right on rattling them off without a care about who's listening or watching. The more practical Scully is more worried about how this will look, trying to make Mulder sound more professional in front of the camera and going so far as to call Skinner to tell him what's going on.

I've always had a feeling Scully was the good girl in the front of the class who ratted out the other kids for misbehaving when the teacher left the room. Oh well, nobody's perfect.

Not only did this episode owe a debt to "Cops" but also to the magic of "The Blair Witch Project" especially in the final moments when Mulder and Scully enter a deserted house with a screaming man and an unseen monster on the loose. But what "X-Cops" did so well was take the cinema verte style utilized by "Cops" and "The Blair Witch Project" and integrate it in perfect "X-Files" fashion.

We're witness to Mulder's off-the-wall hunches, some fine Mulder-Scully byplay, a Scully autopsy and a wonderful character moment where Mulder bonds with the deputy whose afraid to be branded as crazy by his peers, something Mulder obviously can relate to. All shot in "Cops" fashion but clearly with the feel of "The X-Files."

And I haven't even mentioned Steve and Edy yet. How nice to see another couple contrasted against the relationship Mulder and Scully enjoy, an ongoing theme in Season 6. Here it is cloaked in a more humorous way but the parallels are still there - bickering, a fear of abandonment and the emptiness of loss but at the heart, a genuine love for one another that knows no bounds.

Sound familiar?

"X-Cops" had a lot going for it. It had a creativity and an energy about it that most shows in their seventh season can only dream of conjuring forth. But most of all, it was fun. A whole lotta fun.

I've never been a die-hard fan of "Cops," but an episode like this might make me tune in a bit more often. Provided my favorite FBI agents are somewhere in the mix.

"FIRST PERSON SHOOTER"

I have to admit, I never played Cowboys and Indians as a kid. It never really interested me. If I had, I probably would've been an Indian because I really loved Uncas in "The Last of the Mohicans."

I did have a G.I. Joe (with the Kung-Fu grip) but even playing little war games never held my interest for long. Instead I dove into a world of sports and movies, "Star Trek" and "Kolchak The Night Stalker." Those confrontations and the opportunities they presented, both real and imagined, were more to my liking.

Perhaps that's why, as an adult, I can't bring myself to embrace the computer game mentality. I know people who've played "Doom" or "Tomb Raider" or any number of other games where the whole idea seems to be to unleash as much computerized chaos as possible in a specific amount of time, but I can't seem to share their enthusiasm to play their games.

I'm not as narrow-minded as Scully when it comes to their relevance, however.

In "First Person Shooter," she frowns upon such things. She views them merely as an excuse for men to be boys, to whip out their guns (Freud would've loved this episode which was ripe with phallic symbols) and blast away the enemy and ogle an artificially-generated, vivacious women they otherwise would have no opportunity to snare in their lifetimes.

But that's where I depart from Scully. I believe in the power of the imagination, of having a place where you can allow yourself the freedom to be someone you're not or give yourself the opportunity to explore portions of your personality you might not otherwise realize.

Having said that, I do not believe a video game can lead anyone to commit an action they do not already have within their being to commit. No video game ever killed someone. It's the person who must accept responsibility rather than trying to absolve themselves by pointing the finger elsewhere.

These are interesting ideas worthy of debate. Unfortunately, one of the failings of "First Person Shooter" is that it had an opportunity to expound upon such themes and really take a look at the dynamic of the effects of computer games in a paranormal setting.

Instead, it played it safe, preferring to hint at them (sometimes seriously, oftentimes with a wink) and present a simple story about a computer game which takes control of itself and destroys anyone who wanders into it.

In that regard, "FPS" is an episode that is too superficial for its own good. It holds the promise of more, but ultimately isn't as enthralling as it could have been. Or should have been.

This was an episode of moments for me rather than a sustained whole. And in the end I found myself smiling from time to time, but not feeling very satisfied.

For example, I chuckled at Scully's line of "No picking on a girl" at the precise moment Mulder is getting his ass kicked by one while trapped in the virtual game. The overt ogling of Ms. Afterglow (complete with a "Basic Instinct" moment) was too obvious though I did enjoy Scully's bemused look as Mulder practically fell out of his chair watching her leave the room.

I wasn't quite as amused, however, when The Lone Gunmen yelled "You go girl" when Scully was blasting away to save Mulder's life. Instead, I cringed at the juvenile quality of the line. Perhaps that's the rub with this episode. Perhaps you had to be a kid to really enjoy it.

I can just see a group of high school kids talking about it tomorrow in front of their lockers:

"Dude, you should've seen it. There was this really hot babe in a thong (she was sooooo hot, dude) and she's got this .... uhhhhh .... sword and she's killing guys in this virtual computer game. She chopped off one guy's hands and there was blood and everything. So then Mulder goes in and he's wearing these funky shades (I've got to get me some. They ruled.) but when he gets in the game she starts kickin' his ass.

"It was so cool.

"And then Scully comes in (I totally dig her) with this really really really (I mean really) big gun and blasts the thong chick away. But she keeps coming back (she looked awesome in her western outfit) and there's like six of her and she's ..... ummmmmm ... straddling a tank and Scully's blasting away and then somebody pulls the plug and everything's OK and then Mulder says "Now THAT's entertainment."

"It was sooooo cool."

Maybe if I look at "FPS" on that level I would've enjoyed it more. Instead, I was hoping for more from writers William Gibson and Tom Maddox, given how fascinating I found their Season 5 entry "Kill Switch."

That episode was ripe with characters that sucked me in from the get go. From Invisigoth to the Artificial Intelligence which created two of the more memorable moments in the series run: Mulder comforted by Nurse Nancy after having his arms and legs hacked off and Kung-Fu Scully coming in to save the day.

There was a sense of fun and plenty of subtext to go with the seriousness in that episode that was lacking here. This was more along the lines of: "Check out Mulder's shades and did you see the babe in the thong? She was soooo hot." That may work for some people, but it's not enough to justify an episode of merit in my book.

I don't claim to know the first thing about computers games so I'm not sure how technically accurate any of this was. But I honestly wouldn't care if there was something of substance here for me to latch onto. Instead, it was like a pale version of "Kill Switch." Many of the same elements were in place without the payoff.

We had the sexy mysterious babe, Mulder caught up in a computer-generated world of pain and another round of Bad Ass Scully. But this time it fell flat and I found myself waiting for someone to hit the kill switch as Scully kept firing away at "The Goddess" who wouldn't die.

Yawn.

Somewhere buried deep within "First Person Shooter" was an episode that I would've really enjoyed. I just wish someone had dug a little deeper and cleared away a lot of the muck so that I could've seen it.

"THEEF"

Before this season began, I speculated that one of the most interesting themes for this season would be how Scully would begin to process all of the information she had been exposed to over the years. From paranormal phenomena to the existence of extraterrestrial life, it was impossible for her to turn a blind eye any longer to what she had seen so many times before.

In the past, she has been figuratively blinded to the realities around her. In "Theef" she is literally blinded to the truth behind Orel Peattie's power. But it is that temporary loss of eyesight which ultimately opens her eyes again to the truths that are out there.

In the earliest episodes of this season, it was clear Scully's belief system had been shattered. In many ways, she was forced to reconstruct her belief system from scratch to coincide with the information she had begun to process. It came to a head in "Orison," when Scully was pushed beyond the brink of her normal sense of self to commit an action that struck at the core of her very being.

Since then, the instances of Scully's reconstruction have been few and far between. While "Theef," doesn't set out to explore that theme as its central focus, once again we are exposed to a Dana Scully who is no longer quick to reject what she previously would not bring herself to accept.

We see that early on when she is willing to go along with Mulder's belief that some form of witchcraft may be involved with the death of Dr. Wieder's father-in-law. Although her initial autopsy finding appears to refute that idea, Mulder (naturally) continues to press his supernatural-based theory.

Instead of standing opposed to what Mulder believes, Scully stands beside him as the body count mounts, not a firm believer in what Mulder says is the cause, but not willing to totally dismiss it either.

This reaches a climax at the end of the episode when Scully is literally blinded to the events of the paranormal. Peattie's voodoo doll has rendered her helpless, much the same way her belief in science blinded her to the cause of why Mulder's life was at stake. Once again, she is stumbling about in the dark, unable to turn to the strengths she had spent so long building up within herself.

In "Sixth Extinction" and "Amor Fati," she was shaken to the core, unable to resolve her dilemma within the framework of the truths she had built within herself. Here her scientific knowledge fails her again in the face of something she cannot comprehend.

Fittingly, it is Mulder who restores her sight by removing the pins from the doll. Not only does that restore Scully's sight in time to shoot down Peattie, it also opens her eyes again to the realities beyond the realm of her own truths.

Throughout this episode, we are meant to see Wieder and Scully as parallel medical figures. It is their belief systems that are put to the test by Peattie's charmed powers.

Peattie has the simplest of motives - revenge. He believed Wieder murdered his daughter and sets out to extract revenge.

Scully the practical doctor knew what Wieder had done within the realm of modern medicine. Peattie's daughter was dying and while the morphine Wieder used cut short her life, it also put an end to her suffering.

Wieder did what his medical training had taught him to do. That is a decision Scully admits to Mulder she would have made as well.

But was it the only alternative? Was that steadfast belief in modern science the only possible choice?

Having been exposed to so much, seen so much and now having been literally blinded by something she not long ago would have scoffed at, Scully wonders about the possibilities beyond her frame of reference. As she looks down at Peattie in the hospital bed, she wonders if perhaps, just perhaps, there would have been a way to save the girl's life that would run contrary to everything she had been taught.

She cannot bring herself to verbalize this question. But her comprehension is left hanging in the air for Mulder to acknowledge after she leaves the room.

"You do keep me guessing," he says quietly after she's gone.

That one line served as joke between Mulder and Scully early in the episode, but carried added resonance at the end. For Scully, it is all about guessing at this point in her life because the truths she once clung to no longer provide her with the comfort she seeks.

Scully's belief system was not at the heart of this episode. But I felt that theme tugging at me from start to finish.

In many ways, this was a standard revenge story integrated with the theme of modern medicine failing in the face of nature and its magical powers. We see Wieder the well-educated doctor of the year, with all his medical knowledge, failing to save those around him while Peattie's home-cooked remedy's does wonders for the nosy landlady with the aching back.

Dr. Scully is not on trial here. Dr. Wieder is. But the idea that Scully is linked with Wieder in a struggle against Peattie is never far from thought.

On a somewhat-related note, I caught "Fight the Future" this weekend and marveled again at how that story was, at its heart, a love story about Mulder and Scully's. Their bond and the strength they both draw from it was the centerpiece of that wonderful film.

Watching it again made me realize I've missed some of that in recent episodes - no matter how much I have enjoyed most of them. And while it wasn't prominently on display in "Theef," I felt that sense of union here again for the first time in a while.

There was a playful tone between Mulder and Scully early that was nice to see. And the way Mulder spoke that final line, "You do keep me guessing," was filled with a tenderness that brought back memories of his bedside declaration in "Triangle." It was nice to see (and hear) that again and I hope to see (and hear) more of it in the episodes to come.

"Theef" wasn't a perfect episode. Voodoo isn't a terribly original idea and a few plot points were a bit hard to forgive (Peattie must have a pretty good sense of direction to find the cabin where Scully had holed up with Wieder and his daughter; and wasn't it convenient how he left Scully's voodoo doll out in plain site for Mulder to find?).

But there's nothing wrong with a little modern medicine vs. practical magic confrontation. And I definitely enjoyed how Scully had her envelope pushed again. I enjoyed the fact that, at the end, we see her questioning herself once again and I liked the way Mulder took it in with that one perfect line.

"You do keep me guessing."

She most certainly does.

"EN AMI"

Somewhere in the midst of lies, there is typically a kernel of truth. But how do we know where to find that truth when all we have been shown are nothing but lies?

That has been one of the central themes of "The X-Files" and no one represents that idea more than the Cigarette Smoking Man. Each deliciously wrapped lie he delivers contains a nugget of truth, a glimmer of something more and that is what makes his lies all the more tantalizing.

For years, he has tormented and teased Mulder with them. But in "En Ami," he turns his attention for the first time to Dana Scully. Her wall of skepticism is broken down by him and it is her willingness to believe that is put to the test and ultimately turned against her - much the same way Mulder's has been for years.

The CSM comes to Scully claiming he wants absolution for his sins of the past. He claims to be dying from a brain operation (more continuity with the CSM in regards to his actions in "Amor Fati") and wants one final chance to make things right, to leave a positive mark on the world he has tried for so long to corrupt.

What he dangles in front of Scully is the potential cure for not only cancer, but for all human diseases. Scully the doctor is understandably drawn to this possibility, but so is Scully the human being, the woman who was once inflicted with a cancer that the CSM (as he so eagerly tells her) cured her of.

The CSM's desire to find a sense of absolution for his sins is reminiscent of Michael Corleone's quest in "The Godfather 3." What Corleone learned in that film was that there is no escape. You can run from your past, but you can truly never hide. The same holds true with the CSM, although it comes with a twist.

We see him tossing the CD with the alien science into the lake. However, that action comes after he has killed the man who brought that information to

Scully. The CSM's deal with Scully was merely another web of deceit he orchestrated. It was another means to an end, although at the end, the monster who created the web of lies is torn by his actions.

The human element. That is what made this episode so rewarding for me.

Although their writing styles are quite different, William B. Davis, like David Duchovny before him, drew the strength of his script from matters of the heart. They also both show a penchant for good humor (evidenced by Mulder's line "Do you know how many people have *died* in that apartment?" after Scully's landlord mentions how comforting it is to have an FBI agent in the building).

Like Duchovny, Davis is obviously well-versed with the characters he is working with. And like Duchovny, he takes that knowledge and builds upon it. We have seen for some time an attempt to humanize the CSM (going so far last season as to put an actual name on the monster) and Davis takes that theme one step further.

He gains Scully's trust by appealing to the warmth of her heart. He strips away her impression of him as a cold-blooded killer by drawing upon the fundamentally human idea that he would truly like to do something good, to leave something positive behind in the midst of all the chaos he created.

For a woman whose compassion and religious beliefs often overrides her skepticism, playing upon the idea of absolution is precisely the best way to play Dana Scully if you need to win her trust. She sees a dying man in front of her and believes there really is someone there who wants to absolve himself of his evil.

Even though we learn that it was all just a ruse to get his hands on that CD, we also see there is a conflict within the CSM as he tosses that CD into the lake. The monster is truly a man and the man may be trying to reconcile the years of being a monster.

By showing us his human side, the CSM becomes that much more villainous. It is easy to picture a purely evil monster with no sense of conscience committing the actions we have seen him commit. But to know there has always been a shred of humanity within him makes the realization of his nature all the more terrifying.

The human being that is Dana Scully is also on display in wondrous living color. We see her through the CSM's eyes. Professional and stern in her approach but also a beautiful, radiant, angelic figure of good. As we see her arrive at dinner in the dress the CSM bought for her, it is easy to see why he has turned his attention away from Mulder and onto her.

The only thing we're left wondering is what took him so long.

Through the CSM's eyes we see through Scully's protective wall of strength and see the compassion in heart and the willingness to trust a monster if it means serving a greater good. Such trust is not easily won, however, since Scully's devotion to Mulder always comes first.

That is evident as she plants a microphone on herself so that Mulder will not only hear what is transpiring but also be with her in spirit on this journey into darkness. By the way, I think it says something about Scully's social life that she puts a hidden microphone in her bra. Was that the one location she assumes no man will check?

Just wondering.

Scully's union with Mulder is nicely revealed in two other moments. First, when the CSM notes how she is drawn to powerful men, is willing to die for Mulder but cannot bring herself to love him. Although Scully dismisses such talk as pop psychiatry, her wince at the CSM's words reveal they found their way to her heart.

Her reaction displays the inner conflict Scully continues to endure when it pertains to Mulder. She is so willing to trust him, go to the ends of the earth to save him and even die for him, but she remains unable to truly open her heart up to him.

It is so much easier for Scully to be scientific. But her deep-rooted devotion to a logical way of thinking prevents her from truly being one with the man she so clearly loves.

Playing upon these themes shows us that Davis, like Duchovny, is also a shipper at heart. And both of them certainly know how to best present Gillian Anderson in a most alluring light.

The other scene where Scully's heart is stripped bare comes at the end, when she has returned to Mulder with the truth of what she has done. Knowing that she has, even momentarily, aligned herself with his most vile antagonist brings her pain, so much so you can see the ache in her eyes as she reaches out to Mulder with them - a glance he is too hurt to return.

Then again, considering how many times Mulder has ditched Scully maybe he shouldn't be pouting too much.

This wasn't an episode of action. Instead, it was more about reaction. Human reaction. The CSM's reaction to everything he has done. Scully's reaction to having her protective wall exposed and broken down. Even Mulder's reaction to being momentarily deceived by Scully.

These were all human emotions in an episode that struck at the heart of what it means to be human and how even the most vile perversions of humanity can somehow wage a battle to redeem themselves.

No matter how his act of subterfuge played itself out, the CSM is a man seeking some form of redemption. But since he has known nothing but evil for so long it is difficult for him to veer off his chosen path and find the peace he may be seeking.

His willingness to eliminate Cobra represents all the evil he has done before. His decision to throw the CD into the lake rather than have such alien knowledge find its way to vile hands suggests there is a human being who is trying to come to terms with all he has done.

The CSM uses Dana Scully because that is all he knows how to do. But just as Scully's humanity has saved Mulder many times before, here it shines a light on a part of the CSM he had buried within himself.

His own humanity.

In the end, that is what "The X-Files" has always been about. Humanity and the lengths we will all go to preserve it and draw strength from it.

"CHIMERA"

Question: When evaluating a particular piece of entertainment, how important is it to you to have some understanding of the behind-the-scenes mechanisms that went into the production? The answer may very well determine how much you enjoyed the latest "X-Files," offering, "Chimera."

I pose this question because this episode had a particular emptiness for me that lasted from the moment Mulder exited his porn palace stakeout with Scully until the final confrontation with the killer Swamp Thing housewife chick. The emptiness I felt can be summed up in three simple words:

No Dana Scully.

The reason for her absence is simple if you have an inclination for behind-the-scenes information. Gillian Anderson was allowed to essentially sit this one out to prepare her writing/directorial debut - the potentially-fascinating "all things."

That meant reducing her screen time to a minimum and placing the emphasis of "Chimera" on Mulder's investigative prowess. Knowing that made it easier for me to understand why Mulder and Scully had to be kept apart during "Chimera."

Unfortunately, that knowledge did not help me to enjoy the episode.

Now Mulder and Scully have been separated before and that hasn't automatically resulted in an episode of lesser quality. But here, I spent an entire 60 minutes longing to see them together, knowing there are so few opportunities left for that to occur.

For months, I've listened to numerous criticisms of the show's content in what is likely the final season for this wondrous series. I've heard people wondering why a certain episode had to be made, when there were supposedly far more important issues that should be addressed in the final season.

Each time I've heard such remarks, I've scoffed, saying the most important job this show has is to entertain us. Provided they do that, then I believe the powers that be have succeeded and I cannot ask for more.

But for the first time, I found myself longing for more because the series is coming to an end. I found myself wanting to see the type of interaction between Mulder and Scully that we will soon no longer be privy to enjoy.

I found myself saying, "We only have a few episodes left. Why do we have to have one where Mulder and Scully are apart?"

The knowledge of Gillian Anderson's pre-production schedule provided me little solace. I found myself longing for something this episode simply could not provide for reasons that were perfectly understandable.

Instead, what we got were a couple of hilarious phone conversations and another look at the seamier side of suburbia. Perhaps the idea was to correct everything that went wrong with "Arcadia."

Given how messy that episode was, no one should have bothered. I don't even think Steven Spielberg is up to that task.

At least "Arcadia" had Mulder and Scully playing house with engaging results. Here, we get a cheating sheriff and his wife whose jealousy over the fact he's bed-hopping on both sides of the tracks has manifested itself into some kind of Swamp Thing having a really bad hair day that attracts ravens but cannot bring itself to kill Mulder for no apparent reason other than the fact he's the star of the show and he's got to be on Letterman Tuesday night to talk about his new movie "Return To Me."

OK, at least the motivation for the Swamp Thing monster made more sense than the Garbage Thing monster in "Arcadia." But that's not exactly a rousing endorsement.

And did I mention no Scully?

Perhaps if this episode had some spark to it, the fact Mulder and Scully spent 60 minutes apart wouldn't have bothered me so much. But there was little here we haven't seen before.

The idea of stripping away suburban gloss and showing its frightening underbelly isn't unique. Not only did we see that idea examined in "Arcadia" last season, but "Terms of Endearment" as well.

And if one idea was to show how Mulder doesn't quite fit in with this environment. Well, "Dreamlands" spent the better part of two hours dwelling on that theme.

Maybe that's why Mulder appeared so bored by the proceedings he forgot to shave. Or maybe he was so mad the sheriff didn't have the Spice Channel he decided to pretend he was Sonny Crockett for a few days.

Compare his mannerisms here with the enthusiasm he displayed in "Terms of Endearment." There, he had a zest for his job and pounced on the case with high-voltage energy that drew me into the episode from the outset.

OK, he forgot a few things about his profiling background, but why quibble? Hey, everybody forgets a few things about the courses they took in college don't they? I mean, I know I took a calculus test once, but damn if I can remember what question No. 33 was.

In "Chimera," Mulder just went through the motions. He showed up, saw some claw marks, enjoyed a few home-cooked meals, figured broken mirrors meant something but he wasn't sure what (the guy knows every conceivable thing about supernatural folklore, but he's stumped by a few broken mirrors?), unmasked the cheating sheriff, got attacked by the Swamp Thing monster and then saw a naked woman.

OK, it's been a while since he's seen that. But since this was in the line of duty, I doubt he took any pleasure from it. Maybe he just missed Scully. Lord knows I did.

Because of that, for 60 minutes, I had this nagging feeling of been there, done that, why bother?

Perhaps it was so we could unveil the one redeeming moment of this episode - Mulder's response when asked by the sheriff's wife if he had a significant other. His reply, "Not in the widely understood definition of that term" was at least a sign that someone hasn't forgotten what should be the most important theme of this season.

The development of the MSR.

See, even Mulder can't stop thinking of Scully when they're apart. I'm glad I'm not the only one.

Sadly, his response was lost in an episode that was entirely forgettable. But at least there was a nugget of gold buried within that black lump of coal. Oh wait, I'm thinking about "Arcadia" again. Now that, as much as anything, is as strong an indictment of this episode as I can muster.

Should "all things" provide the type of insight into Scully's character that will leave me riveted, perhaps that will ease my lack of appreciation for "Chimera." Then again, it just may make me wonder why they couldn't have given Mulder something really exciting to do while Scully was locked away in a deserted building eating cold pizza and checking out prostitutes.

"all things"

Everything happens for a reason. There are no accidents. There is no random luck involved in the paths we choose.

A woman walks in front of moving car. The driver slams on the brake in time, preventing an accident. But was the woman merely in the wrong place at the wrong time? Or was she fated to be there to prevent an even greater accident? A van headed in the driver's direction.

Fate. Are we governed by it completely? Does it lure us into a false sense of comfort, believing incorrectly that we actually have a say in what we do and the lives we choose to lead?

And at what point must we come to terms with the actions of our past so that we can finally allow ourselves to walk down the path fate has chosen for us?

These are a few of the ideas Gillian Anderson explored in her wonderful writing/directing debut, "all things." This is an episode where Scully must confront her past so she can finally move forward as she finds her own sense of closure on the choice that she made that has caused pain to so many others.

Some may be shocked to learn of Scully's affair with a married man. Perhaps they view her in a perfect light: A figure of good who cannot be tainted by the evil which tempts the rest of us mere mortals.

I, for one, was glad to see Anderson create even more emotional depth for Scully by allowing us to see her as a flawed person. A woman who once made a choice to be with a married man only to walk away, oblivious to the reaction her choice had caused, but haunted by her indiscretion. By exposing the flaws of her character, Anderson has proven once again how perfectly human Dana Scully always has been.

Through a mix-up at the hospital, Scully is forced to confront her past and the married man she once loved. There is an understandably upset daughter who watched her family dissolve because of the affair plus an opportunity for Scully to wonder whether there was another path that would have led her to happiness.

What Scully learns here is that even though we seem to be presented with numerous choices along the way, there is really only one choice we will take that will lead us down our ultimate destiny. Fate rules its hand over us all and we see that clearly in "all things."

Fate led Scully and Mulder to investigate a case of a dead woman in the woods. Fate led Scully to do an autopsy on the woman. And it was fate that placed the results of Daniel Waterston's condition in the folder Scully received instead of the autopsy results she meant to retrieve.

There are no random events. Everything happens for a reason. And here, a seemingly inconsequential X-File reunited Scully and Waterston and led Scully to re-examine herself and look to the past in order to find the answers to her present and most importantly, her future.

It was fate that led Scully to Mulder and it was fate that allowed Scully, through that relationship, to open herself up to a non-scientific way of healing which saved Daniel's life.

Although much of this episode deals with the relationship between Scully and Waterston, at its heart is the bond Scully shares with Mulder. Although Mulder is absent for much of "all things," his presence and importance in Scully's life is felt constantly. This is in stark contrast to "Chimera," where Scully's absence was generally ignored or used for comedic effect.

Interestingly, Anderson, as Duchovny did in "The Unnatural," frames her episode with scenes of Mulder and Scully together. Unlike Duchovny's playful banter in "The Unnatural," Anderson chooses to first focus on Scully's disinterest in her current state of affairs before subtly examining the union Mulder and Scully share.

Some may view Scully's behavior toward Mulder as somewhat rude in the beginning as he's trying without success to get her interested in his latest case. But I see it as a continuation of the confusion Scully has felt since "Amor Fati."

Her entire world has been turned upside down and unlike Mulder, who thrives in the face of chaos, Scully needs the sanctity of order in her life. And she has had precious little of that these days.

This sense of uncertainty not only draws upon the closing scene of "Amor Fati," but also upon the "normal life" discussion Scully had with Mulder in "Dreamlands." In fact, this episode parallels both of those episodes in many ways.

"Amor Fati" was Mulder's journey down the road not taken. "all things" represents the life Scully bypassed when she joined the FBI. A life with a man she once loved who possibly could have provided her with the "normal life" Scully believes she should be enjoying at this point in her life.

Again, that plays upon the idea of normalcy Scully ruminated over in "Dreamlands." But as was the case in that episode, what we, and Scully, ultimately discover here is that she already has the normal life she was meant to have.

Fate has dealt its hand with Dana Scully. Now it is up to her to follow that path and see where that road will take her. In the end of "all things," it takes her back to where she truly belongs: Alongside Fox Mulder. And consummating their relationship in the one remaining way still open to them. Sexually.

The opening teaser shows us Scully getting dressed before the camera pans back to reveal a seemingly naked Mulder in bed. As Scully departs his apartment, the signs tell us she has finally arrived at her fated destination. She has embraced her path and chosen to be alongside Mulder completely.

This was an episode that spoke from the heart. And it's clear Anderson gave a lot of herself to the story she was telling.

As a director, Anderson is clearly interested in imagery. She has some wonderful transitional images, my favorite being the moment where Scully, cloaked in a robe, morphs into a more professionally-dressed Scully walking into a hospital room, only to see herself in the bed calling out to her.

There is also the use of slow-motion to punctuate the emotional resonance of the scene and a surreal sense of movement that perfectly accentuates the confusion Scully is feeling as she is forced to re-examine the choice she made long ago.

And, of course, there was the image of two women kissing which is bound (along with the David Crosby joke) to create even more discussion about Gillian Anderson's personal life although I'm sure she would rather have the attention focused on the fact an intelligent woman of inner strength played a role in helping Scully come to terms with her past and save Daniel's life.

Whereas Duchovny in "The Unnatural" was interested in the power of love and how it can change people (Dales' love for Exley and Mulder and Scully's love for one another), Anderson is more interested in the ideas of fate and spirituality and the way the two can be intertwined.

Anderson chooses a woman in a cap, gray jacket and jeans as Scully's symbol of fate. It would appear Anderson was influenced by the terrific Nicolas Roeg film "Don't Look Now" with the use of a constantly re-appearing figure who represents a predestined path.

In "Don't Look Now," the figure in the red raincoat represented death and Donald Sutherland's ultimate demise. Here, the figure represents Scully's need to slow down her own life pace (evidenced by the near car accident) and open herself up to new possibilities (one of which leads her to a Buddhist temple where she has her vision of the life she has led and the people she has encountered along the way).

But most importantly, that symbol of fate is linked to the person who has become more important to her than anyone else. Fox Mulder. It is no accident the figure Scully chases after departing the hospital for the final time turns out to be Mulder. The path alongside Mulder is the one fate has chosen for her.

At the end, you can see it in her eyes, hear it in her voice that she realizes there is only one choice that can be made. To be sitting on a couch with Mulder is where she was meant to be. And it is in that final moment where Anderson gently reveals the strength of their union.

She does so by focusing on the ease with which they relate to each other. There is a sense of comfort with one another that allows them to theorize on the possibility of what fate holds in store for them. Perhaps I'm a lovelorn fool, but I have always felt such a feeling of powerful romance whenever Mulder and Scully just "talk" to one another.

It rises above their dialogue and reveals so much about how the two of them feel for one another. Credit Duchovny and Anderson for creating a sense of passion without relying on "the traditional definition of that term."

The comfort they feel with one another also allows an exhausted Scully to close her eyes and fall asleep, trusting implicitly in the man she is with, knowing he will protect her from harm should sleep overtake her. Then with one gentle sweep of the hair, Anderson proves she and Duchovny think alike with their vision of how Mulder views the most important woman in his life.

There can be no questioning the intensity of the affection Mulder has for Scully as he brushes the hair away from her eyes and covers her up as she falls asleep on his couch. In that one scene, Anderson's written words and Duchovny's non-verbal actions indicate the ultimate power of their union and the love Mulder has for Scully, one she will soon reciprocate in the middle of the night.

To truly move forward, we cannot be burdened by the events of our past. For years, Dana Scully has been unable to step forward with precise movement because she has been weighed down by actions she regretted committing. In "all things," she is freed of the burden she has felt and free to move down the path fate has chosen for her.

It was left to Gillian Anderson to provide the closure her character needed and the freedom that was necessary for Dana Scully to begin to live her life with happiness. "all things" was a fascinating look at the pain Scully has felt for so long, the confusion she has been trying to overcome and the potential for happiness that awaits her if he slows herself down and allows herself to truly exist.

"all things" showed us that as a writer and director, Anderson has the potential to create something special. Just like the character she portrays.

"BRAND X"

OK, here are a couple things I learned after watching "Brand X:"

1. Smoking is bad.

2. Bugs in the lungs are bad.

All right, I really didn't need to see this episode to know about the latter and since I'm a firm believer in personal choice I'll bypass any debates about the former. Instead I'll just figure out if "Brand X" was worthy of an hour of my time.

And you know what? It was.

This wasn't the most riveting X-File I've ever seen and there wasn't a tremendous amount of heart-pounding tension from beginning to end. About the only real tension came early on when Skinner couldn't stop stammering as he was being yelled at by his boss.

Maybe that's why he kept pointing his gun at Weaver at the end instead of just grabbing him before he lit the killer cigarette. Maybe Skinner was off his game after getting his ass chewed out. Or maybe he was thrown by Weaver's reference about Mulder being Skinner's "boy."

I'm so not going to go there.

But the bugs in the lungs were sufficiently nasty and the story kept me interested until the very end when, surprise, Mulder was saved.

All right, that didn't surprise me. After all, he has to appear in the next episode because he wrote and directed it. So I think having Mulder infected by the tobacco bugs was merely an excuse to get Scully by the bedside of another man she's slept with. Yeah, I said it. And they did it. But I digress.

After the emotionally powerful and satisfying "all things," which took the Mulder/Scully dynamic in a sensual new direction, "Brand X" wasn't interested in intense character or relationship issues. Instead, it wanted to lecture a bit about the evils of smoking (although this lecture was akin to being smacked over the head with a mallet) and provide us with a genuinely eerie ending as Mulder gazed lovingly at the pack of Morleys in his waste basket.

Now that was an ending that packed a lot of punch.

Maybe it's me but when I saw that scene, I was reminded of the moment in "Return of the Jedi" when Luke cut off Darth Vader's hand with his lightsaber and realized how closely linked the path between father and son really was. Of course, if a similar analogy was used here, that would mean that Mulder's father really wasn't his father and his actual father is ...

It's better I stop now.

For seven years, Morleys have been the cigarette choice of evil on "The X-Files." But instead of featuring one devilish Cigarette-Smoking Man in "Brand X," this time the entire brand name is under attack.

In a surprising twist, the folks at Morleys had their plans to create a super cigarette that would be less harmful go awry when, somehow, some bug eggs latched onto the smoke and found their way into human lungs, only to hatch at the most inconvenient of times. Don't ask me how this would happen, but I think it's a sign of growth that Scully bought right into the theory without batting an eye.

Of course, there was one test subject immune to the effects, a rather slovenly fellow named Weaver, who wanted nothing more than a smoke (or 20) a day.

Weaver had a simple life. He hung out in his apartment, watched war movies and lit up as everyone around him dropped dead with bugs pouring out of their orifices. That didn't seem to bother him too much although it sure made Scully flinch.

Speaking of Scully, there was a genuine sense of anguish in her eyes as she watched Mulder slipping away, taking his hand in her own, an action that even made Mulder smile ("It must be bad."). Coming on the heels of "all things," this was a nice way of referencing the landmark events of that episode.

This wasn't a woman losing her closest friend. This was a woman afraid of losing her life partner, the one person she knows she cannot live without. In an episode that merely sought to entertain on a simple level, this was a nice touch.

As was that final shot. I come back to that because it genuinely interested me. How can we watch that scene and ignore the parallels between Mulder and the man who may be his father?

Are we meant to see that pack of smokes as representing the fine line between Mulder and the man he despises? That a single cigarette is a symbol of all that unites them despite the different paths they have chosen?

Mulder has been tempted by the dark side before, only to resist every time. Perhaps we are meant to see that pack of Morleys as a sign that further temptations will await Mulder and one final confrontation with the CSM is yet to come.

In a manner of seconds and with one look from Mulder, this episode added an unexpected dimension of character insight to a rather elementary tale. Then again, maybe he just really wanted to light one up with the little woman safely out of sight.

I've said before that I believe entertainment comes in a wide variety of levels. And one of the things I've always appreciated about "The X-Files" is that it steadfastly refuses to pigeon-hole itself by utilizing a minimal number of story-telling techniques.

For every episode of dramatic power such as "all things" or one as fun as "X-Cops," you can have a basic gross-me-out story such as "Brand X." There wasn't anything ground-breaking here nor was there anything that will take the characters to places we've yet to see them go.

But that didn't bother me. Sometimes, just being entertained is enough. Sometimes, I don't mind just kicking back and watching bugs crawl out of Mulder's nose.

"HOLLYWOOD A.D."

Three things I've learned about David Duchovny after watching his writing and directing efforts the past two seasons:

1. He really knows how to bring out the best in Gillian Anderson.

2. He loves Mulder, not to mention Scully, as much as the show's fans do, even though he's not afraid to poke a little fun at him.

3. After watching "Hollywood A.D." I'm convinced he is a fan of the classic "Star Trek" episode, "The Trouble With Tribbles."

That episode was one of the highlights of the original series in that it not only presented an interesting episode within the confines of the series itself all the while satirizing the very nature of the show. It did so in somewhat broad fashion at times (who can ever forget the bar room brawl between the Federation officers and the Klingons?), much the same way Duchovny paints a broad satirical picture of "The X-Files" with "Hollywood A.D."

"Hollywood A.D." was Duchovny's nudge-nudge, wink-wink writing-directing effort for this season. Unlike "The Trouble With Tribbles," "Hollywood A.D." will not go down as a classic "X-File" (it doesn't even beat out "Jose Chung" or "Bad Blood" as the series' best satire), but Duchovny did not fail to deliver an episode that truly reflected his own wit and intelligence.

All the while remaining true to the spirit of the show that has made him famous.

While the centerpiece of the episode dealt with the laughable movie based on Mulder and Scully starring Garry Shandling and Duchonvy's real-life wife Tea Leoni (adorned in a red wig), the case they're working on was straight out of the paranormal. There's a phony gospel ("Stigmata" anyone?) discovered along with a Lazerus bowl, which may contain an energy powerful enough to raise the dead.

There's also a hippie radical from the '60s who thinks he's Jesus Christ and a Cardinal out to prove otherwise although his chances to become the first American pope take a hit at the end when we discover he has offed the hippie and then himself. And finally, a few dancing zombies.

Never let it be said Duchovny isn't willing to pack a helluva lot into an hour of television.

Unlike "The Unnatural," which was a profoundly romantic poem about the power of the love, "Hollywood A.D." isn't interested in deeply introspective themes or pushing the envelope of the MSR to a new level. That's not to say Duchovny ignores it, however.

One of the highlights is the scene where the cinematic Mulder and Scully finally embrace (in a coffin no less) only to have Scully profess her love for Skinner. That's the breaking point for Mulder, who has been humiliated by what he has seen onscreen but now storms out of the theater, leaving Scully alone across the aisle from Skinner, who's being groped by a Hollywood starlet infatuated with the size of his "flashlight."

It's clear what Duchovny wants here is to have his cake and eat it too. It's impossible to ignore the hidden meaning of the words onscreen that send Mulder packing, but Duchovny still wants us to see it all and laugh, ending the scene with Skinner being fondled.

Nothing too deep, but just enough at the surface to reveal itself before another laugh comes along. So while this effort is not as magical as "The Unnatural," it succeeds in the manner in which it was intended, as an enjoyable romp.

Peppered with numerous in-jokes, a nod to Mulder's porn habit, a hilarious look at Hollywood and references to everything from "Twin Peaks" to "The Larry Sanders Show" and Ed Wood, "Hollywood A.D." (the title itself is an in-joke) is essentially Duchovny's way of telling the show's fans to loosen up a little and enjoy the ride because it's almost over.

I have to admit, however, after seeing how beautifully Duchovny handled the Mulder-Scully relationship in "The Unnatural" and then in the closing moments of "Amor Fati," I was hoping he would push this dynamic even further. Unfortunately, there were no breathtaking "birthday presents" in this episode.

Instead, he maintained the status quo, relying on their considerable chemistry to illustrate the bond they share.

He does deliver one moment of powerful sexual subtext, however. The scene where Mulder and Scully share a telephone conversation (nicely filmed in split screen) while lounging in their respective bubble baths was positively electric as Scully flirts with Mulder as the two discuss the finer points of zombified cuisine.

Something tells me that's exactly how a phone sex call would go between these two. Scully getting frisky and Mulder talking about how zombies are just misunderstood and we really shouldn't take it personally if they start gnawing on our hand.

By the way, where was Mulder's "other" hand during that call?

While that scene had a wonderful erotic chemistry, Duchovny won't allow things to go too far. Instead he stays true to the spirit of his script, going for laughs as Skinner interrupts the call and the screen divides into a triangle to reveal the Assistant Director, like Mulder and Scully, is also sitting in a bubble bath.

Although a part of me wishes Duchovny had resisted the urge to get cute with that scene, the entire "Mulder And Scully Go To Hollywood" segment was the high point of the episode. How could it not be when it begins with Mulder and Scully taking off to Hollywood for a little R&R only to show up wearing their work clothes? From there, it segued into one of the funniest moments of television I've seen in quite some time.

Yes, the joke about which way Mulder dresses, to the left or right, was cute. But watching Scully doing wind sprints in the background as she shows Tea Leoni how to run in heels was funnier than anything I've seen on "Friends" in years.

It would appear Duchovny had some fun making Gillian Anderson run gassers, but he proved again he knows how to make her positively glow onscreen. Just as Anderson lovingly filmed Duchovny's half-naked body in bed in "all things," Duchovny lingers over Anderson's glistening body while she relaxed in the bubble bath before their phone call.

And just like in "The Unnatural," Duchovny affords his co-star the chance to giggle again in their closing scene together which ends with the two of them walking off the sound stage hand in hand. A nice moment indeed. That was one of many nice moments, not to mention several very funny ones, throughout "Hollywood A.D."

In the end, it pales a bit in comparison to Duchonvy's sensational first effort, "The Unnatural," but he does prove himself to be a writer of considerable wit in "Hollywood A.D." and I'm glad he took the time to share some of that with us.

Now about those dancing zombies .....

"FIGHT CLUB"

Ladies and gentlemen, you're about to witness something few people have ever had the fortune to witness. So pay close attention because it may never happen again (which may be good or bad depending on your point of view).

Ahem ......

I'm stumped. I'm speechless. My mind is an empty vessel. I am unable to muster up a coherent thought or an intelligent observation. The reason for this complete and total inability to articulate even the most mundane of thoughts? Simple. I have just been subjected to the most inane hour of television "The X-Files" has ever produced.

Ladies and gentlemen, I give you "Fight Club."

Please, stop hurling profanity-laced tirades my way. This hour of mind-boggling ineptitude wasn't my fault. Honest.

Now I've had my share of horrific television experiences. I have stumbled across "Oprah," I have accidentally lost my remote during an episode of "Roseanne." I have been stricken with back spasms so severe I was unable to turn the channel during an episode of "Two Guys, A Girl And A Pizza Place."

But I have never, ever seen something so sensationally awful produced by a group of people who have turned the television world on its ear for the past seven years.

As each agonizing second past during this episode, I kept wanting to do a really bad impression of Johnny Carson. Ed McMahon was nowhere to be found, but that did not prevent me from wanting to cry out, "So how bad was "Fight Club?""

It was so bad that:

It made "Space" seem like a religious experience.

It made "Travelers" appear to be a thoroughly well-thought out episode that had absolutely no continuity issues.

It made me want to embrace the fainting, screaming Scully of "How The Ghosts Stole Christmas" as an ingenious character twist.

It made me fall in love with Diana Fowley.

It made "First Person Shooter" seem like "Memento Mori."

It made "Hungry" seem like "Triangle."

It really made me hate pro wrestling.

Oh wait, I already hated pro wrestling. Well, I guess I can't blame all the world's evils on "Fight Club" then. No matter how badly I'd like to.

But this much I can say: It was, quite simply, the worst episode of "The X-Files" I've ever seen. Bar none.

I guarantee that throughout his boxing career, Randall "Tex" Cobb never landed a punch any harder than the one I felt while watching "Fight Club." It was like a shot to the head that left me dazed and in searing agony from which there was no escape until the bitter end.

I felt like Malcolm McDowell in "A Clockwork Orange," my eyes wired open, unable to prevent myself from watching the horrors on the screen before me no matter how badly the pain oozed inside me. My cries falling on deaf ears.

Only the pain, the horrific pain ....

As I sit here, I cannot think of a single thing that would make me recommend this episode to anyone with an IQ in double digits. OK, the opening moment between Mulder and Scully with Scully rattling off paranormal possibilities as if she were involved in some wacky game of charades was cute. As was the parallel version of Mulder and Scully who've worked seven years together with no hint of romantic involvement.

Memo to Chris Carter: Stop fighting the inevitable. Second memo to Chris Carter: Don't use this script as a bargaining chip if you're trying to get a new contract from Fox for a possible eighth season.

The idea of twins who create chaos whenever they see each other was interesting. But the story just went nowhere.

It wasn't compelling, it didn't sustain my interest and at no point did I ever care to uncover the mystery behind the events I was witnessing. Oh, and Chris, the copying money idea isn't exactly original. Beavis and Butthead did it once, too. The difference being when they did it, I couldn't stop laughing.

I was probably supposed to be laughing with and not at Mark Snow's "zany" musical score. Instead, I kept wondering if I was watching a Roadrunner cartoon.

And was it me or were David Duchovny and Gillian Anderson sleepwalking through this episode? That would explain why Scully was in such a daze she didn't even bat an eye when Mulder disappeared into thin air. Then again, the fact they showed up at all says a lot about their ability to take one for the team.

Oh, and it doesn't bode well for an episode when it feels like filler material until the next run of commercials arrives. By the way, Sammy Sosa has convinced me to start drinking Pepsi instead of Coke.

Now if only someone had convinced Carter to come up with an entirely different story idea. That would have prevented the pain I'm feeling at this moment.

The unsettling knowledge that an hour of my life has been ripped away from me along with, quite probably, a few brain cells as well. I'm no dummy, nothing that completely and utterly terrible can just exist for an hour without inflicting some type of long-term damage.

Like all television shows, "The X-Files" is not immune to failure. It is the nature of the beast that if you produce 20-plus episodes a year, you're bound to strike out a couple times at least. "The X-Files," as sensational as it has been for the past seven years, is certainly no exception. There have been a few missteps along the way.

But never in seven years have I ever seen an episode so completely devoid of merit that I feel compelled to burn the tape I have it on for fear its very stench could wreak havoc on the other wonderful episodes I have previously recorded.

Suddenly, I have this odd compulsion to see killer kitties and terrifying trees and Mulder wearing a wedding ring. All horrific images from the past that suddenly appear to be Spielberg-esque in their brilliance compared to the hour of excrement I have just laid eyes on.

If it is indeed true that somewhere out in this vast world we all have an identical twin, I have but one wish for mine. I sincerely hope he was spared the hour of torture that "Fight Club" imposed upon me. It was horrible enough to make me want to kick somebody's ass. And I know just the place to start.

"Chris Carter's room please ..."

"JE SOUHAITE"

OK, I have a confession to make. When I was 10, I used to wish that I could be invisible. The idea of moving around unseen, performing superhuman feats, disposing of my enemies, checking out the girls without them knowing (I was 10, cut me some slack) seemed like a really cool thing to do.

Probably the coolest part was that at no point was I ever splattered by a truck or raised from the dead by my brother (like that was gonna happen). What I was too young to realize then is that wishes are tricky deals. The old adage of "Be careful what you wish for, you just may get it," holds true in more ways than we often can realize.

But for many of us, having a wish or two or three at our disposal is a tempting thought. Personal gain or altruistic thoughts? Which would you choose? That's the question Vince Gilligan poses in his enchanting "Je Souhaite," what may be the second-to-last episode of "The X-Files" ever.

But that's another story entirely.

I'll be honest, I've often wondered what I would wish for if given the opportunity. The invisible idea seemed pretty cool when I was 10, but I'm pretty sure (unlike the slow-witted Anson) I would have outgrown such thoughts by now.

If I hadn't, the fact Anson winds up on a slab in the morgue would have convinced me to think otherwise, no matter how excited Scully was to see him there.

That reminds me of something else I thought about when I was a kid. I used to wonder what it would be like to visit my own funeral just to see who would show up and what they would have to say about me.

Would they have kind things to say or would they reveal something darker they always thought about me? And where the hell were all my old girlfriends? But I ... ummmmm ... think I'm starting to digress here.

Back to "Je Souhaite."

After the horrific hour spent with "Fight Club," this was an episode that served as a wonderful reminder of what "The X-Files" can do when it takes a potentially light-hearted subject and treats it with care and provides it with a purpose.

There were moments of humor, but I also enjoyed the idea of existing in the moment and not trying so hard to question what is happening and why. That is certainly something we've seen Mulder and Scully grapple with at times in the past and it has been a real joy to see them simply enjoying their moments together lately.

On the humorous side, it was fun to watch Anson completely foul up his three wishes and his brother botching things even further. I liked the "You Suck" on Anson's boat and the fly hovering around Anson's reanimated body at the dinner table as his brother tried without success to eat, not to mention Anson's painfully loud (and lengthy) scream after he was given the ability to speak again after his brush with death.

Good stuff indeed.

As was having Mulder grapple with his choices after being granted three wishes. His initial thought, like most of us, was to think of something personal, but he quickly realizes (with the help of some nice Nixon and Mussolini visual aids) that may be the problem we flawed humans face when confronted with such a possibility.

We can't think beyond immediate gratification. So subsequently, we wind up being cursed by the desires we crave. So Mulder goes for the home run, peace on earth, only to have that wish granted at the expense of every human being on the face of the earth other than himself.

After using his second wish to wipe out the first (which results in a wonderful exchange with a very confused Skinner), Mulder is forced to ponder his final wish. For someone who has spent his entire life trying to fill his most fervent personal need, it is a nice touch to have him use his final wish to ease someone else's suffering.

He uses his final wish to absolve Jenn of her "curse" of being a genie, giving her what she wanted most, the chance to have a cup of coffee and just watch the world go by. A world that includes Mulder and Scully together on his couch, happy to be with one another watching a Bill Murray classic.

Now that's a wish all of us can enjoy.

"Je Souhaite" was filled with many wonderful moments. An excited Scully saying "bye" to Anson's body in the morgue, Jenn desperately trying to provide a clue about a possible wish Anson or his brother could use that would give Lewis the ability to walk again. Not to mention Mulder's groan as Scully tries to back off her belief that she had seen an invisible body.

But none of those moments topped the final scene of Mulder and Scully together about to watch "Caddyshack" in his apartment. It was sweet and romantic and served as a powerful reminder of how it is possible to get something we wish for by just taking life one moment at a time.

Mulder didn't have to make his wish a personal one to achieve the one thing he wants most. He needn't tamper with fate to have Scully be with him always.

An invitation, a cold one and a video rental is all it takes for Scully to be "relatively happy" and for Mulder to realize his greatest desire. Few things this season have been more enjoyable to watch than Scully's ability to finally express her happiness.

For a show that has often been criticized for its lack of character development and continuity, it has been a true pleasure to watch how Scully has unfolded this season. From coming to terms with her world crashing down around her early in the season to the moment of her personal revelation in "all things" and the relaxed, happier person she has become since then.

Not only has Mulder been "free" since "Closure" and able to move on in his life without being paralyzed by his past, so too has Scully been "free" of the personal demons she was dealing with that often slowed her path. What we've seen in the latter half of this season are Mulder and Scully finally free to walk down their chosen path together, relaxed and comforted by the knowledge that they were meant to be together and the strength of their union will see them past any obstacle.

And neither of them needed a genie's wish to grant them that.

You know, if I was given three wishes, I honestly don't know what I'd choose. But as much as I love "The X-Files," I don't believe I'd wish for creative success by the powers that be if there is an eighth season. "Je Souhaite" proved that just like Mulder, they don't need a wish to be granted to realize something they already have.

"REQUIEM"

It is with a mixture of excitement and a heavy heart that I write this final review of Season 7. The events of the past week have been well documented. "The X-Files" will return for an eighth season, but minus Fox Mulder for the first 11 episodes.

I have expressed my disappointment with this turn of events elsewhere and shall not waste valuable time repeating myself here. But after watching the incredibly enchanting "Requiem," I find my breath taken away by what I have just seen and even more saddened knowing what is to come.

A Mulderless beginning and middle to Season 8.

"Requiem" was a 60-minute reminder of what makes this series so wonderful and what I will miss when "The Scully Show" debuts next fall. It was filled with a passion to explore the unknown, the mysteries that abound in the dark and the necessity to uncover those mysteries rather than turn a blind eye toward them.

But most of all, it was filled with the love that Fox Mulder and Dana Scully share for one another. That feeling of love will remain present when "The Scully Show" debuts, but Mulder's extended absence will be a painful reminder of what is missing.

Such a feeling cannot be replaced when he is absent for so long

Not when they've been this close. Not when the intensity of their love jumped off the screen and plunged deep into my heart and reminded me why I love these two characters together and why their forced separation is not something I wish to see.

It is their union that lies at the heart of this series. And "Requiem" was a tribute to the intensity of that union. From a moment in bed with Mulder gently holding Scully and telling her how he wants her to have the life she could never have alongside him. This moment is filled with shades of both the film from Mulder's perspective and "all things" from Scully's as he reminds her of everything she's lost by being with him.

What Mulder fails to realize is that Scully has made her choice. Her destiny is joined with his as was made clear in "all things."

So even if she cannot go with him in the end, she embraces him tenderly and refuses to let him go alone, sending Skinner off as a physical companion but also armed with the power of her love that she hopes will protect him from harm.

Nothing can ever come between them. Not even a Mulder abduction, which is how this episode ended. Mulder looking toward the heavens, his chosen path finally reaching its inevitable conclusion.

The question then becomes: Did he leave willingly?

Leaving Scully behind willingly is an affront to their relationship. But I would venture a guess as to say Mulder was intoxicated by the events that were transpiring around him and caught up in the moment he has dreamed about since the day his sister was taken from him.

The power of that moment swept him away. Literally. Leaving only a befuddled Skinner behind to confront a reality he also can no longer deny.

In the beginning of the episode, the FBI auditor told Mulder to narrow his vision, to stop looking toward outer space for the answers he seeks. But Mulder's greatest strength has always been his ability to look beyond the normal boundaries and his greatest desire has always been to see firsthand the truths he could never prove to anyone else.

So in this instant, as the alien bounty hunter approaches him and Mulder looks toward the heavens, that opportunity is there. Does he take it willingly or is he being led by the moment? I would say it was the latter. The true pity is that we will be forced to wait 12 episodes to know for certain.

However, that cannot detract from my appreciation of an episode that rivals "The Erlenmeyer Flask" and "Anasazi" as the most breathtaking season finales in this series' history. Where Chris Carter appalled me with "Fight Club," here he enthralled me as he captured the essence of what makes this series great.

Mystery. Danger. And a bond like no other on episodic television. All on display and captured with a poetic quality that was a wonder to behold.

In many ways, "Requiem" was like one big "X-Files" reunion.

The CSM was back, wheel-chair bound and dying, but not about to give up his precious smokes, even if he has to suck them through his neck hole, a visual image far more gruesome than anything this show has ever produced.

Alex Krycek was back as well, looking mysterious and with motives kept delightfully hidden from any of us. We've missed ya, Alex.

The Alien Bounty Hunter appeared as well, doing what he does best, cleaning up the mess around him and offering Mulder a one-way trip to a raise in pay for much less work. The lovely Marita was also back, looking much healthier than the last time we saw her although any explanation for the glow in her cheeks was nowhere to be found.

It was like a smorgasbord of fun with riveting character moments, tremendous pacing and a return to Oregon, where it all began for Mulder and Scully seven years ago. Deja Vu all over again indeed.

But with a twist. This wasn't the wide-eyed Mulder and Scully of seven years ago. This was a mature couple, hardened by the events they've witnessed.

I've said several times that one of the most exciting developments of this season has been the character growth Scully has undergone and we see it on display again here. How refreshing it was to see her here, thumbing her nose at FBI budget restraints to go chase after alien abuctions in Oregon with Mulder.

A trip that leads Mulder down the path he was chosen to walk all along. A journey to the heavens to finally meet the aliens he has chased for an eternity.

Some truths have been admitted. His sister is gone for good. But Fox Mulder's destiny has always been to confront the beings that took her and at the end of "Requiem," he is finally given that chance.

So what are we left with:

The CSM dead at the bottom of stairs, killed by Alex Krycek. A pathetic end for a figure who had become a pathetic shell of what he once was. Watching Krycek step over his body without a second thought was a fitting end as it revealed his insignificance in the grand scheme of things he had long worked so carefully to orchestrate.

But plans for colonization must still remain. And how does Krycek fit into the scenario now? Is he friend or foe and will he and Marita become a darker version of Mulder and Scully, a couple cloaked in darkness, their motives unknown.

What will become of The Lone Gunmen now that Mulder is gone? How can they begin to proceed without him? Perhaps by receiving their own show?

Mulder, of course, is abducted, gone to heaven knows where. Will he return? Of course he will. Right around February sweeps. We'll see you then. Dad.

And most importantly, what shall become of Dana Scully? Pregnant with Mulder's child (clearly putting an end to the "Did they or didn't they" questions after "all things") determined to find Mulder because she "has to."

Her choice of words is telling as it reveals to Skinner the depth of her relationship with Mulder.

Will she partner up with Skinner, whose breakdown at losing Mulder was as touching as the tears Scully shed upon hearing the news the man she loves had been taken from her?

Powerful stuff indeed. And it could set the stage for some interesting ideas for "The Scully Show."

Sadly though, it won't be "The X-Files." Not with Mulder gone for so long. After the beauty that was "Requiem," that will make it even more difficult to wait 12 more episodes for the show I love to return.

The truth has always been out there. And the truth is "The X-Files" has been a show like no other and "Requiem" proved once again there truly is a place for magic and beauty and love on the small screen and I am delighted to have witnessed it for seven seasons now.

Perhaps I will witness it again. Perhaps such dreams will come true. Perhaps those dreams are just 12 episodes away.

"Mulder's Goodbye"

Since "Closure," I've sensed that Mulder is trying to determine the path his life should now follow. He still wants to continue exploring the paranormal, but I think that sense of relief he received when he learned of Sam's fate lifted a burden from him that had saddled him for years.

Now that he is without it, he struggled a bit to determine where his life should go.

The obvious answer is that he wants to be with Scully. Since they became lovers in "all things," the situation has become even more muddled. When Mulder was watching Scully with the baby in "Requiem," I not only sensed that he was thinking about what Scully could not have but also what the two of them could not have if they continued the quest together.

I think Mulder is more concerned about the future now that he has finally stopped chasing his past. His feelings in "Hollywood A.D." seemed to indicate a concern about how he will be remembered and as his relationship with Scully has deepened, it's caused him to ponder that subject even more. I've definitely noticed a change in Mulder since "Closure," which makes perfect sense since that was the end of one chapter of his life and the beginning of another.

There was once a time that chasing UFOs and trying to find his sister was all that mattered to him. But now there's more. He knows of Samantha's fate, he's aware of the alien invasion, but that's not the passion that stirs his emotions any longer.

But I also believe he's uncertain of how to go about any other type of life. He hasn't known anything except chasing UFOs and the paranormal. So even something as intoxicating as spending the rest of his life with Scully may frighten him to a degree since it's unfamiliar ground.

What remains familiar is The X-Files. But he realizes that if he stays so will Scully and he loves her too much to see her deprived of the things he knows will make her happy. So that's what led to, in my opinion, their wonderful scene together in his hotel room in "Requiem."

He was trying to convince her (although his actions would only seem to draw Scully closer to him) that there is another choice out there for her. He was giving her the opportunity to make that choice although his tender way of expressing himself revealed his true desire to have her stay with him.

Of course, what Mulder doesn't realize is that Scully has already made her choice. Her destiny is linked with his no matter what that means giving up or missing out on.

Which brings us to the tail end of the episode. First, we see a relaxed Mulder in his office, apparently resigned to the fact The X-Files will be taken from him. We don't see any frustration or anger by what he senses is about to occur. I think the reason for that is the files are not the sole purpose of his life anymore.

While he still remains fascinated by The X-Files, it isn't where his heart lies. I think he's come to realize what Scully has known since "all things:" There is a life away from The X-Files as long as the two of them are together.

However, he can't resist the path he's walked for so long which enables Krycek to seduce him back for one last chance to "stop it." During his last conversation with Scully, I see Mulder expressing his desire to finally put an end to his past so he can move forward with her, toward what, he doesn't know. But he knows the life he wants to lead must include her so he cannot afford to risk losing her which is why he tells her not to come, thinking incorrectly she could be a target of the Alien Bounty Hunter.

In a sense, Mulder is trying to finally close one door so he can walk through another. That door is a life with Scully that could possibly allow them the luxuries they have denied themselves for so long.

The interesting thing here, in my opinion, is that the Mulder being abducted idea is actually the perfect conclusion for his character arc. It's his destiny to be literally consumed by what has consumed him for so long. It would've been a bold move for Carter to draw that up as the finale for his series and this character but it would have been completely logical since it really is the only ending Mulder could logically know.

However, such an ending would have been emotionally gut-wrenching given how the heartbeat of the show has always been his relationship with Scully. To deny Mulder (and us) that pleasure would be akin to ripping the heart out of the series for good and laughing while the beating heart goes up in flames.

So what we have instead if a temporary abduction and a child born of Mulder and Scully. It will be interesting to see when Mulder returns how his experience affects what desire I believe he has to begin some type of a normal life with Scully. That was the path I believe he was prepared to walk down before he was abducted.

SEASON 8

Chris Carter gambled and lost in the eighth season. And the series he helped craft into a television phenomenon paid a heavy price for his risk taking.

With Duchovny limited to 12 episodes, Carter decided to re-invent his series around a new character. Robert Patrick was cast as Agent John Doggett, with Fox hoping his featured role in "Terminator 2" would appeal to the prized 18-34 male demographic (Fox executives anticipated a 10 percent increase in this demographic due to Patrick's presence).

Some members of Fox's marketing and promotion department were leery of Patrick's ability to replace Duchovny. However, that didn't stop Carter and Fox from trumpeting Patrick's arrival.

Carter said the new character would not replace Mulder, but not only did Doggett take over Mulder's office and position on The X-Files, he became Scully's new partner by the end of the second episode ("Without"). And although Carter insisted Mulder would be the "absent center" of the eighth season during his abduction, the character was virtually ignored in the first half of the season.

The season's third episode ("Patience") ended with Scully stuffing Mulder's nameplate into a drawer and from that point forward, Mulder was rarely mentioned prior to Duchovny's full-time return. Even some of the episodes which featured Duchovny in the first half of the season provided just brief glimpses of Mulder.

"For the character who was key to the success of the show and key to the reason The X-Files (within the show's universe) existed to be so quickly forgotten, to be barely a blip on the screen, was just wrong," said Monica Duff, an Australian fan since Season 2.

Instead, Carter and Spotnitz had a new toy in John Doggett and they were determined to feature him no matter what.

That decision was embraced by fans who thought Mulder and Scully's story had grown stale. Other fans still preferred Mulder and Scully, but believed Doggett's "by the book mentality" provided a fresh infusion of characterization for a series in its eighth season.

"John Doggett is by far my favorite character outside the Mulder-Scully dynamic," said Karen Petrick, a fan since the second season. "Robert Patrick is a terrific actor who, when I heard he had been cast on the show, allayed my fears of having a new actor step into the show. I felt the Doggett-centric episodes from this season, in particular 'Via Negativa,' were very well-written, acted and executed."

Not everyone felt that way, however. According to sources familiar with the show, Anderson wasn't thrilled with the amount of attention the writers were lavishing on Doggett. Insiders said she believed with Duchovny gone this would be her chance to step into the show's spotlight. Instead, the light shined on Doggett, who Carter said spoke with his "voice."

Sources also said Anderson was unhappy the paternity of Scully's unborn child was turned into a season-long tease after being told the paternity would be resolved by Christmas.

Anderson wasn't the only one frustrated with Scully's pregnancy. Criticisms ranged from the haphazard nature of the pregnancy timeline to the idea that a baby had no place on this show in the first place.

"The baby was when the show (took a turn for the worse)," a television insider said. "I thought Robert Patrick did a terrific job of creating a compelling character under difficult circumstances. It wasn't his fault (Doggett) wasn't Mulder. But watching what happened with Mulder and Scully and the baby nonsense was sad to see."

Duchovny felt some frustration as well once he returned full-time for the final six episodes. In interviews after the season, he lamented the lack of resolution to Mulder's abduction and that Mulder was rendered into being a "peripheral" character.

"(Duchovny) was not at all happy with the Mulder return storyline," said one source. "Not just the fact of his under utilization, which definitely came through in his interviews, but he was unhappy with the Mulder being resurrected storyline and the introduction of the SuperSoldiers."

Not only that, but Duchovy offered to write and direct an episode that would have built off the scenes of Mulder being tortured in the season's opening two episodes. Carter nixed the idea because it was not about Doggett.

Sources close to the show said Duchovny also did not care for the paternity tease since it prevented him and Anderson from establishing any proper dramatic foreshadowing. The two stars were also reportedly unhappy the relationship between Mulder and Scully was not explored more fully since Duchovny planned to leave the series at the end of the season.

Instead, Carter and Spotnitz continued to sidestep the relationship. Only at the end of the season did fans receive something of substance when a kiss between Mulder and Scully in the season finale cemented their relationship and offered the definitive word on the baby's paternity.

"The final scene was meant to say that Mulder and Scully had consummated their relationship and this child was a result of that," Spotnitz said. "That was the conclusion."

At least Duchovny and Anderson shared a kiss. All Nick Lea got was a kiss off.

Lea, who played the nefarious Alex Krycek, had numerous discussions with the writers over the years about Krycek's constantly shifting characterization. At times, they listened. Sources said Lea approached Carter and asked that some moments of kindness be added to the fifth-season episode, "Patient X," so

Krycek wouldn't appear to be torturing a Russian boy infected with "the black oil" for his personal gain.

"A couple of things were added," one source said. "Namely the scene where he gives water to the kid on the boat and the line 'I'm going to take good care of you' which was intended as an expression of sympathetic concern."

Far too often, however, Krycek was simply a convenient plot device. Although there had been discussion within 1013 of doing a Krycek-centered episode in the seventh or eighth season, it never came to pass. By the eighth season, Lea had grown weary of trying to make sense of his character and when he learned Krycek would be killed in the season finale, sources said Lea welcomed the news.

Lea and Mitch Pileggi (who played Assistant Director Walter Skinner) had reportedly been lobbying for Skinner to be the one to eliminate Krycek and that wish was granted. However, sources said Lea was unhappy with Krycek's confusing death scene and asked Carter if the scene could be re-shot to provide more clarity. Carter turned down that request.

So Krycek exited as an enigma no one - not even the actor who played him - ever truly figured out.

"Everything has an end," Lea said in a message on his official Web site the night "Existence" aired. "I felt that K wasn't getting a fair shake anyway. It's not that fun to just play a villain, without any reasoning behind it. I wanted more in-depth ideas about the character and it never came. It kind of stopped being fun to play."

The show stopped being fun to watch for many fans, especially when Mulder wasn't in it. Their discontent was reflected in the ratings. The 12 episodes which featured Mulder averaged 13.93 million viewers (the season average was 13.53 million, down from the Season 7 average of 14.2 million) and six of the episodes ranked higher than the season average. The nine non-Mulder episodes averaged 13 million viewers and only three ranked higher than the season average.

What's more, the five episodes with the most viewers all featured Mulder, while four of the five with the lowest amount of viewers were sans Mulder. It was not uncommon for Fox affiliates around the country to receive calls from viewers asking one burning question each week: "Will Mulder be in this week's episode?"

The Powers That Be had clearly underestimated the viewers' loyalty to Mulder and Scully. While Carter had long insisted the strength of the series rested with its "scary stories," for many fans, the show had always been about Mulder and Scully.

As a fan, I felt disconnected from the show I loved for seven seasons. Mulder and Scully's world was suddenly populated by drab characters and inane stories, the nadir being "Badlaa," an episode I dubbed "Butt Munch" since it was about a genie who invaded his human hosts by crawling into their rectums (Anderson called it "The Butt Genie").

"The X-Files" was quickly becoming a show I had no interest in watching. And I wasn't the only fan who felt that way.

"I didn't like the treatment of Mulder on his return because at that point it should have included what he had been through," said Deborah Young, a fan since the pilot from Ohio. "I also didn't like the way that they made Scully seem so off from her normal character. Then when she did get Mulder back, they didn't advance the story of Mulder and Scully reconnecting."

"Season Eight was a season of lost opportunities," said Jenny Morris, a fan since Season 1. "One of The X-Files' greatest strengths over the years has been its ability to tell multilayered stories, but this was lacking (in the eighth season). They could have had their precious MOTWs, but with a backstory of what was going on Mulderwise."

In an interview I conducted with Spotnitz after the season, he said the writers were taken aback by such comments.

"I was surprised that there were a number of online people who somehow thought we were not honoring the character of Mulder during those periods when we didn't have David Duchovny's services as an actor," he said. "They questioned whether Scully loved Mulder or cared about him because she put away his nameplate and it never occurred to us that people would interpret it that way because it seemed so clear to us how Scully felt about Mulder.

"It's very hard to write episodes about looking for Mulder when A) You don't have David Duchovny as an actor or B) Because you don't have this actor, people know you aren't going to find him. So I think we were a little limited in our ability to dramatize the search in those episodes when we didn't have David."

Perhaps, but even after Duchovny returned, 1013 made questionable use of his screen time. Anderson and Duchovny were allotted a mere 20 minutes when they were alone together in the final six episodes. What had long been the norm had suddenly become a novelty.

"Season 8 was nothing more than game playing," said Randi Peterson, a fan from Ohio. "They played with the characters we had grown to love, destroying them in an effort to make the 'Next Generation' look better than the old. Worst of all, they played with the fans. By bringing in this new team, they caused a rift in what had been a tightly knit group of very dedicated fans and the ratings began to show their displeasure."

Ultimately, I decided to watch all of the episodes, but only review the ones in which Mulder appeared. I had no desire to analyze the character of John Doggett and his immersion into "The X-Files." For me, the show had always been about Mulder and Scully. Their relationship had provided the foundation on which the series had been built and the fuel that had driven it so well for so long.

Mulder and Scully *were* "The X-Files" for me. And my reviews in the eighth season would reflect that belief.

"WITHIN"

All right, I couldn't stay away. I tried. I honestly did. But I just couldn't. I realize I spent many an hour issuing strong proclamations about how I would possibly refrain from reviewing the new season of "The X-Files" given how disheartened I was about what was to come:

A season nearly bereft of Fox Mulder.

A "manly man" introduced to make the girls shriek and the women swoon.

The essence of the series ripped asunder as if it meant nothing now that the opportunity to "reinvent" things was at hand.

None of that excited me. In fact, it infuriated me. Given all that, I had decided it was best for me to step away and put the reviews on hiatus. I actually felt a kinship with Fox William Mulder. As Mulder would go, so would I. But then I realized, I've come this far and if this show that has meant so much was about to go down in flames, I was going to jump into the fire and fry along with it.

Going out with a blaze of glory? I'm not that optimistic. Call it the unavoidable side of human nature that causes us to stop and look at a traffic wreck on the side of the road. We gasp at the gore and are repulsed, but we continue to stare.

So I'm back. But for how long? Perhaps I'll only return when Mulder does and when the spirit of "The X-Files" returns and graces us once again with its presence.

I can't guarantee I'll be back for the entire ride. But I have returned for the moment, backing away from my earlier declarations and venturing into the unknown, not entirely enthused about the prospects that await me, but determined to see how this hand is played out.

And if my appearances do parallel Mulder's, all I ask is that you lay off the probing and stay the hell away from my cheeks. I mean it.

Now onto "Within."

"Why do I get the feeling they'd be happy if they never found Mulder at all."

If ever there was a phrase that sums up Season 8, that was it. Although the words come from the lips of Dana Scully, they might as well have been uttered by the multitude of fans who remain in an uproar over the "reinvention" of the series.

Do The Powers That Be really want Fox Mulder around anymore? That is a legitimate question to pose based on how heavily Chris Carter has promoted the arrival of John Doggett and how he intends to "reinvent" the show around that character and his new relationship with Scully.

Such reinvention is, of course, an insult to the essence of the series. Fortunately, it won't truly begin until Episode 3 when the practicality of a season without Fox Mulder will be put to the test. The first two episodes, however, will focus on Mulder's absence and how it impacts those close to him.

Namely Dana Scully.

One of the joys of "Within" lies in showing how Scully longs for the man who means more to her than any other. We feel her pain clearly thanks to the brilliance of Gillian Anderson. We can only watch helplessly as Scully seeks comfort from her torment by crawling into Mulder's bed, a familiar place indeed, clutching his shirt as if that fabric will bring a piece of him back to her.

It briefly becomes her sanctuary from the nightmares of him being tortured at the hands of aliens that haunt her dreams. Mulder's absence causes her to ache and suddenly her life has lost its meaning, its center. There is a moment at the beginning of the episode where Scully does nothing but stare at her reflection in the mirror. Through the despair of her gaze, we feel how truly alone she is now that Mulder is gone.

She walks the halls of the FBI alone. Life passes her by, but she moves as if in a daze, her focus gone, nowhere to be found. She heads instinctively toward the one place where she hopes some sense of meaning can be found, only to find Mulder's office being torn asunder by the bureau's best, who have been assigned to find their spookiest colleague.

It is in those moments when "Within" achieves magical heights and reminds us of why "The X-Files" is so special. They are also a wonderful reminder of how powerful a non-verbal actress Gillian Anderson has become.

Wisely, Chris Carter envelopes "Within" with Mulder's spirit. He may be gone, but he is constantly felt. Although he is glimpsed only in Scully's dreams and in a tease at the end, he is never allowed to stray far from our thoughts.

His absence provides the framework for the entire episode. We share in Scully's emptiness because it is ours as well. Mulder's absence has not only altered the course of Scully's life, it has altered the course of the show itself. We cannot watch without realizing clearly what has transpired to bring us to this place.

In many ways, "Within" was a winner. And yet, something gnawed at me for the entire hour.

"Within" had the proper Xs and Os of an ideal X-File. The creep factor was high (thanks to Scully's rather unpleasant Mulder imagery). The conspiracy factor was on overdrive with mysterious envelopes being slid under doors and Gibson Praise arriving out of nowhere (much like Scully's "realization" that Gibson was somehow linked to Mulder. She must've been watching "Murder She Wrote" reruns during her brief stay in the hospital).

149

And the us against them element was firmly in place as Scully and Skinner (and to a lesser extent The Lone Gunmen) drew a line in the sand against the forces of evil represented by Doggett (for now) and Kersh, proud owner of a move up the FBI's food chain.

But for all of "Within's" strengths, it somehow felt empty. It was an episode missing something vital. Its heart.

What it lacked was the power of Mulder and Scully together. We were deprived of that interaction since David Duchovny's fleeting scenes were (sadly) limited to a few seconds of dream-induced torture and a final scene in the desert.

Had Carter been smart, he would've constructed his script with a scene with Duchovny that featured one moment of Mulder-Scully interaction. By giving us a glimpse of what we were missing, it would have made the pain of Mulder's absence that much stronger.

Instead, we were left with some dental work that would make Dustin Hoffman squirm and a chubby-faced Mulder, who looks like he's made one too many runs to the border for a chicken burrito supreme, hijacking Gibson Praise, who apparently is once again the key to The X-Files.

By denying us any Mulder-Scully magic, it merely reinforced how it cannot be replaced, no matter how badly Carter may try with the introduction of Agent John Doggett. Robert Patrick is steely-eyed and determined as Doggett, and his character has interest, mainly because Patrick brings a quiet intensity to the character that rivals Gillian Anderson's. There is no question the two of them work well together in this episode.

But Doggett isn't Fox Mulder. And that's the rub. That one undeniable fact will be the most difficult obstacle "The X-Files" will have to overcome in the weeks ahead.

"Within's" strengths were derived from its focus on Mulder and how it impacted Scully and fueled her desire to find him. Once Mulder is spirited away (again), will the episodes without him work on a comparable level? That is a question that cannot be answered yet although speculation is sure to run rampant in the weeks to come.

In many ways, "Within" reminded us why we tune into "The X-Files" every week. However, it also reminded us why the road ahead will be so difficult. Fox Mulder may be gone, but he will never be forgotten.

Or replaced.

"WITHOUT"

"He went over the edge."

And just like that, he's gone. No more Mulder. And no more X-Files. Not for awhile anyway. At least not for me.

"Without" marked a pivotal moment in that it will be the final episode in which special agent Fox Mulder is a central component in the storytelling process for the foreseeable future. Beginning with next week's episode ("Patience"), the show will be "reinvented" to focus on John Doggett and his dogged pursuit of The X-Files as Dana Scully's new partner.

Yawn.

With that in mind, shouldn't "Without" have been an episode that grabbed us, made us desperate to follow this new series path and brazenly dare us to avoid what's about to come next? Shouldn't it have been all that and more? Was that just too much to ask?

Apparently it was.

Instead of delivering the goods, "Without" was aptly named in that it was without substance. This was an episode that amounted to nothing. Zero. Zip. Nada. Looking for even the slightest clue about what has become of Fox Mulder and why he was taken?

Don't look here.

Looking for a deeper examination of the powerful union Scully shares with the man she loves? Outside of a brief tearful exchange with Skinner, there wasn't any reason to believe Scully had a personal investment in finding Mulder.

I kept waiting and waiting for something, anything, of substance to be provided in this episode. Perhaps the slightest glimmer of something that would provide me with a reason for Mulder's abduction and why he is being tortured by aliens after so many years of being Untouchable Human No. 1.

Remember the days when Mulder meant so much to the aliens project they didn't dare lay a hand on him? Well, let's just say their attitude has ... ummm ... shifted.

Apparently, the only thing he's good for now is to have his cheeks stretched wide while being gawked at by multiple versions of The Alien Bounty Hunter. Oh, every once in awhile he gets to scream "SCULLY!" and apparently his suffering is so powerful that not only can Scully feel it, but now so can Gibson Praise.

So why then didn't I feel anything?

In a season that has forced me to have the lowest of expectations, it's possible "Without" may have generated a new low. This was Chris Carter's attempt to keep Mulder involved in the storytelling process even though he's barely around?

Consider it a huge disappointment.

Oh yeah, the "He's out there," and "You're so close" really had me captivated. Whatever. Yeah, he's out there all right, stripped down to his FBI briefs with needles poking into his cheeks like some sort of crazy S&M project gone bad. For a second, I thought The Alien Bounty Hunter was going to brandish a whip and a smirk, saying "You've been a bad bad boy Mulder."

All of which begs one simple, obvious question. Why?

Why should I care what's coming next when I'm given no reason to be invested in the present? Why is it so difficult to involve the star of the show in the storytelling process instead of utilizing lackluster references and pointless debates?

I mean, what did we learn here? That Kersh is a bad ass who's willing to sabotage anyone who gets within sniffing distance of The X-Files. Ummm, we've known that for some time now.

That Gibson Praise is a special little boy the aliens have now decided they'd kind of like to get their hands on? Nothing new there. That Scully has seen things she cannot explain and refuses to enter the desert without first donning a push-up bra? Sorry, been there, done that.

Where was the sense of mystery? Where was a single reason that would make me want to continue to keep watching this series when Fox Mulder isn't around? Would it have been so difficult to provide at least a single one or even make an attempt to do so?

This wasn't taking "The X-Files" in an exciting new direction. It was like being dropped in the pool for the first time and frantically splashing about only to realize you haven't moved an inch. This wasn't an episode that pushed the series in a bold new direction. It merely laid the groundwork for the "reinvention" of the show which basically consists of Scully becoming Mulder and Doggett becoming Scully without the push-up bra.

How very clever.

About the only new development we witnessed was the apparent decline of The Alien Bounty Hunter. Is this guy/thing losing his/its edge or what? He knows how to sneak into places without being seen, but he sure is found pretty easily these days.

First Doggett has little trouble tracking him down in the desert and then Scully finds him in a hospital that sure wasn't filled with any sick people or doctors. By the way, here's an important tip for you Alien Bounty Hunters: When trying to escape, don't call out to the people who are chasing after you. It defeats the purpose of trying not to be found.

So much for the idea of intelligent life outside our galaxy.

You'd also think somebody on that ship would've created a transporter by now instead of spending their afternoons pulling Mulder's cheeks apart. I'm beginning to think they spent a little too much time watching "The Story of O" on that ship in the desert instead of old "Star Trek" re-runs.

So let's see, Mulder is still "out there" and Scully is "so close" and Skinner needs some eye drops in the worst way. That must mean it's time to go hunt Batman or something. Oh, and Gibson is now in a foster home for alien-human hybrids or something, which should make it really difficult for the aliens to find him since I'm sure they're not just going to give up the hunt now, right?

Yeah right.

If "Without" was Chris Carter's attempt to prove that he could keep Mulder an active participant in the proceedings despite limited air time, he failed. And if it was meant to generate proof that the series can thrive without the Mulder-Scully dynamic, consider that a failure as well.

All it did was remind me why the show is a hollow shell of what it once was as long as Fox Mulder is strapped to an alien table and why "The Doggett and Pony Show" holds absolutely no appeal to me whatsoever.

"THE GIFT"

"How much damage will be done to her good name? And Mulder's ... For what?"

Imagine if you will, a present has been handed to you. It's not everything you've ever desired, but it has a wonderful essence to it, a magical quality that intoxicates you and pulls you in deeply. It is a present that reminds you of better days gone by and presents you've received countless times before but had come to fear you may never see again.

Now imagine that at the center of this present was a lie, a falsehood you know you cannot accept, an untruth so damning and egregious you realize with all your heart it defies all logic to accept what it's telling you. And yet without the lie, there can be no present.

Knowing that, would you still accept it? Would you embrace the lie in order to be captivated by the present?

That is the dilemma I find myself grappling with as I sit here after "The Gift" has come to an end. In many ways, this was an episode that brought back the intensity, magic and the power of "The X-Files" that I have been missing throughout this most mundane of seasons.

A sense of mystery filtered its way throughout. Powerful connections between past and present as we watched John Doggett finally become something more than a generic TV cop, a transformation sparked by the beauty and inner harmony that is Fox Mulder. For the first time this season, I became invested in his pursuit of the truth as he found himself fueled by Mulder's passion.

For one of the few times this season, Mulder truly became "the absent center." He was there, literally being seen in flashbacks, and symbolically as every step Doggett took matched the ones Mulder had taken several months before.

Using Mulder as his spiritual guide, Doggett became a part of "The X-Files" for the first time. Because of the emotional investment I felt as I watched him enter this mysterious world of Indian beliefs and soul suckers, the bullet that struck him in the back had significant meaning.

It carried with it a powerful sense of emotional resonance as I watched Doggett being killed and buried, only to be reborn as his death provided eternal peace for a creature Mulder believed would lead to his salvation.

It was all there in an episode that was a standout in this woeful season. There was so much to appreciate and rarely has a episode title been so aptly named. Indeed this was a gift, a reminder of what this show used to be about.

Yet to fully appreciate it meant I had to accept a lie. An untruth brought about in an effort to create a needless sense of drama.

In order to accept the beauty of "The Gift," I had to accept the idea that Fox Mulder was dying a year ago despite an entire season's worth of evidence to the contrary. Worse than that, I had to accept the fact that he would possibly keep such information from the person closer to him than anyone on the face of the earth.

Dana Scully.

A year ago, Mulder was not dying. There was no terminal brain condition only he knew about. A year ago at this time, he was not keeping this a secret from Scully, whom he had grown closer to and who had shared his most deepest and intimate confidences. But a year later, all that has changed. What we once knew as truth has suddenly been replaced by a lie.

Now we're told Mulder was dying. He suddenly was keeping this a secret from Scully and was traipsing off to Pennsylvania on the weekends in an attempt to find an Indian "soul sucker" who could cure him of this disease he once never had.

Coming face-to-face with the soul sucker, Mulder could not bring himself to be spared of his disease we know he never had. Instead, he attempted to take the soul sucker's life in order to spare this creature of the pain it felt by continually being forced to absorb the diseases of others. It was, a quintessential Mulder moment framed by a lie that had no basis in character logic or continuity.

In that instant, the humanity of "The X-Files" was restored by the person who had come to represent it most strongly: Fox Mulder. The sense of compassion that had been missing this entire season was suddenly back again in the guise of the man whose passion and love for the unknown had fueled so much of what we'd seen before.

But at what price did the return of this humanity cost us? What were we now being asked to believe about a character we had once known so well? "How much damage will be done to her good name? And Mulder's ... For what?"

As Skinner's words swim about in my head, I sit here wondering how much more damage will be done to Mulder's character the remainder of this season, and for what? We've already seen considerable damage done to Scully's character as we were asked to believe she would abruptly stop her search for her "touchstone" after a mere two weeks and shove his memory away in a drawer where she would never have to be bothered with it again.

Until she had to start pulling genie's out of people's asses.

Now we are forced to believe the unbelievable. That which we can contradict with our own eyes and with voluminous amounts of evidence, not to mention no less than three trips to the hospital a year ago. That which we know is a falsehood and yet if we are to appreciate the beauty we are being given, we must embrace the lie that provides its context.

Can I do that? Can you? More importantly, should we? Should we accept the lie that provides the impetus for what we are seeing now and may see in the future?

Or should we toss it aside and not let it dominate our appreciation of everything else "The Gift" had to offer? Should we ignore the troubling warning signs this episode may be signaling? Should we show as little interest in this lie as Langly does about wearing pants around the house or as Scully does about keeping Mulder's apartment clean and his fish fed?

By the way, is there a reason why Scully wasn't involved in a search for Mulder? Too busy buying form-fitting tops? Off paying rent on an empty apartment she apparently doesn't visit anymore? Does it strain credibility so much to think she and not Doggett would have checked out all these cell phone calls Mulder was making and followed up on the lead herself?

Touchstone? What touchstone?

Or maybe there was another reason. Since we now have a date stamp for Mulder's abduction (May) and since "Redrum" was set in December that must mean Scully's absence from "The Gift" was due to the fact she is finally giving birth.

Right? Yeah right.

So here I sit, torn between the lunacy of the damning lie and all it represents and the ethereal quality so much of "The Gift" possessed. Here I sit, wondering if perhaps Mulder's spirit is watching me the same way it looked down upon Doggett at this episode's conclusion.

Perhaps he isn't wondering what happened to his nameplate. Perhaps he is awaiting my decision, wondering if I will accept the lie or cling to the facts I know cannot be refuted.

In the end, "The Gift" offered me a present I cannot fully accept because I cannot accept the lie at its center. Because it is built upon a lie, "The Gift" does not completely succeed. What it does, however, is offer me hope that if the lie is soon put to rest, perhaps there will be more to come that overcomes the missteps of the recent past.

I cannot embrace the lie, but I will embrace the hope that "The Gift" provides. It is not all I would normally ask for, but in a season marked by character blunders and misbegotten storytelling, it is a start.

"PER MANUM"

"There you are, I've been looking all over for you."

That's what I've been saying to "The X-Files" for much of this season. "I've been looking all over for you." All season long, there's been this impostor in place of the show I once revered. An alien show that bore little resemblance to the greatness that came before and was misguided in its attempt to carve out a unique identity for itself in the process.

Perhaps, though, the tide has begun to turn a bit. I haven't quite found "The X-Files" yet. Like Mulder, it remains somewhere "out there," missing from view no matter how badly I try to locate it.

However, "Per Manum," like "The Gift" before, provides me with another indication that the truth is indeed out there and I may rediscover the show I once loved before it is lost forever.

"Per Manum" is hardly a classic X-File. But in a season marked by unadulterated boredom and ridiculous plotting, it is a sign the connection to what made the show great not so long ago has not been completely forgotten and may indeed be rediscovered in time.

Many of the elements of "The X-Files" were in place. Dark foreboding terror. An overriding sense of paranoia. The fear of the unknown. A feeling of isolation, first a pregnant woman feeling a sense of invasion as a group of doctors remove an alien baby from her womb. And then, primarily, with Scully feeling desperately alone with Mulder gone, although looking quite svelte for a woman in her 10th month of pregnancy.

Oooops, I mean 14 weeks. Sorry bout that.

Then again, in the world of "The X-Files," giving birth seems to have its own set of rules. Haskell tells his wife in the teaser, "Don't start without me" as she's screaming in agony. Yeah, that's pretty much how the process works.

"Just hold it in ma'am until Duffy's done watching the Lakers game."

Where "Per Manum" works is in displaying the overriding terror and fear of isolation, particularly with Scully, who has nowhere to turn except within. She cannot bring herself to reveal her pregnancy to Doggett (nicely played by Robert Patrick as he struggles to earn his partner's trust and untangle the web of mystery that continually surrounds him). With Mulder gone, she is alone and frightened, wondering if the baby she's carrying is something inhuman, something that has her possibly marked for death.

For one of the few times this season, we are shown something we should be seeing continually, how alone Scully truly is. Bathed in darkness as she recalls previous moments with Mulder, her life is in a state of upheaval and she has no idea when she will see the light again.

Where "The X-Files" has always worked is in connecting a sense of isolation with a fear of the unknown. The inability to trust anyone. Mulder and Scully were alone in their quest and they never knew what was lurking just around the corner. Their only sanctuary was with one another. What gave them strength, besides their incredible bond with one another, was their sense of humanity.

Here, Scully fears her basic humanity could be used against her for a nefarious purpose she has yet to fully understand. The fear that she is carrying a baby of inhuman origin works quite well and feeds off the memories of her own abduction and the horror that went along with that traumatic event.

The episode's greatest strength, however, lies with the return of what this season has so badly missed: Mulder and Scully together.

Mulder is first seen standing outside an elevator looking for Scully. It segues to a moving scene where he tells her about her taken ova and how he kept the news from her because he could not bring himself to cause her any more pain.

This scene is punctuated by a powerful moment when Mulder holds open the elevator doors, afraid to let Scully leave, only to let them close knowing he could not stand in her way to find the truth. Their final moment together is their most touching as Scully tells him of the failed IVF attempt only to have Mulder gently hold her and tell her not to give up searching for "a miracle."

In these few fleeting moments together, we are provided the unquestioned high point of this season.

There is a wonderful magic watching the two of them interact again. The electricity and warmth between them practically leaps off the screen as they take so little time together and transform it into something much grander and meaningful.

What David Duchovny and Gillian Anderson have together is something Anderson and Patrick could never capture or duplicate. There is an elegant grace with which Duchovny and Anderson interact. They are like lifelong dance partners, so at ease with one another's movements they can anticipate where the other is going and feed off their unified steps in the process.

"The X-Files" thrived for so long because of this wonderful dance, this beautiful union. And it has felt empty this season with that union removed for so long.

Interestingly, while much of the episode's strength lies with Scully's characterization, that is also where its greatest failings reside.

It strains credibility to hear Scully tell Mulder she cannot accept the fact she can no longer have children when we were given little indication in the past seven years this was a significant part of her life's plan.

It is also maddening to watch Scully being dumbed down again. Here, she allows herself and Mrs. Hendershot to be taken to 1) An Army hospital (Hey Scully, remember when they were the bad guys?) and 2) Whisked away by complete strangers led by the big dude from "My Bodyguard" in a van merely because they claim to know John Doggett. Something tells me if Scully had a gun with her at the time, she would've given that away too.

Even more frustrating was how little thought we are provided with Mulder and Scully's decision to have a child. This is a life-changing event and apparently all Mulder needed was his lunch hour to think it over and forget he was dying (maybe) and Scully figured it'd be a quick hop to the hospital and then it's time to start shopping for cradles and pacifiers.

Alien colonization plan? What alien colonization plan?

And I'm sure Scully's tearful exchange with Doggett about how she couldn't reveal her pregnancy because "they" would use it to stop her from searching for Mulder wasn't meant to be funny, but I laughed. Ummmm Dana, when's the last time you actually looked for your "touchstone?"

Realistic character development has not been one of the show's strengths this season.

Also, the lack of a time stamp prevents us from gaining any type of feel for when Scully decided she needed to have a baby so bad and Mulder decided to take aim in a cup. By failing to offer us a timeline we can trust, it prevents us from trying to place these actions within the context of what came before, a tremendous failing from a storytelling perspective.

In the end we have learned nothing of consequence other than Scully and Mulder's IVF attempt did not work. Scully may or may not be carrying an alien baby and Mulder may or may not be the father.

So what we have is yet another tease. A lot is thrown at us, but as we cipher through it, we come away with nothing. It's the same old song and dance, but one that's grown a bit tired.

At some point very soon, Chris Carter and company are going to have to step up to the plate and end the games and deliver on all the questions they have so brazenly posed. The viewers who have stood by this series since its inception deserve that much.

And then some.

Unfortunately, no answers were forthcoming in "Per Manum." But what was delivered was an episode that restored another missing piece of humanity to a season nearly devoid of that attribute. And most of all, it provided a few tantalizing glimpses of what this series has always been about and where its true heart and strength resides.

Mulder and Scully. Together.

"Did Mulder Long For His Abduction?"

I have firmly believed for some time that, from a thematic point of view, the most appropriate way to end Fox Mulder's journey was an abduction.

Logically, it made the most sense. He had spent much of his life chasing that one particular moment. He not only was interested in abductions, but on some levels he was envious of their experiences, longing to understand what they knew, what they felt when those moments occurred.

158

Even after learning the horrors of the alien project, I don't believe Mulder had lost his curiosity for what an abduction experience would be like. He had grown wiser and the boyish enthusiasm was gone, but the connection he longed to feel with abductees was still a part of his overall makeup.

Given all that, it was fitting then, I believe, that his journey should end with the final realization of all he had sought. Thematically, it was precisely the type of way Mulder's story should conclude.

He should literally receive what he had craved for so long. An abduction.

From a television and (possibly) cinematic point of view, however, that's not a direction Chris Carter could realistically take. The uproar he would receive by simply removing Mulder from the premises would be akin to killing him off. Fans of the show would not stand for it and Carter knows that.

As bold and daring as it would be, there are also the practical realities of television and cinematic marketing that would take precedence. It's similar to how George Lucas could not conceive of killing off Han Solo even though Harrison Ford argued (logically) that it was the most appropriate way for that character's story to end in "Return of the Jedi."

So rather than ending Mulder's journey in such a way, Carter has (wisely) chosen to make the abduction an extension. But by having Mulder disappear with the aliens and go to who knows where, it leads to yet another potentially fascinating question.

Could Mulder possibly be enjoying his abduction?

Granted, being strapped naked to a table, having probes shoved into your mouth and saws slicing and dicing away at your skin isn't the way most people enjoy spending a weekend. And I feel safe in saying Mulder isn't finding any real enjoyment from those moments.

But consider this: For so long the moment that haunted his life was the disappearance of his sister Samantha. That singular event in his childhood not only shaped the man he would become, but the path on which he would travel.

Mulder not only needed to find Samantha, he needed to know exactly what happened to her after that fateful evening when she was lost for good. But on a subconscious level, perhaps he not only needed to know what happened, but experience it as well.

To completely understand the gravity of that moment, he had to experience it for himself. And I think somewhere deep within Mulder's being, he has always known that.

I think it's safe to say that Mulder not only felt the burden of losing his sister for so many years, but was haunted by his inability to prevent her from being taken. That was reinforced when he believed he had "lost' her again in "End Game." When he broke down in front of his father, it spoke volumes about the guilt he not only felt at that particular moment, but in every waking moment since the day Samantha was taken.

Perhaps as a form of punishment, Mulder feels the need to be exposed to everything his sister was exposed to. A form of retribution for his failure (in his eyes) to prevent the suffering she endured.

In "Closure," Mulder was able to learn more about what happened to his sister and begin to say goodbye. Perhaps, though, by matching her suffering and experiencing more of what she experienced, in some way he can further free himself from the pain he has felt for so long.

I pose this point because I'm curious to know how this abduction will change Mulder upon his return. Knowing we have only a handful of episodes that will deal with his return, it would be nice if Carter was using David Duchovny's time now more wisely, allowing us glimpses into Mulder's pysche as a way to understand how his abduction has begun to shape him.

And most importantly, how it has brought him even closer to the sister he lost so many years ago.

We know this experience will change him. I'm curious to know not only how it will change him, but if he is, even in the most remote of ways, enjoying the change and the enlightenment this experience has provided.

"THIS IS NOT HAPPENING"

"Excuse me, I'm confused."

You ain't the only one Scully. For most of this season, Chris Carter and Co. have confused the hell out of me with their re-writing of history, their botched characterizations and their fascination with boring stand-alone episodes, the nadir being an episode which featured a little guy who got his kicks crawling up people's asses.

Talk about going where no man has gone before.

Color me confused, but week in and week out I kept wondering where in the hell was "The X-Files?" Turns out I didn't have to crawl up anybody's ass to find them although I could've sworn that's where Carter's head has been buried most of this season. Turns out all that needed to be done was reach in a drawer and remove a nameplate that had come to symbolize all that had been lost this season.

All it took to steer the series back on the right track was the return of Fox Mulder. Well, sort of.

The search for Mulder came to an end in "This Is Not Happening." Unfortunately, we didn't see a lot of Mulder here, which, sadly, has been par for the course in terms of David Duchovny's screen time thus far this season. We catch him spread-eagled on the alien S&M rack again, appearing to Scully as a ghostly apparition and lastly in the woods, where he's found dead as a doornail.

Sure he is. This guy is harder to kill than Rasputin. Call me crazy, but I have a hunch that whatever death No. 347 (give or take a few hundred) holds for Fox Mulder is bound to be a short one.

Unlike most of the episodes this season, what we saw at the end of "TINH" was a logical continuation of everything that came before. There was a steady stream of progression, as Richie chased a UFO in the teaser paralleled Scully's desperate chase to find Mulder at the episode's conclusion.

Everything in "This Is Not Happening" built toward the moment in the woods where Mulder is found dead. This was an episode that moved from Point A to B to C in an intelligent and well thought out manner. This was the episode Mulder's abduction has demanded for so long.

It wasn't just about the search for Mulder, but also the potential consequences of that search. For the first time, Scully was forced to confront a reality she had denied was a possibility. That the search would end with Mulder's demise.

This was an episode in which many things happened, and yet nothing felt rushed or cluttered. We not only saw the first signs of a new plan by the aliens, but also the return of the one man who can stop them. But most of all, we saw the most important thing this season has lacked: Scully's fear that she may never see Mulder alive again.

Scully's angst was placed in the spotlight here and not surprisingly, Gillian Anderson was radiant from start to finish. From an early attempt to seek comfort with Skinner (in a moving homage to "Closure"), to a near breakdown as she conducted an autopsy on a returned abductee to her final breakdown after finding Mulder, each moment was a carefully layered piece to the puzzle of Scully's agony and the pain she has felt since losing Mulder in the Oregon woods.

With each movement, Scully's fear she may never see him alive again registered cleanly. With each step forward, the strength of her relationship with Mulder began to slip away. The anguish she felt in the episode's final scene was heartbreaking. And if we are to believe that she and Mulder are lovers, then the pain she felt is that much more pronounced.

She has lost something more than a partner. Something more than a friend. In that final moment as she cried out to the heavens, we watched her lose a part of herself as well.

Anderson was so breathtaking and the theme of separation was so pronounced that would have been enough to satisfy a full hour. But the reinvention of "The X-Files" also continued with the introduction of Agent Monica Reyes, who will not be replacing Gillian Anderson should there be a ninth season next year. No really, she won't. See how easy it is to buy into the party line?

Carter would be so proud of me.

Reyes likes to smoke Morleys (hell, who doesn't on this show?), has a history with Doggett, but is his polar opposite in terms of how open she is to extreme possibilities. She's like Melissa Scully with a badge.

Turns out Reyes was part of the search for Doggett's missing son, which was first referenced in "Invocation" and is brought up again here as a way to provide context for Doggett's obsession with finding Mulder, an obsession which apparently got quite a workout in the three episodes Doggett spent searching for him. Oh wait, "for months we've been searching for a break."

We have?

By chasing after Bat Man, Metal Man, Ghost Boys, Dimwit Twins and Butt Munch? It's staggering to think that type of investigating prowess didn't turned up Mulder before now.

Turns out Doggett wants to leave the past in the past as he gazes deeply into Reyes' eyes. Turns out the two of them may be asked to carry "The X-Files" forward should there be a ninth season. Turns out they are pleasant enough characters, but every time they were onscreen I kept wanting to return to what was really important.

The search for Mulder.

Far more interesting than the arrival of the new female agent was the return of Jeremiah Smith, the alien healer who frightened the CSM silly in "Talitha Cumi" and was last seen fleeing for his life in "Herrenvolk." He has returned to thwart the aliens plans again, this time using his healing touch to restore life to abductees who have been dropped off by the aliens after being sliced and diced for reasons unknown.

He saves Teresa Hoese, but is unable to use his powers on Mulder. First, he's thwarted by Doggett's FBI raid of the farmhouse where he has been hiding out. And, finally, he's stopped by the aliens, who beam him up before Scully can bring him out to the woods to save Mulder.

And in a wonderful contrast of themes, Scully's first confrontation with a UFO comes on the heels of potentially losing Mulder forever. Knowledge is provided while something is taken away.

Some may look at the final scene and feel it's unfair to punish Scully further, that it isn't right to add yet another layer of torment to her tortured soul. I would counter by saying Mulder and Scully's relationship has always been built upon a sense of loss as much as the knowledge they've accumulated.

I find it fitting that finally, Scully is forced to confront the one realization she has suppressed (mostly due to shoddy writing) since Mulder's abduction. The realization that Mulder may be dead and everything he has meant to her and everything they shared will be lost forever.

This is a painful reality and we see the agony Scully is enduring throughout this episode, only occasionally brimming above the surface. Repression is

Scully's middle name and she continually tries to bury those nagging fears as the evidence builds toward a conclusion she does not want to face.

In the end, when she finds Mulder dead and is unable to save him, the pain is released and her agonizing scream is full of loss and torment, as if her very soul has been ripped away and left to die in the woods alongside the man she clearly loves.

I cannot forgive Chris Carter for the mindless way he has handled much of this season. I can't forgive his ridiculous attempts to re-write history and alter the behavior of established characters.

But "This Is Not Happening" was the episode that finally built off the beauty "Requiem" set up. This was the type of episode we should have been seeing all season long. "TINH" proved Carter still understands what made his show so great.

It isn't "scary stories," and monsters who lurk in the dark and crawl up your ass. It's honest-to-goodness human emotion and characterizations that grow out of feelings we all can relate to.

That's what made Mulder and Scully so enjoyable to watch. It's what has made them so real for so long. And it was the return of this human emotion that made "This Is Not Happening" the first gem of Season 8 and a reminder of the wondrous heights this series can attain when its creator is properly motivated.

"DEADALIVE"

"I'll say it again, this is insanity."

I'll say it this way. This was mechanical. How about wooden and convoluted? Or listless and mundane? Or ... well you go ahead and pick a description.

Just don't use uplifting. Or emotional. Or magnetic. None of them would apply to the return of Fox Mulder in "DeadAlive." And that is something I honestly cannot believe.

Given how much emotional drama there was for Chris Carter and Frank Spotnitz to mine here, it's incredible their script simply didn't do justice for the single most important moment of Season 8 to date. Mulder and Scully's reunion.

I wanted to like "DeadAlive." Dollars to donuts, I really did. I mean there was so much on the surface that should have been so appealing and so rewarding.

Political maneuvering in the guise of Kersh toying with Doggett's future and that of The X-Files. The return of Alex Krycek, lurking ominously in the darkness, sending those vicious nanobots surging through Skinner's bloodstream. Ma Scully returned as well, apparently having finally gotten around to checking the messages on her answering machine. And a full-blown pregnant Scully, all weepy and teary-eyed as she first puts Mulder in the ground and later takes part in his resurrection.

Oh, and did I mention a pretty important reunion?

So why did I feel unmoved? Why didn't I feel this episode truly built off the wondrous climax that marked "This Is Not Happening?" Why did I feel as if it did a nice job of setting up plot points without providing the emotional drama with the one moment I've been waiting to see since "Requiem?"

Given how I spent an hour watching Butt Munch's Ultimate Anal Exploits, I deserved something more than a routine episode, didn't I? Didn't I? And yet I found myself watching "DeadAlive" and feeling two distinct impressions above all others: Confusion and Lack of Interest.

1. Confusion as in: "Why are the aliens shedding?" Before, the black oil just enslaved us and did that really cool oily stuff in our eyes. But wait, then it actually was creating little aliens inside us. Fair enough. Oh wait, now we're apparently being put on the alien S&M wrack so duplicate humans can be created who are really aliens who like humans after they've gotten all lathered up and shed some skin?

Huh?

Can somebody place a call to Krycek for me because I'm fairly certain at this point he's the only person who knows what the hell is going on here. Oh wait, apparently Skinner is omnipotent as well. How else could he have known that taking Mulder off life support would save him?

Lucky guess? Oh wait, he had to do it. He did? Really? Huh?

2. Lack of interest: As in I couldn't give a dollar for any donut Doggett may lose if Kersh jerks him around on The X-Files. I don't care that he's being demoted. I don't care how much rope Kersh gives him or if he hangs himself with it or if the fish are biting or he can't see the forest for the trees or any other analogy I'm given. I just don't care about the guy enough to feel any empathy or sympathy or whatever for his plight.

God bless Robert Patrick because I can tell he's really trying. But he continues to feel like a square peg stuck in a round X-File hole. He doesn't belong in this world any more than he belonged in Mulder and Scully's reunion scene.

But more on that in a bit.

That's not to say the episode was devoid of fine points. There were moments I found especially rewarding. I'm a sucker for Krycek intrigue although for the life of me how a guy who should be on the FBI's Most Wanted list can roam up and down the FBI elevator without a care in the world is beyond me.

At least the last time he wore his Jesus of Nazareth disguise which obviously allowed him to not only get past security, but walk on water too. Oh, was I the only one who found it unnerving the way he smiled and called Skinner, "Walter?"

Most of the moments I truly enjoyed, though, were turned in by Gillian Anderson, who powerfully displayed the agony of a person who has lost not only someone dear to them but a part of themselves as well. I especially liked the quiet and often subtle ways she showed Scully's connection with Mulder.

Note the way she reached for her pregnant stomach the second Doggett exits Mulder's hospital room after Mulder was dug up and brought back to the land of the living. Note also the connection Scully made between holding Mulder's hand while she held her stomach with the other as if the life force that runs through her and her unborn child could somehow infuse Mulder with life as well.

Those were nice touches that once again illustrated how effective Anderson is at speaking volumes through non-verbal means. Without saying a word, Anderson was able to convey Scully's feelings of loss and her desperate need to cling to the most important person in her life.

Which brings us to the single moment that should have defined this episode. Mulder's return from the dead and his reunion with Scully.

Once again, everything was in place for a sensational scene. Scully teary-eyed and elated. Mulder groggy, yet witty enough to toss off not one but two clever remarks. None better or more meaningful than "Anybody miss me?"

Yeah Mulder, a lot of us missed you. More than you'll ever know.

So why did the scene fail to move me the way I hoped it would? Why did I feel so much of what Scully felt at the end of "This Is Not Happening" and so little of what she and Mulder were feeling here?

I wasn't expecting a passionate embrace. I certainly wasn't expecting meaningful forehead kiss No. 1,013. However, I was expecting something more than a couple quips, tears from Scully and then fade to black.

What I was expecting was something that represented what these two people meant to one another and what their separation had meant. And I certainly wasn't expecting a completely inappropriate entrance from Doggett, sporting a hound-dog look like he'd just lost the cheerleader to the quarterback of the football team on Prom Night.

Whatever possessed Carter and Spotnitz to soil this moment with Doggett's intrusion is beyond me. This was a moment that should have served as a powerful reminder of what these two people mean to one another and the seven years they have spent on their united quest. It was not the time or place to remind us how horribly Mulder's abduction had been dealt with early in the season.

And if anything or anyone has come to symbolize the ineptitude of the first half of Season 8, it's the character of John Doggett.

Ultimately, "DeadAlive" set the stage for what may be the countdown toward the end of Fox Mulder's time on The X-Files. It stands to reason we will be given more insight into why the aliens are shedding, perhaps a clue as to why

Krycek wants Scully's baby dead as well as the aftereffects of Mulder's abduction as he reconciles what has occurred to him with all of the changes he is about to encounter (note the camera angle in the reunion scene did not allow him to see Scully was in the family way).

David Duchovny captured much of that uncertainty in a single faraway glance as Scully's head rested on Mulder's chest at the end of this episode. Another wonderful non-verbal moment and a reminder of how talented Duchovny can be even while given little to work with.

So there is clearly a lot to come and in many ways, "DeadAlive" did a nice job of putting several events in motion at once. And yet, it left me wanting more. I wanted to feel the joy Scully felt at Mulder's return just as I felt her anguish when she believed Mulder to be dead.

Instead, all I felt was a sense of relief that Mulder was finally back and maybe now things can really get down to business. First up: Bitchslapping Doggett.

"THREE WORDS"

Imagine you've been abducted by aliens, strapped to an S&M table and poked, prodded and anal probed until your cheeks turned blue. Then when the poking, prodding and probing was done, you're tossed into a field of someone else's dreams, left for dead and buried for three months before a miraculous resurrection.

The first sight you see upon your awakening is the woman closer to you than any other human being on the face of the earth. Your "touchstone." You laugh, she cries and you ponder your return into a world that has aged but left you in stasis.

Oh, and you happen to notice she's just a tad bit pregnant which is really odd since the last time you saw this woman, she was barren, had failed to get pregnant via IVF and had less success on the dating circuit then the kid with the big nose, bigger glasses and pocket protector who sat behind you in math class back in the eighth grade.

My question to you is this: Would you bother to ask this woman how she suddenly happened to get pregnant while you were away? Of course you wouldn't. Not if you're Chris Carter and Frank Spotnitz and you are hoping to turn Fox Mulder into an idiot in "Three Words."

"Three Words" marked Mulder's full-fledged return to the world he had been removed from in "Requiem." And it's too bad Carter and Spotniz blew the biggest issue confronting Mulder and Scully because they did so well with everything else involving his return.

When first we see Mulder, he's reliving the memories of the alien S&M routine he endured, the scar on his chest a physical symbol of the damage that has been done. But not to worry, the physical signs of his torture will soon be gone, Scully and his doctor tell him. And remember that terminal brain disease Mulder never had last year? That's gone too in case anybody really cared.

And we know who you are, Chris.

So Scully takes Mulder home. A deceased fish provides another symbol of the death that enveloped his world while he was gone. Then he happens to notice that Scully's put on quite a bit of weight since the last time he spooned with her in an Oregon hotel room.

Mulder is happy that Scully's got her big wish and is about to be a mom. He says he doesn't know where he fits in and Scully tries to say something but can't because Carter and Spotnitz didn't write another line for her that would've allowed this situation to be put to bed (so to speak).

Instead, Scully hems and haws and we get nothing.

Then it's off to solve the big case which apparently involves the CD soundtrack to the film. Oh and Kersh wants Mulder off The X-Files and Mulder doesn't like Doggett, which proves he didn't lose his good taste while being buried alive.

Then Absalom breaks out of prison, takes Doggett prisoner and is shot by men who don't ask questions or ask questions but don't want the answers or who demand answers for why they're shooting first without asking questions.

Something like that.

Oh, and the big guy from "My Bodyguard" sets Doggett up so that Mulder will be killed. Only Doggett figures it out (WHEW!) and the "My Bodyguard" guy has a growth in his neck which tells us he's really an alien because they're on like Phase 3,452 of their human invasion plan and the best way to spot the transformed aliens is the growth on their necks. And that's really bad news for anybody hanging out in a watch tower in France.

Oh, and did I mention Mulder isn't the least bit curious about how Scully got pregnant?

At least The Lone Gunmen, no doubt thrilled to be rescued from their train wreck of a television series for one night, were curious. Langly asks about Mulder's role in Scully's "blessed event." Mulder, though, looks confused as if he missed the day on reproduction in health class. Scully looks ambiguously pensive and then it's back to the big case.

And that's what's really important here, isn't it? The big case.

Well, here's the kicker people, I might have cared a lot more about the big case if Mulder and Scully had actually had the one conversation they should have had in his apartment.

"It's really too bad your fish died, Mulder, but aren't you the least bit curious about how I got pregnant?"

"Nope, but boy the place sure does look tidy Scully."

Apparently the 1013 game plan is that it's quite all right for Mulder to avoid the big question he should be be asking and for Mulder and Scully to look like a couple of embarrassed teen-agers than it is to look like the two intelligent people we came to know and love for seven seasons. Intelligent people don't treat miraculous events like a barren woman getting pregnant as if it were the pile of magazines under daddy's bed they're forbidden to look at.

Intelligent people wait until mom and dad are out of the house and then sneak into the bedroom and see what the big deal is with the magazines. Oh, and they don't ignore pregnant women who supposedly couldn't get pregnant or a date to save their life.

But then as long as we keep the action going, why stop and worry about those pesky little characterization problems, right?

It's clear Carter's agenda is to prolong the ambiguity about Scully's pregnancy for as long as he can and if Mulder and Scully end up looking like a pair of dolts in the process, so be it. The thing that Carter seems oblivious to is that the interesting question isn't whether Mulder is the father, but what is it about this baby that makes it so important and possibly even worth killing as Krycek apparently wanted to do in "DeadAlive."

Unfortunately, Carter is treating the mystery about Mulder's "involvement in the blessed event" with all the subtlety of a bad soap opera. And that's too bad because he and Spotnitz did a fine job of nailing every other aspect of Mulder's return in "Three Words."

The entire episode felt strained, but I believe that was intentional. I saw it as a reflection of the unease surrounding Mulder's re-investment in the world he was taken away from. It was as if he wanted to hit the ground running, but the world wasn't ready for him to get up to speed just yet.

His moments with Scully felt tense and even awkward. Scully was struggling to verbalize her feelings about everything she had endured (personally, I think she was trying to come up with a really good lie so that Mulder wouldn't discover she stopped searching for him after two weeks) during his abduction. Things can't be the way they were before. Too much has changed. For the both of them.

So we didn't see the Mulder and Scully of old. Not completely. We saw two people trying to deal with this traumatic event and trying to re-discover the pace and sense of one another they had known before.

Mulder's idea of pacing was to move forward quickly and step over anyone whose presence is deemed unworthy, most notably Doggett. Scully was more restrained in her desire to see Mulder get back into the swing of things. Both were in character and the conflict of pace led to a sense of unease between them. And that was nicely done and felt real.

But while Carter and Spotnitz did a nice job of exploring all of the other changes Mulder encounters upon his revival, they skipped past the most important one - Scully's pregnancy.

It strains credibility to think Mulder would not ask how she got pregnant. It's possible, I suppose, that Scully would not tell Mulder she believes he's the father because she fears that might lead to sensory overload as he's trying to process everything he's endured. I can buy that.

What I can't buy is Mulder apparently not the least bit interested in finding out how Scully got pregnant. Sorry guys.

It's too bad Carter and Spotnitz did not have the courage to provide Mulder and Scully the forum to truly discuss where Mulder "fits in" with all of that statement's implications. It's too bad they didn't have the courage to allow Mulder to ask the one question he should be asking. Instead, they were too busy piling on more layers to the alien conspiracy and mistaking ambiguity about Scully's pregnancy for genuine human drama.

I enjoyed the former, but was thoroughly annoyed by the latter. And in the end, that prevented "Three Words" from signaling Mulder's return to "The X-Files" in grand fashion.

This was an episode that had tremendous promise and Carter and Spotnitz almost got it right. Sadly, they failed to invest themselves fully and intelligently in Mulder's return. That one misstep prevented this episode from reaching its full potential and unfortunately, left me with the impression that the brain disease Mulder never had removed some of his common sense before it went into remission.

"EMPEDOCLES"

Pop quiz hotshots. Got your thinking caps on? OK, here goes.

Remember "The X-Files?" You know, the show that starred two characters named Mulder and Scully? The one about the paranormal-obsessed FBI agent and his constantly skeptical partner and the relationship they fostered over time, one born out of respect that grew into something more powerful, more enduring and possibly even more intimate?

Remember how great that show used to be?

Now think about what that show has become. With only five episodes until the possible end of the Mulder-Scully era, the two are reduced to mere footnotes in "Empedocles." Their interaction is given so little investment it's as if they've been transformed into two of the red shirt guys who get axed in the first few minutes of every episode of "Star Trek."

"Empedocles" was the latest attempt by 1013 to reinvent its series around John Doggett with a sprinkling of Agent Smiley Reyes tossed in for good measure. Perhaps there is a segment of the show's fan base who just can't get enough of this dynamic duo and want more, more, more.

For me, it's just more smiling. And more odd accents. More furrowed brows, pained expressions and less of what "The X-Files" used to be about. Mulder and Scully.

At this point in the game, Doggett should be placed firmly in the background while Mulder and Scully, in perhaps their final moments together, are front and center. Instead, the heart and soul of the series is given three measly scenes in "Empedocles."

Three scenes. That's it. I'm telling you, there are episodes of "Star Trek" where the red shirts get more love than 1013 gave Mulder and Scully in this episode.

Their first scene was an awkward moment in which Mulder comes to Scully's apartment bearing gifts, not the least of which, as Scully observes, is a "nice package." Scully gets the better end of the quips as Mulder is left to joke that maybe the pizza delivery boy is the father of her child.

See, we're all supposed to be laughing heartily at home because we don't know who the daddy is. And see, it could be the pizza boy. Or maybe it was Mr. Roper hearing Jack and Chrissy grunting and thinking they're having sex when really they're fixing the sink.

Isn't ambiguity a hoot?

Scully wonders if they've been caught up in an episode of "Mad About You." I wondered why anybody would want to channel Paul Reiser and what the hell happened to the real Mulder and Scully.

Mulder's joke is bound to generate a lot of discussion about whether he is the baby's father. For the "joke" to work, we have to assume Mulder and Scully have talked about how the baby was conceived and Mulder believes he's the father and merely teasing Scully. The alternative is to assume Mulder and Scully are a couple of dolts who believe the best way to talk about the baby is to ignore it completely.

Like Scully's alleged search for Mulder earlier in the season, this is a conversation that obviously occurred off camera which only serves to reinforce the idea that the best work 1013 has done this season has been conjured up by the show's fans. I'm thinking a lot of us ought to be put on 1013's payroll given how hard we've tried to make sense of some of this nonsensical storytelling.

To believe Mulder and Scully have not discussed the baby's origins by now would mean they are complete idiots. Why Chris Carter would render his characters intellectually impotent is beyond me, so I refuse to allow that to happen. Hence, the off-camera discussion.

Fortunately, the second and third scenes were far more rewarding.

In the second, Mulder visits Scully in the hospital after she suffers an abruption. There is a moment when Mulder places his hand on Scully's pregnant stomach. It is Mulder's first physical gesture in relation to Scully's pregnancy and it is a poignant one. The look of joy on Mulder's face revealed a man not just happy for Scully, but for himself as well, a realization of where he fits in with this new development.

In "Requiem," we saw Mulder prepared to close one door of his life and open another, a door represented by his blossoming relationship with Scully. Here for the first time is a physical acknowledgment of Scully's pregnancy and the look on his face shows us the Mulder we saw in "Requiem" has returned and is prepared to pass through a door into a world that has changed dramatically since his abduction.

Memo to Chris Carter: If your plan this season was to reveal that Mulder and Scully were never romantically involved, you probably should have told David Duchovny and Gillian Anderson to stop acting as if their characters are in love. It's making your ambiguity look really stupid.

In their third scene together, Mulder and Scully enjoy a pizza and Mulder gives Scully a present, a rag doll his mother used to have. Is the doll just a gift given from one partner to another? Or can it be seen as a symbolic connection between the family Mulder once knew and the family he is about to start with Scully?

It's impossible to watch those two scenes without seeing the beauty of the Mulder-Scully dynamic and the evolution it has undergone this season. It is clear the processing Mulder was undergoing in "Three Words" has taken root. He has grown more comfortable with his rebirth into the world he was taken from and the world he shared with Scully.

After the stilted first scene, there is a relaxed feeling between the two that reveals a Mulder who is beginning to fit in and find his personal niche again. He is no longer defined by his work on The X-Files. Instead, he is defined by where he fits in his world with Scully.

Even while he is on the case with Reyes, there is a sense that Mulder is not truly committed to it, that he knows he doesn't belong in the field, chasing after visions and trying to help Reyes and Doggett make sense of what they have seen. His place is alongside Scully. It is no surprise then that only in his moments with her, do we see the real Fox Mulder.

And only then, do we see the real X-Files at work.

Sadly, that in a nutshell was all we got from the heart and soul of "The X-Files." The rest of the episode had something to do with visions, Doggett's dead son, the return of Agent Smiley and the possibility that evil can be randomly transferred from body to body.

An interesting, idea. Too bad it was done much better on an episode of "Star Trek" in the '60s. Trust me, a possessed Scotty carrying a bloody knife is far cooler than a possessed Bo Duke with glowing eyeballs. Or was it Luke Duke?

Whatever.

To be fair, the X-File itself wasn't half bad. The problem is, at this point in the season the focus should be on Mulder and Scully, not Doggett's further immersion into The X-Files. Instead, we are victims of an agenda (centering episodes around the two stars of tomorrow) at the expense of logical storytelling (providing us closure with the story of the only real stars this series has ever known).

Perhaps I would have become more invested in this particular case if I hadn't gotten a bad case of the willies watching Doggett's continuing efforts to stalk Scully. Ever since his hang-dog expression upon seeing the depths of Scully's feelings for Mulder at the end of "DeadAlive," Doggett's obsession with Scully and darkness has given me the creeps.

In "Three Words," he was lurking outside Scully's apartment late at night. Then in "Empedocles," he spends an awful lot of time hanging around her hospital room in the dark. Instead of spending so much time wondering who Scully's husband was, the bitchy ER nurse should've called the cops and had Doggett's ass hauled out of Scully's room.

When he's not stalking Scully, he's taking his apparent sexual frustrations out on Mulder. In a scene that will never be shown on "Inside The Actor's Studio," Doggett roughs up Mulder for having the audacity to wear a leather jacket when it wasn't Casual Friday at the FBI.

At least I think that's why he was mad. I couldn't make anything out over Doggett's ranting and raving and totally wacko behavior. Doggett's yelling and screaming at Mulder played about as realistically as Adam Sandler doing a rendition of Hamlet.

"To stalk Scully or maul Mulder? Dollars to donuts, that is the question."

Like Sybil on her worst day, "Empedocles" had a bad case of the split personalities. In trying to prep for the future while remaining connected to the past, 1013 tried unsuccessfully to balance Doggett and Reyes with Mulder and Scully.

That only served to remind us how Doggett and Reyes pale in comparison to the magic Mulder and Scully possess. It also resulted in an episode that didn't really work because its separate parts never added up to a convincing whole.

Instead of focusing its attention on bringing the Mulder and Scully story to a satisfying conclusion, 1013 is attempting a balancing act, trying to merge the future with its past. That approach is not only emotionally unsatisfactory but dramatically insufficient since neither story is given the attention it deserves.

There is but one story that deserves our attention right now. Perhaps in the final four episodes, 1013 will remember where its priorities should reside and put the stalking and the smiling on hold.

"VIENEN"

"If I didn't know better, I'd say this was a Mulder stunt."

If I didn't know better, I'd say the return of the black oil has given me hope the concluding act to the eighth season of The X-Files will end on a high note and not be bogged down by the ineptitude that has marked much of this disappointing season.

After watching "Vienen," I can honestly say that for one of the few times this season, it felt good to be an "X-Files" fan again.

"Vienen" marked the return to the feel of "The X-Files" for the first time since the wondrous "This Is Not Happening." Since then, the episodes have been marked by routine fare ("DeadAlive"), botched handling of the revived Mulder's reaction to Scully's pregnancy ("Three Words") and a horrible mismatch of the past and future of the series with Mulder and Scully reduced to being guest stars on their own show ("Empedocles").

But "Vienen" got it right.

The episode saw the return of the black oil. For those keeping score at home this was the fourth season version. You know, the one that hops from body to body and acts as a mind-controlling agent.

In addition, there was the backdrop of political intrigue, a heightened sense of paranoia with evil all around Mulder and Doggett on an isolated oil rig (shades of the classic horror film "The Thing") and culminating in a moment that has been foreshadowed since Mulder uncovered the truth behind his sister's disappearance.

His departure from The X-Files.

Eight years ago, The X-Files were not only Mulder's obsession but, in many ways, the very reason for his existence. His powerful yearning to discover the elusive "truth" drove him to the ends of the earth and helped him form a bond with Scully that provided the additional strength he needed to persevere.

Eight years later, Mulder's focus has shifted. A new priority has taken prominence in his life, as his relationship with Scully has replaced the gaping hole in his being that was created the night Samantha was taken from him.

The X-Files are no longer is his reason for being. The answers he now seeks are closer to the heart. And they are symbolized by his growing relationship with Scully, which may have gotten the short end of the stick in terms of screen time in "Vienen," but not in dramatic impact.

Even though they were separated for most of the episode, the Mulder-Scully dynamic was still at work in a powerful way. This was Mulder and Scully at their best: Giving great phone with Mulder on the oil rig unearthing the unearthly explanations and Scully in the lab using her scientific knowledge to put the rest of the puzzle together.

Did I mention these two give phone like nobody's business?

It certainly doesn't hurt when the dialogue has significant meaning. Consider the way Mulder ended their first conversation. "When he gets old enough, you tell the kid I went down swinging."

Here's a perfect example of why I was so frustrated with the first half of the season. In just 13 words, 1013 advanced the MSR and enhanced Mulder's characterization in regards to his relationship with Scully by leaps and bounds.

It was a simple line and yet think about what it potentially signifies. It plays off the dramatic events in "Empedocles," particularly the tummy touch scene in which Mulder, perhaps for the first time, bonded with the child he now realizes is his. What this line represents is Mulder considering the future he plans on having with Scully and her child.

Strike that. Their child. It's virtually impossible to view that scene in connection with the two final moments Mulder shared with Scully in "Empedocles" and think there is any other possibility for what Mulder now believes.

Once again, I think it bears out how effective something simple can be in terms of characterization and dramatic content. Think about what could have been done earlier in the season to enhance the Mulder abduction storyline and Scully's characterization had there only been enough intelligence to realize how so much could be gained by doing so little.

We don't need the grand dramatic gestures to further the story and the characters in interesting ways. It's a lesson 1013 should have learned earlier this season, but one that served "Vienen" and the MSR well here.

David Duchovny played that moment perfectly, with a hint of sorrow in his voice as he briefly pondered the possibility he may never see his child. And Gillian Anderson's reaction was perfect as well, as she revealed with one quick look the thought of what losing Mulder a second time would mean to her. Damn, these two give great phone.

How good was this episode? It actually made me enjoy watching Doggett carry on for an hour. Perhaps it was Duchovny's ability to bring out the best in the actors he works with. Or perhaps it was Mulder's character bringing out something interesting in Doggett (which occurred in "The Gift" when Doggett tapped into Mulder's humanity to reveal his own), but for one of the few times this season, Doggett wasn't an annoying pain in the ass.

Too bad I can't say the same about Kersh. Is there ever going to come a time when this guy becomes something other than the bureau's official buttplug? OK, he hates The X-Files. He really hates Mulder. He's the only guy on the show who isn't hot for Scully. We get it. So close the damn files already and stop bitching every time an alien shows up, will ya?

Compared to this guy, Diana Fowley was an intelligently thought out character with a rich history and well-defined motivations. Then again, I did like the way he hissed the word "assistant" when referring to Assistant Director Skinner, who by the way did a very good job of standing and sometimes sitting in this episode.

Am I the only one who remembers when Skinner actually had some balls?

Back to Doggett. I almost felt bad for the guy when he found out Mulder had sneaked off to the oil rig ahead of him to begin the investigation. Well, almost.

He still looks constipated half the time. Then again, he was probably just PO'd that his Stalking Scully Schedule got screwed up.

Wednesday night: 8-9 p.m. Watch Dawson's Creek. 9-9:15 Freshen up. 9:30-10:45 Rifle through Dana's unmentionables. 11:30- Sleep contently.

As for the basics, the black oil is back, but not everyone is susceptible to its charms. If you're lucky enough to be born of a certain Mexican Indian descent, you get to avoid having a rather nasty oily pick me up ... ummmmm ... oooozed down your throat.

Of course, the flip side is you might get turned into a human steak tar-tar. So it's kind of like having a blind date with Rosie O'Donnell behind Door No. 1 or a date with Kathy Lee Gifford behind door No. 2. I'll take the slow painful death behind Door No. 3, Monty.

All right, the Indian immunity angle was a little like Spock having that weird second eyelid thing, but I bought it. Then again, I'll believe just about anything Scully says when she's wearing a lab coat.

In many ways, this episode was the official passing of the torch from Mulder to Doggett. The continued unease between the two was there from the start with Mulder locking the door to his old office and rifling through a case he believes has alien origins and Doggett is convinced is unworthy of his time.

Forced to work together, the wall Mulder had wisely put up against Doggett is slowly worn down by his need to rely on Doggett's help even though he does not believe Doggett has the necessary tools to understand and defeat the foe they are up against. But by the end of the episode, Doggett sees with his own eyes the effects of the black oil and in that instant, Mulder believes Doggett has seen enough to take responsibility for something that he never would have considered giving up eight years ago.

The X-Files.

A shocking decision? Hardly. See here's the thing: This isn't your parents' "Spooky" Mulder. Times change and people change. And Mulder has changed.

He no longer needs the sanctity of the X-Files and that dingy office in the basement to find the answers to all the questions that are posed to him. Since "Closure," I believe Mulder has been prepared to walk out of that office and never look back, his life headed in a new direction. One not consumed by extraterrestrial possibilities, but of more earthly concerns and desires.

In "Vienen," he finally walks out, with no regrets because he realizes the time has come to close one chapter of his life and truly open another. The one earmarked by Scully's presence and their unborn child.

For the first time, Mulder literally turns his back on The X-Files, prepared to move forward and leave that office to someone who has the necessary passion to uncover the answers that so many want to keep hidden. "Vienen" marked Mulder's official departure from The X-Files. It also marked the show's return to a level of entertainment that has often eluded the series this season.

Let's hope it stays there from here on out.

"ALONE"

As the eighth season of "The X-Files" nears its conclusion, I think the time has come for me to share a little secret with everyone. So pull up a chair, come a little closer and listen up.

I am responsible for the success of this series.

Oh sure, Chris Carter deserves credit for creating this series. And the show would have gone nowhere without the amazing contributions of David Duchovny and Gillian Anderson in front and behind the camera. And, of course, there are numerous other writers, production people and actors who deserve plaudits as well.

But let's not kid ourselves, I'm the one who deserves the credit for this series becoming a powerhouse television drama. If it weren't for me tuning in every week, this show would have sunk to the nether regions of the TV landscape years ago.

Don't believe me? I never watched "The Michael Richards Show" once and you all saw how that turned out.

OK, so I've had a little help with "The X-Files" from several million other viewers, but that's beside the point. What isn't is the fact that without the fans, a television series cannot exist. Without viewers, all the sensational work amounts to little more than a test pattern on your TV late at night.

Without us, there can be no show.

At times this season, I have honestly wondered if 1013 had lost sight of that. Many of their actions indicated they had lost touch with their fan base and rather than paying heed to what they were saying, they often went out of their way to insult and ridicule them.

But with "Alone," Frank Spotnitz takes a positive step toward mending the wounded relationship between 1013 and its fans. By naming a character after the late Leyla Harrison, the fanfic writer who recently died of cancer, Spotnitz shows an abundance of class as well as a keen sense of how best to pay tribute to the people who have fueled this show's success.

The fans.

In "Alone," Leyla Harrison is an accountant at the FBI who has processed Mulder and Scully's travel expenses over the years. Like us, she's a huge fan of their adventures. Like us, she knows about flukemen, liver-eating mutants and shape-shifting aliens. Unlike us, she gets a chance to be invited into TXF world when Doggett needs a new partner after Scully takes off on maternity leave.

Scully departs after sharing a hug with Doggett and a gift, the Apollo 11 key chain Mulder gave her on her birthday in "Max." OK, so Seinfeld would sneer at her and Mulder chided her for being a re-gifter, but it was a nice symbolic attempt by Scully to pass on the idea of teamwork to Doggett. It was Scully's way of not only thanking Doggett for his support, but also to express the idea that no one person can exist in that basement alone, a realization Scully knows all too well.

I have to admit I find it odd the things 1013 remembers. They forget an entire season's worth of episodes that contradict the asinine idea that Mulder was dying last season, but they can remember a key chain from Season 4.

Incredible.

More incredible was the fact Scully allowed Doggett to cop a feel with that hug she gave him as she said goodbye. Don't think Doggett wasn't appreciative either. The guy was happier than a teen-ager who just saw a naked picture of Jessica Alba when he thought Scully was coming back to his office.

Has that dude got it bad or what?

So off Scully and Mulder go to Lamaze class. But not before Spotnitz interjected some needless pregnancy ambiguity as Mulder goes from behaving as if he knows he's the father in "Empedocles" and "Vienen" to wondering if Scully is having a boy or girl only to have Scully flash an enigmatic smile.

See Mulder doesn't know the baby's sex and if he doesn't know, that means we don't know either. Isn't ambiguity fun? Well, assuming your idea of fun is an alien anal probe, yeah I guess it's a blast.

I can't tell you how thrilled I am that 1013 is dragging this pregnancy thing out until the last possible minute. Will somebody please phone Krycek and have him tell us what's going on. That guy knows everything.

Then again, if I were Doggett I'd be really worried that a tape of him dancing around in his house wearing Scully's matching black lace bra and panties might pop up in Kersh's in-box sometime soon. As I said, Krycek knows everything.

But let's get back to the case. With Scully gone, in comes Harrison and her enthusiastic XF views that conflict with Doggett's by the book approach. Doggett's love for Scully is so blinding and his feelings so devastated by her departure he's oblivious to the fact that Harrison is really cute. So instead of giving her some ... ummmm ... guidance, Doggett brings Harrison along as they go searching for some lizard-man thing who blinds his victims with venom before killing them.

At least it's not a Butt Munch.

Doggett looks stern. Harrison quivers. And soon the both of them turn up missing. Pretty soon, it's Mulder to the rescue because ... well he's Mulder and the show's a lot cooler with him in it. Don't believe me? Try watching "Salvage" again.

Gleefully impersonating Kersh, Mulder gets the lowdown on a scientist who Mulder believes has bred the lizard-man thing. Trouble is, the good scientist didn't breed one, he's become the lizard-man thing.

The lizard-man thing is on the prowl, about to have a blinded Doggett and Harrison for a late-night snack. Mulder shows up and, saves the day because ... well he's Mulder and the show is a lot cooler with him in it.

That leads to a quick trip to the hospital where Doggett and Harrison's temporary blindness is cured and Harrison is given the key chain, a symbolic gesture that again links the fan base to the characters we have loved for so long. Then it's up to Harrison to pose a question that some inquiring minds have wanted to know for three years now:

How in the heck did Mulder and Scully get back home from Antarctica in the movie?

As Harrison watches, Mulder and Scully bicker lovingly. Scully denying the existence of the spaceship ("No, no, no, no, no remember I was unconscious.") and Mulder enduringly providing the point to her counterpoint ("Apparently you're still unconscious.").

While poking a little fun at fans who have a tendency to over analyze things to death (who me?), we also were given a classic moment of snappy Mulder-Scully repartee. It speaks volumes to the brilliance of Duchovny and Anderson that in that brief moment together, they provided us with something so meaningful and so much more enjoyable than Butt Munches, Batmen, Ghost Boys, Metal Man and the like.

In that instant, we were again reminded of where the heart and soul of this series truly resides: With Mulder and Scully.

All the while, Doggett is left alone, an outsider disconnected to their world and the memories they share, the intimacy that belongs only to them. In that instant, his reality is clear. He'll never be a part of the world Mulder and Scully, and by extension the fans (represented by Harrison), share. He will always be on the outside looking in, an observer not a participant to the magic we share with one another.

Knowing that, he walks off. Alone. A man with no true home. No true place in our X-File world. Of course, the upside is that with Mulder and Scully in the hospital having a lover's tiff, it gives Doggett plenty of time to sneak off to Scully's apartment and ... ahem ... lounge in her bed for awhile.

"Alone" won't make any Top 10 lists in "X-Files" history anytime soon, but it was an enjoyable marriage of the past and present of this series. It wasn't as strong as "Vienen," which featured excellent work from Duchovny and Robert Patrick together, but it was far better than most of this season's fare.

In the end, Doggett is saved by the things he cannot possess: Mulder's intuitive leaps and Scully's scientific knowledge. Two of the things that have made this series so great in the past paved the way for its future star to carry on tomorrow.

More importantly, "Alone" was a fitting homage to a renowned fanfic writer and a population of fans who have stood by this series for nearly eight years, often enamored and sometimes irritated by what they have seen, but loyal to the core. Through the character of Leyla Harrison, we were invited into Mulder and Scully's world, given an opportunity to share our enthusiasm with them and see up close the dynamic that has made them and this show so wonderful.

It was a fitting tribute and Frank Spotnitz, in his first stint as a director on the series, is to be commended for it.

Unlike Doggett, we will never be alone no matter how this series may end. Like Harrison in that final scene, we will always have our images of Mulder and Scully together. Like Scully cleaning out her office and seeing Queequeg's tag, the Apollo key chain and the "Dreamland" coins, we have memories that can never be taken away from us, reminders that will be as powerful tomorrow as they are today.

Memories of a show that has moved us, thrilled us and taken us to places we will never forget.

The future of "The X-Files" is unsettled, but "Alone" served as a pleasant reminder of what has come before and why the journey to this point has, for the most part, been so wonderful.

"ESSENCE"

"We're almost at the end."

And if "Essence" is any indication, it's going to be one hell of a dash to the finish line.

There have been moments this season when I admit I lost almost all of my hope in "The X-Files." Beset with foolish plot developments, boring characters and stories that made episodes of "Family Matters" look Wellesian in nature, I wondered if there was any chance this series could even begin to reach the levels of greatness it not so long ago enjoyed.

I believe I've been right to question the lackluster work 1013 has done this season. The folks there squandered golden opportunities for drama with their endless tease and ridiculous attempt to thrust an unwanted character into the limelight at the expense of the two stars who made this show sensational in the first place.

At times, I've felt as if my hope was lost and the series along with it. I honestly wondered if 1013 was so busy pulling genies out of their ass they'd completely lost touch with the essence of what made this series great.

And then I watched "Essence" and I remembered precisely why this series has struck such a powerful chord in my very being. This wasn't simply a good X-File. This was fantastic television, as intense and gripping as anything I've seen on the small screen in quite some time.

It's episodes like this that make me wonder if there are two Chris Carters. One of them writes dreck like "Fight Club" and believes ambiguity equates to genuine drama. The one who goes out of his way to try and destroy the heart

179

and soul his series by conjuring up asinine plot ideas such as Mulder dying right when there isn't a shred of evidence to support such an idea and then lying to Scully about it.

Then there's the other Chris Carter. The one who created this wonderful series eight years ago and penned the quintessential X-File at the end of last season ("Requiem") and returned the series to a momentary level of greatness once again with "Essence."

Watching "Essence" almost made me glad I sat through the insufferable foolishness of episodes such as "Butt Munch," "Metal Man," Ghost Boy" and "The Dimwit Brothers Take D.C."

Almost.

This episode packed one hell of a punch. It had Mulder in super-protective mode, determined to do everything in his power to protect Scully and the baby. It had religious symbolism galore as the speculation over the baby's conception carried with it powerful religious implications.

It even had the old Skinner, who apparently found his missing testicles and wasn't about to let anyone push him around anymore. And it had Doggett doing what Doggett seems to do best: Grimace, tell everyone everything is "crap" and shoot stuff.

However, the true beauty of "Essence" is that it brought "The X-Files" full circle after eight years. Eight years ago, "The X-Files" were all about Mulder. They were fueled by his sister's abduction and his relentless desire to find the "truth."

Eight years later, "Essence" provides an emotional transference. Now it's all about Scully. More importantly, the baby she is carrying. A baby that may hold the key to stopping the aliens' plans to reclaim the planet that once belonged to them.

This is a baby a whole lot of people are keeping tabs on. There's Duffy Haskell, ably assisted by Kate Winslet's mom from "Titanic." This time, she isn't rowing out to sea with Kathy Bates, but brought in by Ma Scully to help poor, secretive Dana make it to term without any undo stress.

Like ... oh, I don't know ... a decapitation. Or another baby shower.

Don't even try and tell me any of those women ever met Scully before. The reason for her obvious discomfort was not so much having Kate Winslet's mom thrust upon her, but rather that her life is so devoid of friendship her mom had to place a casting call ad in "Variety" for extras on an episode of "Friends."

"Wanted: Several white females, mid-30s with no distinguishable characteristics such as an actual personality. And positively no little bumps on the back of your neck." I wonder if this is how Ma Scully got Bill hitched. Finding some nameless woman to come take him off her hands for good. That would explain why he always acted like he had a bug up his ass.

But I digress.

Oh, remember that sweet kid Billy Miles we met eight years ago? Well Billy's not Billy anymore. He's an alien replicant with a Henry the 8th mean on like you wouldn't believe. Not only is he hacking off the heads of every doctor connected to the alien-human hybrid birthing project he can find, but he's out to put the kibosh on Scully's pregnancy as well.

I have to admit, Billy gave me the willies. Maybe it was the fact he can slice a guy's head off with his finger (I think I saw Luke Cage Power Man do that once in a comic book) or maybe it was his glare of evil, but there was tension in his every step. His every movement was danger personified.

It's taken eight years, but Carter finally delivered an alien that scared the living hell out of me.

And that was one of this episode's strengths. Watching Anti-Billy on the prowl made me fear the damage he would inflict if he found his way to Scully. Their nervousness became my nervousness. Their fear became my fear.

This was an episode enveloped in paranoia and overflowing with dramatic tension. To make an episode where the characters are in danger work, you have to fear for their safety. And every time Anti-Billy appeared, he brought with him the possibility of terror.

Unfortunately, this was not a perfect episode. There was the little matter of Alex Krycek and his maddening lack of consistent characterization. You remember the last time we saw Krycek, don't you? Doggett and Skinner sure do. Doggett got his butt kicked by the one-armed man and Skinner wet his BVDs when Krycek told him to kill Scully's baby.

Well, guess what? Alex doesn't want the baby dead anymore. He's a good guy now, crunching Anti-Billy under his car and saving Mulder and Scully's hides. Are you saying you don't understand this 180-degree turn of events? Well sheesh it's so simple. He ... ummmmm ... well there's ... and I guess ...

Oh the hell with it. I guess he's just a good guy now. Stop it with the stupid questions like logical plot devlopement.

Apparently, he's so gosh darn lovable the news he wanted the baby dead doesn't even generate a flinch from Mulder and Scully. OK, Doggett scowled at him. But that's because he knows if Scully is gone, he'll have to find another woman to stalk. And there's nothing worse than putting in a good six months of stalking, only to have to start all over again.

I mean, what are the odds he'll find another red-head with a profound love for black bras? Who will he stalk next if Scully's gone? Agent Smiley? Ewwwww.

Then again, how sad is it that Doggett is the only one having a logical reaction to Krycek's duplicitous nature? I know I'm in trouble when I start saying to myself, "Hey guys, shouldn't you listen to Doggett?" Of course, I'd be in more trouble if I actually answered that question and started talking to myself.

It's reached a point with Krycek that whenever I try to figure out what he's up to, I feel like I'm back in college knocking back several beers and listening to my buddies try to decipher the "real" meaning behind the lyrics to Led Zepplin songs.

"No dude, I'm tellin ya 'If there's a bustle in your hedgerow, don't be alarmed now, It's just a spring clean for the May queen' is deep man, real deep.

No it's not deep. It means nothing. There is no May queen. There is no hedgerow and nobody's bustling. It doesn't mean a damn thing so get your face out of that bong and let's go find some girls.

Then again, maybe Krycek is the May queen and Carter is bustling in your hedgerow and we should all be alarmed because we're eight seasons into this thing and the only thing I know about Krycek is that he's done more for prosthetics than Pam Anderson has done for breast implants.

Oh Lord this is just like college. I've wasted too much time thinking about this. I've got a serious headache and the girls left hours ago with the guys from Alpha Beta Dumbass.

What I do know about Krycek is that he is Carter's mytharc mouthpiece. He's used to conveniently gain Mulder's trust and provide us with those pesky little alien details that don't make much sense. And in "Essence," he springs quite a doozy.

Scully's baby is not only special, it's "more human than human" and its birth could signal the existence of a higher power. And that, my friends, apparently scares the beejesus out of the aliens, which is why they want it dead. It doesn't scare Mulder, but that's because he knows he's the father. Of that, I am more certain than ever before.

Ignore the "your baby" and "my baby" dialogue that seems stilted since it's in Doggett's presence and exists merely to extend Carter's precious tease. Instead, concentrate on two stronger clues.

The first is provided in the voiceover, where Mulder ruminates over the possibilities of how Scully's baby may have been conceived. By considering sex as one option, it tells us Mulder and Scully have slept together. If they hadn't, there would be no reason for Mulder to consider it a viable option.

Skinner thinks Mulder and Scully have been doing the naked pretzel and he's determined to win the FBI's "Is Fox The Father" pool (First place is $800. Second place is a free lunch with Kersh), so he asks a question somebody should have asked months ago. Mulder says Scully's baby is her business, but note he does not deny the speculation that he is the father, he merely shifts the conversation toward his inability to answer how a barren woman was able to conceive.

Since he does not have an answer, we can rule out IVF as a possibility, leaving us with some form of immaculate conception, natural reproduction or possibly a combination of the two.

Mulder does not have an answer to the question of how Scully was able to conceive. Nor does he have Scully at episode's end. She's in a car with Agent Smiley heading who knows where.

The episode ends with more aliens about and Mulder and Scully separated. The look of anguish on Mulder's face speaks volumes. The woman he loves and the baby he swore he would protect are literally headed away from him, his ability to protect them diminished by their absence.

So where do we go from here? Scully and Reyes separated from Mulder and Skinner (oh yeah Doggett too) with aliens lurking all about. And quite possibly, a concluding act to the Mulder and Scully story that not long ago, I had wondered if I was ever going to receive.

Thanks to "Essence," I've become a believer again.

"EXISTENCE"

"Nobody down here but the FBI's most unwanted."

And so it began. The first meeting of Fox Mulder and Dana Scully. Who knew where it would take us when we first tuned in eight years ago? All we knew at the time was these fresh-faced kids and their crazy UFO stories sure were fun to watch.

Who knew what wonderment was to come? Who knew it would end like this? With an episode that was emotionally compelling and featured a final scene wonderfully fitting for these two great characters and the world we have been fortunate to share with them.

That is what "Existence" provided. The logical conclusion to the story that has always been at the heart of "The X-Files."

"Existence" gave us more aliens on the loose, the return of MyBodyguardAlienGuy, more religious imagery, a dead Krycek and a baby special not because he was the second coming of the savior. Instead, little William Mulder II was special because he was, ultimately, completely human and a product of something far more wondrous than mankind's next hope to thwart an alien invasion.

He was the product of Mulder and Scully's love for one another.

"Existence" picked up where "Essence" left off, with Scully and Agent Smiley off to Georgia (home of Doggett's birth, awwww) to escape the aliens while Mulder and the rest of the crew remain back in D.C. to deal with the back from the dead Anti-Billy Miles and the alien plot to harm Scully's baby.

It doesn't take long for the action to heat up. Anti-Billy pops up at the FBI again and gives Skinner a chop to the head, while Doggett is told by MyBodyguardAlienguy that Scully's chip is responsible for her pregnancy. Meanwhile, back in Bethlehem ... errrr I mean Georgia ... Agent Smiley is giving Scully the creeps by pretending to be a whale and touching her.

183

All of a sudden, I'm wondering if I turned on the Spice Channel and I'm watching No Men Allowed Night (ummm I was told they have shows like that). But then a game warden shows up to stop Smiley from more touching and whaling and I realize I'm still watching "The X-Files."

Undeterred, Smiley begins to give in to her previously hidden lesbian impulses by coming on to Scully. She tells Scully she looks beautiful. I have to admit Smiley's right. Scully does look pretty damn good. But then Smiley crosses way over the line by asking Scully if she'd like to sip champagne by the fireplace in their lingerie.

OK, that didn't happen, but I'm pretty sure Doggett not only gave Smiley explicit instructions about where to take Scully, he also told her to hit on her and see if she could work out a post-pregnancy threesome. Smiley's sapphic sensibilities are put on hold when Anti-Billy arrives, only to be gunned down by the helpful game warden.

Back in D.C. the men are all straight and in a shocking development, Krycek's a bad guy again. One episode after saving Mulder and Scully from Anti-Billy, he's now in league with MyBodyguardAlienguy and the equally bumpy Agent Crane.

Yeah I know, I can't follow that anymore either.

Krycek tries to kill Mulder, but commits the No. 1 crime of idiot celluloid killers. He spends an endless amount of time jabbering instead of shooting. Krycek says he saved Mulder countless times. He calls him his brother. He thinks Mulder looks really hot in a red speedo.

Blah. Blah. Blah. Blah.

Krycek blabs and then Skinner shows up and shoots, pumping Alex full of lead in a display of ferocity no doubt inspired by the fact Skinner has endured an entire season minus his testicles. Mulder appears shocked and decides he has to get the hell away from this lunatic. He has the convenient excuse of wanting to save Scully, but I know he's really afraid Skinner's about to go postal and he wants to get the hell out of Dodge ASAP.

Speaking of Scully, she's really thirsty, there's a nice picture of Jesus in the background (see the baby is supposed to be the next savior, get it?) and suddenly there are aliens everywhere. The game warden is an alien. Anti-Billy Miles is back from the dead again and suddenly Bethlehem ... errr I mean Georgia ... has turned into a "Night of the Living Dead" movie.

Back in D.C., Doggett spots MyBodyguardAlien guy and Crane outside Kersh's office. Pretty soon, they spot him in an abandoned FBI hallway (doesn't anybody work at that place?) and Doggett insists he'll use force as they come striding toward him like extras in a bad Frankenstein movie. Doggett's idea of using force is to turn and run away like the Knights of the Roundtable in "Monty Python and the Holy Grail."

Run away! Run away!

Fortunately, Doggett runs into Skinner, who is so pumped with testosterone he could kick Mike Tyson's ass and have enough left over for Riddick Bowe. Soon they're driving and being chased by MyBodyguardAlien Guy and Crane. Skinner shows Doggett he's no wimp by running over Crane, only that doesn't stop Crane from keeping up the chase.

Meanwhile, Scully is still surrounded by the Night of the Living Dead aliens. For some reason, this only makes Smiley smile even more. The fact that she's turned on by all this really bothers me and Scully sure doesn't seem thrilled about giving birth to a closet lesbian with alien-fetish tendencies.

The aliens are watching. Scully is screaming. Smiley is yelling "Push! Push! Push" and trying to submerge the feeling that she hasn't been this excited since cheerleader tryouts during her freshman year in college. Back in D.C., Skinner drives Crane into a wall and then Crane is run over by MyBodyguardAlienguy who conveniently crashes into another wall as his car explodes.

Whew.

Back in Bethlehem, Mulder suddenly arrives in what has to be the speediest helicopter on the face of the earth. He just followed a light in the sky (see there was a light over the manger ... oh, never mind). The aliens leave. They just drive off without saying a word, which is pretty much what I did after paying good money to see that lousy Bo Derek "Tarzan" movie back in high school.

Yeah she's naked a lot, but what the hell was Richard Harris thinking?

Anyway, Mulder rushes through the cars of aliens and into the manger to find Scully. Cut to Doggett and Smiley in Kersh's office where they tell him he's under investigation, thus setting the stage for the events in a ninth season I won't watch.

Back at Scully's, The Lone Gunmen come to see the baby bearing gifts. See there are three of them and they're wise and they have gifts and we're supposed to think the baby is really Jesus. Me? I'm thinking Carter has just set an all-time TV record for the amount of biblical references crammed into a one-hour episode.

Turns out the baby is neither Spanish or the next Savior. He's just a little human bundle of joy. That makes Mulder and Scully feel so good they can't keep their hands and lips off each other in an ending that was perfectly in tune with the evolution of their relationship the past few years.

As enjoyable as I found "Existence" to be, it wasn't on par with "Essence." It lacked the dramatic power and tension of "Essence" as well as the evil of the Anti-Billy Miles stalking everyone in sight. It also had moments of utter confusion.

For example:

1. Does anyone have any idea what in the hell Krycek was up to? Did anything he said before being blown away make the least bit of sense to anyone

not named Chris Carter? Didn't think so. I'll bet Nick Lea doesn't have a clue either.

2. Why did the aliens just give up so easy? OK, the baby wasn't the next savior and so it wasn't a threat to them after all. But why just drive away? Was there an alien board meeting they couldn't be late for?

3. Why did MyBodyguardAlienguy run over the suddenly important Agent Crane and is there a reason why I should even care?

4. How in the hell did The Lone Gunmen get out of the building they were trapped in at the end of their season finale and has anyone told them their series got canceled?

More questions than answers. But the answers that were provided left me feeling good about this episode. Very good.

It wasn't the taut high-wire act of "Essence," but it was an enjoyable race against time with the tension of Scully's delivery nicely paralleled against the actions of the boys back in D.C. who were uncovering the real truth before Mulder's race against time to find the woman he loves.

After watching "Existence," I'm even more convinced Carter has an evil twin. But I'm thrilled the good Carter prevailed in the end. The one who created this series eight years ago and not the one who made me queasy with his bizarre plot decisions this year.

By the way Chris: Mulder wasn't dying last season. You know it and I know it. So cut the crap and edit that lunacy out of all future airings of S8 episodes. Oh, and you're still not forgiven for "Fight Club."

The evil twin, meanwhile, has been banished to the nether world, to be tortured by images of Diana Fowley, Butt Genies and Kathy Griffin for all eternity.

From his eternal dwelling in the fires of Hades, the evil twin was unable to view the concluding act of "Existence" which consisted of affirmation of the child's origin, confirmation of Mulder and Scully's intimate turn in their relationship and a tender kiss between two lovers.

"The truth we both know."

Indeed we do. Many of us have known the truth for some time. We were just wondering if Carter would follow through on everything he had set up in terms of Mulder and Scully's relationship.

In the final moments of "Existence," Carter followed through with grace and elegance. And thanks to the magic between David Duchovny and Gillian Anderson, the scene will serve as a defining moment in the Mulder/Scully dynamic.

There was tenderness and humor (nice touch by Carter to pay homage to Duchovny's joke about Scully being in love with Skinner in "Hollywood A.D."). But most of all there was confirmation of the relationship Mulder and Scully share and affirmation of their shared "truth" - their love for one another.

Scully tells Mulder she named the baby William after his father (not hers) and we can deduce the "truth" behind that statement. Mulder's fragmented family was the impetus of his blinding obsession (one even Doggett has picked up on in their short time together). By naming the baby after Mulder's father, this is Scully's way of telling us who the father of her baby is and her way of telling Mulder this is his chance to repair the damage his tortured soul experienced by creating a family of his own.

Together, they will start anew. The baby is their united source of hope for a better tomorrow for the both of them. The son has become the father with a chance to do right where his father went wrong.

A baby alone does not a relationship make. So Scully, serving as she always has as the voice of the audience, asks Mulder what further truths they should know. Mulder responds with a kiss, one Scully welcomes by pulling him closer as the camera pans away and the episode comes to a close.

With this kiss, we have Carter's affirmation of the relationship his two main characters now share. This is not the kiss of transcendentally platonic friends. This is the kiss of two people in love with the baby cradled between them serving as a symbol of their love. This was more powerful than words could convey. This was Mulder's way of confirming where they had been before his abduction and where they would always be for all eternity.

Together. On an intimate level. Never to be torn apart again.

This was the ending Mulder and Scully deserved. One filled with hope. The baby symbolized a living representation of their own humanity, which has been their greatest strength and one of the show's strongest themes since its conception.

There is going to be a ninth season of "The X-Files," but for me "Existence" marked the end of the series. Most importantly, it's come to a fitting end. With Duchovny leaving and the Mulder/Scully dynamic no longer the centerpiece of the series, it will cease to be "The X-Files" and become something else entirely.

To be honest, that's not a series I have any interest in watching, but that's not important. What is important is the show I have loved for eight years has come to a fitting end. In the end, we saw Mulder and Scully together with their new baby a living embodiment of their love, plus a final kiss that signified the tremendous power of their union.

The series has ended the way it began. The two of them together, about to chart a course into a new world, uncertain of its possibilities or what truths and revelations fate has in store for them.

It is a journey they will make together and that is the way it should be since "The X-Files" has always been about Mulder and Scully. Their relationship. The strength of their union and their ability to trust no one but one another.

It is fitting then that the final image we have of this series is of them together. The last moment we may ever see of them together is filled with the tenderness, devotion and love that has made their relationship, and this series, so remarkable over the years. It was the perfect final scene and the ideal culmination of an eight-year relationship that has taken us to the boundaries of humanity and beyond.

Sealed with a kiss.

THE EVOLUTION OF A RELATIONSHIP

We all have our favorite Mulder and Scully moments, scenes that bring a smile to our face, ones that make us think fondly of the series we love and the characters we have warmly embraced. Each of us could probably easily recite a dozen or more at the very least without hesitation if asked to name the moments we cherish most.

But which moments transcend the realm of personal taste? Which moments provide us with a glimpse of this wonderful relationship and how it progressed over the course of so many years? I've given some thought to this and compiled a list of moments I believe are not only wondrous examples of the Mulder-Scully partnership, but testaments to its unique evolution.

IN THE BEGINNING: SEASONS 1-3

"The Pilot:" To look at how this relationship has evolved, we obviously have to go back to where it all began. Not so much the introductory scene between Mulder and Scully. While charming, that's not the one I find to be most significant. Instead, I believe the scene in Mulder's hotel room in Oregon is the one that truly laid the foundation for this relationship. Not only are we given insight into Mulder's quest, but Scully is enthralled as well. She (and we the viewer) can feel Mulder's passion for his beliefs and the intensity with which he relays the mission he is on is seductive. In fact, you could say Scully is seduced by Mulder's words and the powerful way Mulder intently describes his past, present and where he believes his future is headed. In that instant, Scully is hooked. And so are we.

"One Breath:" Arguably the greatest episode in the series' run. The key scene here, in my opinion, comes near the end when, for the first time, we see Mulder place someone else above his quest. Mulder is forced to make a choice between facing the men responsible for Scully's abduction and being with Scully in what may be her final moments on Earth. When he chooses Scully over his quest, it is a significant moment and a powerful indication of how deeply the two of them have grown together. For so long, nothing else mattered to Mulder than uncovering the truths he so desperately sought. But now, for the first time, the truth became insignificant. Something else, make that someone else, finally mattered more than the path he had been on. It's a significant moment for Mulder and for the relationship between Mulder and Scully.

"Wetwired:" The strongest foundation of the Mulder-Scully relationship had always been trust. Above everything else, the trust they had in one another was vital. That's one reason why this episode is a standout. It flips the characters around, lovingly encasing Scully in paranoia. And when Mulder insists to Scully that "you are the only one I trust," there is a powerful resonance in his words. It represents how no matter where they go, they are always in that basement, alone, but always together with the world a separate entity. That is the plea Mulder is making as he tries to talk Scully out of her delirium. They may question everything and everyone around them, but they need not question one another. Their trust, their faith in one another, has become their united lifeforce.

THE RELATIONSHIP DEEPENS: SEASONS 4-6

"Memento Mori:" One of the brightest lights in "The X-Files" universe, this episode is devoted to the bond Mulder and Scully share with one another. Confronting her cancer, Scully spends much of the episode pouring her feelings into a diary, attempting to convey to Mulder the wide range of emotions she was confronting. Mulder, meanwhile, is spent unearthing the mysteries he hoped would reveal the reasons behind Scully's illness. Although they spend much of the episode apart, they are never truly alone. Although he cannot hear Scully's words, they propel him along all the same. And as was the case in "One Breath," Scully draws strength from Mulder's beliefs. At the end, both are left to ponder their demons, physical in Scully's case, emotional and psychological for Mulder. Both are left to ponder the truths that can save both of them. Truths they can only find together.

"Fight the Future:" In many ways, the film is a two-hour case study of the Mulder-Scully relationship. But the pivotal moment comes in Mulder's hallway after Scully has told him she will be leaving. Scully is wracked with self-doubt, questioning her place alongside Mulder, convinced she is yet another obstacle in his dogged pursuit of the truth. Mulder's response is crucial. For the first time, he extends the nature of their relationship beyond the aspect of trust. When he tells her that she has made him a whole person, he is pulling Scully inside him, filling the gaping hole created the night his sister was abducted, the night Mulder lost a part of himself as well. Mulder can't go on without Scully because she has become as essential as "the truth" had always been. The elusive truth was the fuel that drove Mulder's quest. But Scully had now provided the soul he needed to not only persevere, but to survive.

"Triangle:" An homage to "The Wizard of Oz" or a riveting peak into Mulder's subconscious as he tries to decipher the true meaning of his relationship with Scully? How about both? Although Mulder is confronted with several people from his life (ala Dorothy), I think there is an interesting examination of his growing relationship with Scully as well. The ship could be seen as a metaphor for Mulder and Scully's relationship and when the Nazi's board the Queen Mary, one could argue this is Mulder's subconscious mind at work, creating a hurdle that represents Mulder grappling with his deepening relationship and true feelings for Scully. What he needs to truly take that next step and articulate his feelings is the belief in him that only Scully can give him. That comes at the end when Scully alters the course of the Queen Mary (symbolizing Mulder's desire to alter the course of his relationship with

Scully). Mulder has been given his sign and after a kiss shrouded in darkness (again Mulder's subconscious mind at work, the darkness possibly representing his trepidation in pushing things further with Scully), he is snapped back to reality where he can finally convey the feelings he now has for Scully. Scully saved the ship in Mulder's dream state and allowed him to open another door to his present.

FROM THIS POINT FORWARD: SEASONS 7-8

"**Requiem:**" Much of this episode is about looking to the future while feeling the past nipping at Mulder and Scully's heels. From an FBI audit which threatens the future of The X-Files to, more importantly, the progression of the Mulder-Scully relationship, it's clear a new chapter is being written. Mulder seems resolved to move to another place in his life. He wants something more for Scully, something more for himself and his growing relationship with Scully symbolizes the change in his life. He is prepared to move forward, but before he can, he believes he must put an end to the past that had driven him for so long. The irony of Mulder's abduction is that it came at the precise moment in his life when he no longer needed it or was driven to embrace it. His "quest" no longer sustained him entirely. There was something more in his life to draw strength from. He seemed resolved to the fate of The X-Files. None of that truly mattered anymore. But before he could truly take that next step with Scully, the one he was now truly ready to make, he was taken from her.

"**Existence:**" The pivotal moment comes with a kiss and the enigmatic words that symbolize the evolution of their relationship. "The truth we both know" is Mulder's way of confirming to Scully his love for her. There was no longer anything to fear from the "possibilities" that may come with taking that next step together. With a kiss, Mulder and Scully embraced not only one another, but the new direction their relationship was taking them. A relationship eight years in the making.

SEASON 9

The eighth season of "The X-Files" ended with a kiss, a moment between Mulder and Scully that would have never seen the light of day were it not for Duchovny and director Kim Manners. Carter's original ending for "Existence" was a forehead kiss between Mulder and Scully. Duchovny and Manners nixed that, believing the time was right for something more intimate between the two questing heroes.

"The scene that was produced was the scene we all thought was the best," Spotnitz told me after the season came to an end. "We ended up with the right scene."

The kiss left many fans content with how the season had ended, if not enamored with how the season had unfolded. When Duchovny departed, many fans hoped the show would end with him. Alas, "The X-Files" would continue for one more season although without Mulder and Scully at its core, Fox's once-proud network centerpiece quickly plunged into the depths of ratings despair.

The ratings decline was precipitated by the confusing way 1013 attempted to explain Duchovny's absence. When I spoke to Spotnitz during the summer hiatus, he was confident the explanation would prove worthy of Mulder's character.

"I think we've got a way that's going to be completely true to the character and completely true to the series," he said.

The "in character" decision consisted of Mulder simply leaving Scully and their son after being warned his life was in danger. Given how Mulder's life had been in danger numerous times since the show's inception and he had never abandoned Scully before, many fans believed this turn of events was a rather questionable way to explain Mulder's absence in the ninth season.

"There was a lack of any thoughtful explanation of what had become of Mulder," said Elizabeth Martinez, a fan since the second season from Little Rock, Ark. "1013 again demonstrated their lack of imagination in how to deal with Mulder's absence and Scully's way of dealing with it. It was another instance of bad and stupid storytelling choices."

"Having Mulder abandon his family was totally out of character and lacked imagination on the writers' part," added Gayle Jones, a fan from Arkansas who began watching in the fourth season.

With Duchvony gone, Annabeth Gish was elevated to a co-starring role as Agent Monica Reyes and Cary Elwes ("The Princess Bride") snared a reoccurring role as a possibly corrupt assistant FBI director. Former "Xena" star Lucy Lawless was also cast as a Super Soldier in the first two episodes of the season. Hamstrung by Anderson's desire not to do any pre-season publicity and aware of the overwhelming lack of interest in Doggett by many members of the fan base, Fox turned to Lawless as a means of generating interest in the new season.

It didn't work.

The first two episodes were a disaster. Only 10.6 million viewers tuned in for the premier with a dismal 9.4 million watching the following week. As the season progressed, the ratings only got worse. Episodes such as "Hellbound" (7.8 million viewers), "Underneath" (7.3) and "Release" (7.8) were a far cry from the 19.8 million viewers who watched during the show's peak in the fourth and fifth seasons.

The show suffered a 30 percent drop in viewership from the eighth season and its overall ranking was No. 63, compared to No. 31 in Season 8. What the eighth season had foreshadowed, the ninth season was proving conclusively: "The X-Files" simply did not work without Mulder and Scully together.

It didn't seem to be working for Anderson either. After stating numerous times how she was "physically and mentally exhausted" by the show's demands, Anderson stunned many observers by signing on for an extra year prior to the start of Season 8.

Publicly, Anderson said she extended her contract so that she would be more adequately compensated financially. Privately, some television insiders speculated that Anderson's camp assumed the pending actor's strike would prevent a ninth season from ever occurring. When the strike was averted, Anderson was stuck with one more season on a show she had admittedly grown tired of doing.

Meanwhile, sources said her relationship with Carter had cooled since the start of the eighth season. During the early stages of Season 9, she reportedly spent much of her time in her trailer, appearing on the set only to film her scenes.

Then again, it wasn't as if she had all that much to do. Although Spotnitz insisted Anderson's role would not be diminished in the ninth season (his answer was an emphatic "No" when I posed the question to him in an interview before the season began), that is precisely what happened as the series began to focus more of its attention on Doggett and Reyes.

The problem with that plan was many fans simply did not care about the new lead characters. Their personal investment resided with Mulder and Scully first and foremost and their disinterest in Doggett and Reyes was reflected in the show's sinking ratings.

"Although I liked Doggett, the new characters were just 'too normal.' They lacked the uniqueness and intelligence of Mulder and Scully," said Margie Stratfull, a fan from Sacramento, Calif. "Mulder and Scully's flaws, along with their chemistry and intelligence, helped make them so endearing."

With viewers tuning out in droves, sources said Fox execs became more involved with the show's content and direction. "Underneath" had so many problems Fox seriously considered pulling it completely before finally allowing it to be aired later in the season.

"Carter didn't have to pitch stories since Season 1, so he was upset by having to do that," one source said. "Spotnitz didn't even know they had to do that, so he was upset by it. Carter and Spotnitz had their way for so long they couldn't imagine being accountable to anyone. They thought they were fighting for their show, but Fox just wanted to make sure the shows made sense because they were the ones paying for it."

That issue became paramount since the eighth season marked the first time in the history of the show that Fox didn't make its money back in repeats and profits on the secondary market. Given how expensive each episode was to produce, that revenue was vital for Fox in terms of allowing "The X-Files" to remain on the air.

With the show sinking in the ratings and morale on the set suffering, speculation began mounting late in 2001 that the series would be canceled. Around that time, sources said Carter and Fox executives began making overtures to Duchovny about returning for the season finale. The talks continued in earnest until late January when Carter announced the show would conclude at the end of its ninth season.

Shortly thereafter, it was announced that Duchovny would return for the series finale and also direct and co-write a pivotal mytharc episode, "William." That episode would feature the return of Jeffrey Spender from the dead (which was the genesis of Duchovny's idea for the episode) as well as one of the most controversial moments in the series history: Scully's decision to give her and Mulder's son up for adoption.

Duchovny's return was greeted enthusiastically in most quarters of the fan community and by Anderson, who admitted she greatly missed their on-screen partnership. Although many fans had grown disenchanted with the series or had stopped watching altogether, the opportunity to see Mulder and Scully one final time was alluring.

That excitement was tainted for some fans, however, after "William" aired. Not long after 1013 shocked and angered many fans by killing off The Lone Gunmen in an episode titled, "Jump The Shark," watching Scully part with her son was even more difficult for those fans to stomach from a characterization and storytelling perspective.

"Making baby William an oddity that was constantly placed in harms way and then shipped off like some puppy that the owners (writers) couldn't handle, which in turn made the Scully character look like a fool, was the worst decision ever made," said Nicole Jenkins, a Florida fan since the pilot.

Sources close to the show said the decision wasn't wildly embraced within 1013 either. The episode was based on Duchovny's Season 8 idea about a mysterious, disfigured person with connections to Mulder who enters Scully's life. According to producer John Shiban, the idea to give William up for adoption originated with Carter and Spotnitz.

Duchovny, Anderson and Shiban (all parents) reportedly were not thrilled with the idea. They grudgingly consented only after Carter revealed his plan to end the series with Mulder and Scully on the run, hardly in the best position to raise a child.

Duchovny's return left fans and industry insiders speculating about how much creative input he would have with the series finale given his disenchantment with how Mulder was handled the prior season. Although Duchovny said publicly he did not have a hand in writing "The Truth" (Carter had sole writing credit), sources on the set said he played a key role in the episode's development.

"He was very involved with the Mulder and Scully scenes," a source said. "He spent a lot of time working with Kim Manners on blocking and shaping the scenes. He had a lot of input."

Duchovny's influence extended off the set as well. Although Nick Lea reportedly told associates he would never work with Carter again given how frustrated he had been with Krycek's lack of development, he returned for the series finale as a favor to his friend Duchovny. When it came to "The X-Files," for many, Duchovny had become the straw that stirred the drink.

Like many fans, I planned to stop watching the series after Season 8. Without Duchovny and Anderson at the show's core, I had no desire to tune in every Sunday night. I avoided most of the season, only watching a few episodes and only reviewing "Trust No 1," "Providence," "William" and "The Truth," since all dealt strongly with the Mulder-Scully dynamic in some way.

Duchovny's return in "William" and "The Truth" managed to infuse the series with some much-needed energy, wit and occasional brilliance and for that I was grateful. But when the series ended, I was more relieved than anything else. Looking back, I believe all of the damage that had been done in the eighth season robbed me of much of my emotional response to the series.

Once I learned of Duchovny's return, all I hoped was that the series finale would allow Mulder and Scully to exit in a way that was fitting given all they had experienced together. "The Truth" was the series had ended for me long before the final scene would air on May 19, 2002. But I wanted to see Mulder and Scully again and be reminded why this series had proven to be so meaningful to myself and millions of others.

Thankfully, "The Truth" gave me much of what I had missed the previous two seasons.

"TRUST NO 1"

I've been a "Star Trek" fan for as long as I can remember. Kirk. Spock. McCoy. The original gang. I couldn't get enough of their stories and, OK please keep this between you and me, I know all of the episodes by heart. It's true. Really.

So imagine my surprise when, on my sixth birthday, I got model figures of my favorite "Star Trek" characters. Kirk, Spock and McCoy in my own home. It was a "Trek" fan's dream come true and this little "YoungBound" couldn't have been happier. But something was amiss. The model figures looked like Kirk and Spock, but they didn't quite act like the ones I'd seen on TV, the ones I'd seen in all my favorite episodes.

To be honest, when they talked, they sounded like me, which wasn't what I was expecting at all.

At one point, I made the Spock model make out with my sister's Barbie, hoping this unbridled display of human emotion would snap him back to Vulcan-like behavior. But all that did was piss off my G.I. Joe with the Kung-Fu grip.

So there I sat, proud owners of model figures of my favorite "Trek" characters and yet something wasn't quite right. No matter how much these model figures looked like Kirk, Spock and Bones, I realized it wasn't really them. They weren't the characters I'd come to know and love. They were just imitations. I felt as if I'd been promised something the models could not deliver.

Which brings me to "Trust No 1," the first episode of the ninth season of "The X-Files" I have seen.

Yes I watched it. I have no spine. I have no inner strength to stay true to my word, to stay true to who I really am. I feel like the ninth season version of Mulder. You know, the one who runs away, cowers in fear and calls Scully, "Dana."

He calls her Dana now?

When the hell did that happen?

Is this still "The X-Files?"

Yes I watched and I'll be honest, I have no idea what "Trust No 1" was supposed to be about. It said Scully and Mulder were in love. Well I knew that already. Thanks to the opening Carterlogue, we also received more confirmation that Mulder is William's father. I knew that already, too.

So what was the point of the episode?

Was it to show us that anyone can stop by Dana Scully's House For Nefarious Characters and steal ... errrr ... watch her baby? What the hell happened to Scully? Why do I get the feeling that when she stuffed Mulder away at the end of "Patience," she shoved her brains in that desk drawer at the same time?

Seriously, how many people have to walk into her apartment or try and break in to bring harm to her or the kid before she STOPS LETTING STRANGERS SLEEP ON THE COUCH? Who is this person? What the hell happened to Scully?

And why is Mulder calling her Dana?

So anyway, there's a weird couple and they fight and then get to chill with Scully and tell her some Shadowman (memo to 1013: Stop casting actors we've seen before on the show. It makes the characters look stupid if they don't recognize them. Or in Scully's case, it makes her look even more stupid - if that's possible) is part of this whole SuperSoldier thing and somehow Mulder has to know about it.

Memo to anyone who still believes there's a point to the mytharc: Wasn't Mulder originally going to be a SuperSoldier? Isn't that why he was abducted and tortured? Wasn't Billy Miles turned into a SuperSoldier after being abducted by aliens? Didn't there used to be aliens on this show?

What happened to the aliens?

And why is Mulder calling her Dana?

Seeking answers, "Dana" meets the Shadowman. He knows all about her, all about her fear of clowns, how the carpet doesn't match the drapes (do the clowns know about this?) and how ... on "one lonely night" she invited Mulder to her bed.

Yup, that's right. The moment when Mulder and "Dana" took their relationship to a more intimate place all began just cuz "Dana" needed someone to scratch her loneliness itch. Gee, how ... romantic.

Of course, I've seen "all things," so I know this "lonely night" nonsense is just that, nonsense. I know the moment of intimacy began not because Scully was sick and tired of being horny and alone, but rather because she had come to a point in her life where she realized where fate had placed her and, most importantly, whom fate had placed her with. That is when Scully and Mulder became united in the only way they hadn't experienced before.

I loved "all things." I loved what it said about Mulder and Scully and their relationship. I loved Scully back then, too. Does anyone know if she's coming back? I miss her.

Stepford Scully apparently forgot all about "all things" and that pivotal moment in her life. Stepford Scully reacted the way someone would after hearing the truth. Like Shadowman, "I was surprised, too." But not that Scully invited Mulder to her bed in a fit of loneliness, but rather that anyone actually would believe this crap.

I thought twisting and contorting characterization and the MSR was the motto of the eighth season. Apparently, it's still in vogue. How wonderful.

Now that I think about it, if this Shadowman really knows everything about Mulder and Scully, maybe he could tell us why in the hell Mulder was calling Scully, "Dana." And maybe he could tell me why Agent Reyes The Lesbian Whale Singer wasn't wearing a bra. Shouldn't she be wearing a black one like Scully? Isn't that standard FBI issue? Or did she and Doggett The Stalker steal them all on their last late-night romp through her unmentionables?

Another memo to 1013: Doggett The Stalker and The Lesbian Whale Singer are actually much more appealing when they're not onscreen very often. Go figure.

Anyway, Scully "sends" for Mulder as if he's her plumber and she needs her pipes unclogged (hey this "one lonely night" business is starting to make sense now). But, GASP! There's a big shootout at the train station (I saw this in a John Wayne movie once), people die and Mulder rides on by, only later we seem him running away from The Stalker, which proves he still has some good sense left, and Shadowman gets sucked into the rocks or something because he's afraid of iron.

Or maybe it's really small pebbles. Honestly I have no idea what the hell is going on with this show anymore.

"Dana" then wraps things up by doing the dumbest thing in the entire episode and that's no small feat. After being told how every move she had made, including e-mails to Mulder, was being monitored, SHE E-MAILS HIM AGAIN! Gee, there's a good way to keep those plans a secret, huh "Dana?" What the hell happened to the woman who was more paranoid than Mulder? When did she start acting like Chrissy on "Three's Company?"

And why is Mulder calling her Dana?

I admit it. I didn't understand any of this. So I figured the only way to make sense of "Trust No 1" and understand and fully appreciate its immense beauty (because it had to be there and I was just too blind to see it, right?) was to call the man in charge. So I placed a call to the Surfer King himself.

CHRIS CARTER: Hello?

UNBOUND: Hey Chris, it's me 'Bound.

CC: You're not allowed to talk to me.

UB: Yeah, whatever. I just have one question. What was "Trust No 1" supposed to be about?

CC: Mulder and Scully love each other.

UB: I knew that.

CC: Ummm, Mulder's the father of Scully's baby.

UB: I knew that, too.

CC: Ummmm, I have more scary stories to tell and the series could go on indefinitely.

UB: Is that a threat?

(pause)

CC: That's not your name blacked out on the opening credits, you know.

UB: Yes, I'm aware of that.

CC: It's Glen Morgan's.

UB: Figures. Umm Chris?

CC: Yes?

UB: What happened to the aliens?

(click)

As I heard nothing but dead air on the telephone, I was left to ponder the dead hour of television I'd just witnessed. Were there some nice moments where Scully's desire to be with Mulder were on display? Yes there were. Of course, if someone would explain to me why in the hell Mulder left in the first place, we wouldn't have to sit through another Scully-tear fest although Gillian Anderson plays angst like nobody's business.

So what were we left with? Let's see, there's something funky about Willie, Mulder is still a deadbeat dad and a coward and the father or son have to die because the Super Soldiers are afraid of iron or really uninspired episodic endings. Yes, Carter and Spotnitz offered us the first actual on-air confirmation that Mulder and Scully slept together, but they wrapped it in a statement that made no sense to anyone who had seen the characters or the show before.

And given some of the bizarre word choices in those e-mails ("Dearest Dana?"), my guess is Mulder didn't disappear because of some Super Soldier threat, but rather so he could begin his new career as a senior writer for Hallmark Cards.

After watching "Trust No 1," I find myself wondering how a show that once was so great could be reduced to bizarre characterizations, incomprehensible story arcs so that even an episode that strives to aim for the acknowledged heart and soul of the series misses the mark badly.

I can't help but wonder if Carter and Spotnitz penned "Trust No 1" because they truly wanted to show us the bond between Mulder and Scully or because they are keenly aware of the fan revolt that occurred during Mulder's absence last season as well as the declining ratings this season and are desperately trying to win back viewers any way they can.

Yes, Mulder and Scully are the heart and soul of "The X-Files." But not the Mulder and Scully I watched in this episode.

Call me crazy, but a Scully who babbles one minute about not trusting Shadowman and then invites a total stranger into her home isn't a Scully for me. And call me "hysterical," but watching Mulder run away from The Stalker, while amusing on a number of levels, doesn't appeal to me because the Fox Mulder I knew wouldn't run in fear of anyone or anything. He'd face "the future" and fight it with Scully by his side.

That's "The X-Files" I remember, not this model imitation I witnessed in "Trust No 1." Just because it walks, talks and sometimes acts like "The X-Files" doesn't make it "The X-Files."

Yes I watched. The boys at 1013 suckered me into seeing what all the fuss was about. I watched and now I am left feeling empty. Mulder was mentioned a lot and Scully was around a lot, but I feel as if I never saw them once throughout the entire episode. And that only serves to make me wonder:

199

What happened to the aliens? Why is Mulder calling Scully "Dana?" And does anyone else miss "The X-Files" as much as I do?

"PROVIDENCE"

"If you want to see the boy, you'll bring me the head of Fox Mulder."

With words like that, how could I resist? How could I possibly hope to refrain? How I could possibly refuse the temptation to dip back into the waters of "X-Files" reviews after hearing such a threat?

The end is near my friends. We know this to be true. A once-great show on its last legs is attempting to build a head of steam toward an uncertain conclusion. Hope springs eternal and bears the form of David Duchovny, whose absence removed not just Mulder from "The X-Files" equation, but Mulder and Scully as well.

And without that, "The X-Files" ceased to exist. Don't believe me? Check out the ratings. I haven't seen anything that frightening since I caught a glimpse of Rosie O'Donnell in a bustier in "Exit to Eden."

The horror. Oh dear God, the horror.

So I look longingly for a light at the end of the tunnel, knowing that in a matter of time a reunion will take place and perhaps a chance for a return to the show I once loved. Until then, Josepho's words haunt me. They fill my head with contemplation. They demand my attention and although I wait with bated breath for what is to come in the future, I cannot resist taking a peak at the present.

And what is it I see? Scully being told she must give Mulder head ... errrr give Mulder's head ... to a madman. Is it any wonder I had to check "Providence" out?

The first thing I had to do was turn the volume on my television up to 50. Why in the hell was everybody whispering? What was the big secret? That nothing in this episode made any sense?

Here's a news flash for Chris Carter and Frank Spotnitz: In space, nobody can hear you scream and if no one's tuning in to watch your television series any longer, nobody can hear you whisper either.

SO SPEAK UP DAMMIT!

And isn't this lovely, Scully doesn't trust Skinner again. Hey, that's a fresh story idea ..... during Season 5. Didn't we put an end to all this foolishness back with "Redux II?"

So let's see, William The Super Freak (Copyright Unbound I ©2002) has been kidnapped by a UFO cult who believe the kid is some kind of savior who will help facilitate an alien invasion. And WTSF's father has to die or WTSF will follow in his footsteps and stop the alien invasion.

I guess this is meant to tell us that Mulder is WTSF's father. Since I saw the end of "Existence" I already knew that. I was actually more stunned to hear there might be aliens on this show again.

Go figure.

Scully spends most of the episode with the ever-present glint of a tear in her eyes. Apparently, that is now a standard part of every mytharc episode along with one seriously impressive push-up bra. Somehow, Scully finds a way to fight past the tears and enlists the aid of Reyes to try and find her son.

Now I realize Carter and Spotnitz wanted you to focus on the search for WTSF, but to me, this episode wasn't about aliens, UFO cults, Super Babies or shady members of the FBI.

Nope, this episode marked something far more monumental in the history of the series. This was Scully and Reyes' first date. OK, nobody had dinner and there wasn't a movie, but you can't fool me, this was a date. Why else would Scully spend so much time in leather?

Sure, Reyes tried to throw everybody off the scent by showing some concern for Doggett, who spent most of the episode in a coma, thus marking some of his best work yet since he's been on the show. She even went to a hospital chapel and prayed. But while Follmer may think her prayers were for Doggett, I'm convinced she was praying that once this series came to an end she might find a new gig on "Queer As Folk."

Scully and Reyes spend the rest of the episode gazing lovingly at one another and courting under the guise of trying to find WTSF, who like his mother sure knows how to cry. Only his tears lead to a smorgasbord of UFO cultists and the departure of an alien spacecraft.

Take that mom.

Scully and Reyes confirm the love that can never be spoken by holding hands briefly before finding WTSF, alone and crying. Scully holds WTSF, Reyes comforts Scully with a gentle caress, Doggett's hearing voices in his head (he thinks it's Reyes, but really it's millions of Nielsen television families chanting "You're no Fox Mulder. You're no Fox Mulder"), a bumpy neck is pulling Kersh's strings and I'm sitting here wondering why Scully cried at Doggett's bedside but didn't shed a tear when she believed Mulder was dead.

Oh well, out of sight out of mind I guess.

Either that or maybe Scully's as tired of hearing that Mulder is dead as everyone else is. The look on Gillian Anderson's face didn't exactly register concern or a heart that had been broken upon hearing the news. Instead, it was more like "He's dead again? Oh brother."

Speaking of out of sight, where in the hell were all the answers this episode was supposed to provide? Let's see, Mulder's dead. Oh wait, no he's not. WTSF is some kind of alien leader. Oh wait, maybe that's a false prophecy.

Scully's been concerned about her son's origins since the moment he was conceived? Ummm, where the hell was all that concern last season?

No time for concern when Butt Munch is on the loose I guess. Would it just kill these people to give us even one answer an episode from here on out? Just one?

Watching "Providence," I couldn't help but be reminded of my first day of Spanish class my freshman year in college. I'm sitting next to this really hot brunette and the professor walks in and starts talking in a foreign language. OK, I should've figured that was gonna happen, but the point is I had no clue what the hell he was saying and what any of it meant.

You know, now that I think about it, my professor looked an awful lot like that bumpy neck who was controlling Kersh. Hmmmmmm.

As this series winds down, you would think Carter and Spotnitz would be in a hurry to resolve some of the myriad of questions they've posed. Instead, "Providence" was just more of what we've come to expect the past two seasons. Sixty minutes of urgency marked by often incomprehensible storytelling.

One of my complaints about this new version of the mytharc is it has become so diametrically opposed to its past. Am I the only one who remembers when this was a "global conspiracy?" Somehow, that seems to have gotten lost.

Even by tossing back in a hint of an alien invasion, the threat is no longer global. It's been placed squarely in the lap of an infant. And that's a rather radical shift in my opinion.

By placing such a heavy emphasis on WTSF, it removes the more pressing concerns that always provided the nasty undertow of the conspiracy, the idea that every one of us was being threatened by unseen forces, that all of our lives hung in the balance. Now the only thing that seems to matter is saving the kid.

And frankly, I'm not so sure I care about the kid.

I'm not sure I care because Carter and Spotnitz have failed to make the connection between this kid and why anyone believes he's a Super Baby. Does it have something to do with Mulder's experiences in "Biogenesis?" Is it at all connected to Scully's own abduction experience? Is it some combination of those two factors?

If so, then why doesn't someone come out and say it? Oh wait, no one can actually say that because we cannot have direct verbal confirmation that Mulder is actually WTSF's father. Raise your hand if you're tired of this song and dance?

Listen up people: Viewers have tuned you out and you're in a race to the finish line. It's time to stop creating new adjuncts of your mytharc and start providing some conclusive answers. It's not so hard. Storytellers do it every day. No really, I've seen them do it. Honest.

"Providence" should have marked the beginning of the show's push to the finish line. It should have begun to steer us on the course toward whatever conclusion Carter has planned for his series. Instead, it was another muddled attempt to create drama by piling on more unnecessary questions on top of ones that may never be answered.

How many days until Duchovny returns?

"Mulder's Sense Of Family"

The idea of trust has been arguably the pre-eminent theme on "The X-Files" since its inception. But providing an undercurrent to that theme has been the theme of the shattered family and the lengths people will go to in order to repair the damage done within.

We see it clearly in Mulder's family. Torn apart by a decision made by Bill Mulder. When Bill Mulder made the decision to turn his daughter over to the Consortium, it not only spurred into the motion the quest that would soon provide the lifeblood for his son, it also marked his failure as a father.

Bill Mulder failed his daughter, his wife and his son. And the ramifications of his actions would be felt for many years afterward. But now, it may be that the Mulder family is about to come full circle.

If the child is indeed father to the man and if Scully does give William away for adoption, it may not only pave the way for Fox Mulder to return, it also may provide him with the opportunity to succeed where his father failed. Bill Mulder failed to save Samantha. But now Fox Mulder may be given a chance to do what his father could not.

And if he can indeed save his son, it would bring the Mulder story to a fitting conclusion. Where once it was defined by failure, now it would be defined by salvation.

David Duchovny has defined Mulder as a questing hero, an almost mythological figure. It is my belief that one of the most powerful aspects of Mulder's quest has been the subconscious desire to repair the damage done to his family the night his sister was abducted.

For years, it tormented him. It drove him to the brink of insanity and beyond. It wasn't until the events of "Closure," that he was able to accept his sister's demise and move forward, to stop being burdened by the past and to embrace whatever the future may hold.

That future now includes a son who may be taken from him and the woman he loves.

"WILLIAM"

"I'm afraid. I'm afraid to believe."

So am I. I'm afraid to believe what I have just seen. I'm afraid to believe the events that have just passed before my eyes could actually have occurred to a character I once loved.

203

I weep for Dana Scully. I weep for the character I once knew, the fiercely independent and intelligent FBI agent who was Fox Mulder's equal and who provided one half of the most fascinating partnership I have ever seen on television.

I weep for her because I miss her. And after watching "William," I've begun to wonder if I will ever see her again.

("Mulder, it's me.")

The legacy of the past two seasons of "The X-Files" is not a proud one. It has been filled with the most egregious of characterization sins.

We've been told about a brain disease that can be disputed with the most elementary of episodic evidence. We've seen Scully ignore the abduction of her "touchstone" and embrace a partner she had no reason to trust. We watched Mulder and Scully clumsily tap dance around the paternity of their unborn child like Mr. Ed on crack and saw Mulder turned into a coward and a deadbeat dad right in front of our very eyes.

("I've heard the truth. Now what I want are the answers.")

The answers we were provided the past two seasons mystified many of us. All the while, we wondered if it could get any worse. If the destruction of these two beloved characters could be more complete. Then "William" comes along and possibly pounds the final nail into Dana Scully's coffin.

("Don't think! Just pick up the phone and make it happen!")

"William" marked the official return of David Duchovny to "The X-Files." Although glimpsed briefly in a reflection in Scully's eye, Duchovny's central role with this episode was behind the camera, where he served as the director and a co-writer along with Chris Carter (who wrote the teleplay) and Frank Spotnitz.

As a director, one of the qualities I admired most about "The Unnatural" and "Hollywood A.D." was the way Duchovny brought Scully to life. When Duchvony shined his directorial light on Scully, she positively glowed. And there are some wonderful moments in "William" where, under Duchovny's expert hand, Gillian Anderson brings Scully to life once more.

("It's not that Mexican goat sucker either.")

Hearing her sing "Joy to the World" to William takes us back to a moment in the woods with Mulder in "Detour." But the most powerful moment comes during an almost erotic examination of a sinister figure known as The Breather.

Grappling with the possibility The Breather may be Mulder, Scully finds herself literally drawn to him. Inches from his face, her lips close to his, Scully's longing for Mulder manifests itself when she literally sees his face in her mind's eye.

In an instant, Duchovny deftly shows us the emptiness Scully feels with Mulder gone and displays the intensity of the union Mulder and Scully share with one another.

("Shut up Mulder, I'm playing baseball.")

But where Duchovny the director succeeds, Duchovny, Carter and Spotnitz the writers often fail. By co-writing "William," Duchovny has become complicit with the continuing saga of Stepford Scully, who has stumbled and bumbled her way around "The X-Files" the past two seasons. Sadly, further evidence of Dana's Demise was on plentiful display in "William."

Scully's Home For Wayward Psychos is open again for business as she allows The Breather to take a little nap on her bed. What better way to allow this nutjob access to her son than to put him just a few feet from the kid's bedroom? At least she wasn't dumb enough to let the potential psycho hold her son.

Oooops ...

The Breather, meanwhile, looks like he raided the wardrobe for Vince Gilligan's Brady Bunch episode. As he laces up his Zips, we're left to wonder if he may be Mulder.

Doggett believes he is which tells me he lied about reading every one of "The X-Files." If he had, he'd know there's no way in hell The Breather could be Mulder because even though Fox has had some serious haircut issues, he'd never try to pass himself off as Ringo Starr's long-lost son with a whacked out moptop.

("Believing is the easy part, Mulder. I just need more than you. I need proof.")

So The Breather (aka The Fifth Beatle) has Doggett fooled which, to be honest, is about as impressive as exhaling. All of us watching the episode know The Breather isn't Mulder because ... well ... we looked at him. My grandmother, who has a 10-inch black-and-white TV and only one good eye, called me and said she could tell The Breather wasn't Mulder and so could her cat.

OK, I made that up. My grandmother didn't really call me and I can't verify what her cat does or does not know. But c'mon, look at him. OK, look at him again. Now blink and look at him a third time.

Does this guy look anything like Mulder? He doesn't even look like Denise from "Twin Peaks" for cryin' out loud.

Apparently, simple eyesight wasn't scientific enough proof, so a DNA test is run. Although initial results prove a DNA match between The Breather and Mulder, soon a nation of viewers (or a ratings share of 6.6 for the overnights and 6.4 for the final) discovers that really isn't the case. Instead we learn he's Jeffrey Spender, whose body was never found after the CSM put a cap in his ass in "One Son."

Turns out Jeff was a tad bit pissed by CGB's rather stern method of parenting and made it his mission to thwart his father's plans. He does so by injecting William with magnetite. He also tosses in another nugget of information, confirming once and for all the CSM is Mulder's father.

I'm so disgusted by what Scully does in this episode I don't even want to think about how stupid I've always thought that storyline is.

Spender tells Scully the kid is now normal and no longer the key to the aliens' plan for colonization. He adds a little caveat, however, telling Scully the aliens will never rest until they get their hands on William whether he's "normal" or not.

This just in to the aliens: You had a great chance to nab him when Scully was giving birth to him in "Existence." Why the hell didn't you grab him then? Were you frightened by Reyes' Whale Singing and lustful feelings for Scully?

OK, I'll cut them some slack there. That freaked me out, too.

So knowing how much danger William is in, Scully does what any mother and competent federal agent trained to protect and serve would do. She lets the kid be someone else's problem. Apparently those late-night feedings were a real bitch.

("I want you to close your eyes and say, there's no place like home. There's no place like home.")

Although the return of Spender provided a fascinating subplot (the vengeance he sought against his father was a nice extension of the shift we saw his character making before his apparent demise in "One Son"), the heart of this episode clearly resides with Scully and William. The dramatic centerpiece is Scully's decision to give him away.

She believes it's to protect him, but the Dana Scully I used to know would immediately recognize the folly of such an idea. The men, aliens, Super Soldiers or whoever the hell is pursuing William have proven time and again they can find whatever it is they're seeking and act with terminal intensity.

The safest place for William is with his parents since they are the only ones equipped to deal with the threats posed against him. And yet, Scully blindly ignores all of this and gives him away, not only sealing her son's fate, but also risking the lives of other innocent people who will come into contact with William because once the forces of evil that want William find him (and they will find him), chances are they won't leave any witnesses behind.

In other words, it's adios Ma and Pa Kettle.

By giving up her son, Scully has not only handed him a death sentence, but effectively snuffed out the lives of everyone who comes into contact with the boy as well. All of this made me wonder if Scully is putting an example of this ludicrous behavior on the final for that class she supposedly is teaching.

Then again, who knows if Scully is still a teacher. She spends less time in the classroom than Tia Carrere on "Relic Hunter."

("I won't let you go alone.")

The adoption, of course, could be a ruse. Few things are what they seem on "The X-Files." By focusing on a white buffalo mobile (the white buffalo symbolic of "a great change" in "Paper Clip") in William's new home,

Duchovny provides a possible clue that all is not what it appears to be here either.

It is a visual link to the Anasazi, which could in turn be a link to Mulder given his connection with them many years ago (not to mention Duchovny's personal connection to the episode "Anasazi," which he co-wrote). If William is to return to Mulder and Scully, the answers may lie with the Anasazi and it's possible this theme will be revisited one final time.

Yet if there is a tie to the Anasazi, why do these words from Albert Hosteen haunt me? "My father taught me when I was a boy that this is how life is. That for something to live, another thing must often be sacrificed."

Has William been sacrificed so Mulder could return to Scully? Or is this adoption the result of a writing staff which introduced a pivotal plot line at the end of the seventh season and then had no idea how to logically handle it?

Rather than use this child as a means to represent the evolution of Mulder and Scully's relationship, he was rendered a silly plot device the past two seasons. William never felt like Mulder and Scully's son because he was 1.) never directly referenced in such a manner and 2.) he served only to further whatever particular storyline was needed at the moment and not as an emotional and dramatic foundation by which Mulder and Scully's relationship could evolve.

As I said, it's possible what we have seen in "William" is not indicative of what will occur when the series ends. But for now all I feel is a sense of sadness. Unlike The Lone Gunmen, who perished needlessly in "Jump The Shark," Scully isn't really dead and because she's alive, there's no way of knowing what further damage will be done to her.

The boys at 1013 can no longer strike at TLG, but they have three episodes left to tamper with Scully. And that's far more terrifying than any of the "scary stories" Carter has long insisted were the lifeblood of his long-running series.

("If I leave now, they win.")

Directing a mytharc episode for the first time, Duchovny again shows a nice visual flair. He uses shadows and darkness to good effect, provides quick, but meaningful images (the fleeting glimpse of Mulder's fish tank in Scully's apartment is understated yet compelling) and the torture sequences with The Breather leap off the screen in powerful jolts of visual pain. He also elicits strong performances from the entire cast.

Unfortunately, the episode is undone by Scully's critical decision, one that strains credibility and defies characterization. The episode failed to completely succeed for me because I could not connect with the most essential moment of the story.

Duchovny did a masterful job of luring me back to the world of "The X-Files." But when Scully gave away William at the end, I felt disconnected because Scully had become a stranger once again.

I want to trust that when this series concludes, we will have been told our initial appraisal of the situation was incorrect. That there really was more going on here than we had believed. I want to believe Carter, Spotnitz and Duchovny would not destroy this character and that she (and Mulder) will be returned to us in the end.

Yet having seen so much destruction the past two seasons, I can't help but draw upon the words Scully spoke many seasons ago. The words symbolize my feelings about what I have watched of late and the trepidation I now feel for the final days of this once-proud television series. So when 1013 asks me to believe, I have but one response.

"I'm afraid. I'm afraid to believe."

"THE TRUTH"

It began in the basement and ended with Mulder and Scully in bed in a Roswell motel room. Bet you never saw that coming, did ya?

So now my friends, we have finally reached the end of the road with "The X-Files." For some, the show ended one, two, three even four seasons ago. Yet many of us returned at the end, curious to see the conclusion Chris Carter would provide for a series that had such a wonderful beginning, a glorious middle and far too many fragmented moments of lunacy the past two seasons.

We came to see if Carter could do something he has often had difficulty doing in the past - provide true closure when his series needed it the most.

"The Truth" was the two-hour culmination of nine seasons of "The X-Files." A momentous occasion to say the least. One so great it sparked the return of David Duchovny, who had wisely avoided the bulk of this season, sparing himself (but sadly not the character of Fox Mulder) the embarrassment of being a part of this ship while it sprung numerous holes and sank into a sea of ratings despair.

Were it not for Duchovny's return and the anticipation of seeing him and Gillian Anderson together again, "The Truth" is nobody would have given a damn about the end of this series. But Duchovny returned and that gave Carter a tremendous advantage when it came time to pen his penultimate episode.

I'll give Carter credit for not writing a series finale like Xena's where someone lost their head (would it have been so bad if Doggett at least got a really bad razor cut?). And he didn't pull a lame "it was all a dream" scenario out of his ass the way the creators of "St. Elsewhere" did when they butchered the end of their beloved show.

Wisely, Carter stayed true to the foundation of his series and ended it in a fitting manner - with Mulder and Scully alone, yet together on their united quest to fight the future. In that sense, Carter succeeded by not bastardizing his series the way he often did the past two seasons.

What else did we learn from "The Truth?" Well, we found out very clearly that Mulder and Scully love each other and are determined to be with one another. We also learned the mytharc is a jumbled mess, incomprehensible to even the handful of people still trying to figure the damn thing out.

In other words, we discovered nothing we didn't already know in an episode that should have told us everything we needed to know. Or at least something we didn't already suspect.

That's not to say the episode was without merit. On the contrary, watching Duchovny and Anderson work together given meaningful moments (something 1013 often refused to give them last season) served as a wonderful reminder of how powerful these two acting forces are and how magical their chemistry remains.

Duchovny was brilliant, especially during the scene where he's being tortured and asked what he's thinking about. "My son ... his mother" is his response, reinforcing the powerful shift in Mulder's life that has now become a vital component of his quest.

Anderson and Duchovny later shine during two visits in Mulder's prison cell. The first begins with a classic "Mulder it's me" before shifting into a wonderful reunion between two characters who missed each other greatly and two actors who radiate in one another's presence. The second has Duchovny effectively showing Mulder's torment at denying Scully's request to share with her the information he has unearthed.

The return of Mulder also meant a return of Mulder humor. First he lifts a line from "Silence of the Lambs" when he says to Scully, "I could smell you coming Clarice" during a visit with Scully and Skinner in his cell. Then he jokingly offers Skinner a little lovin' after sharing a passionate kiss with Scully.

It's amazing anyone actually thought this show could work without this guy.

The focal point of the episode finds Mulder on trial for the alleged murder of Super Soldier Knowle Rohr, who Mulder may have killed during a tussle in a government facility where Mulder had gone in search of the elusive "truth." We're not privy to everything Mulder uncovers, but judging from the look on his face, I'm betting he finally learned what Scully did with his nameplate in "Patience."

That's nothing, Mulder. You missed her crying in Doggett's arms two days after meeting the guy. And here you thought only the aliens knew the meaning of pure torture.

Not only is Mulder on trial for murder, he's pulling a Haley Joel Osment, seeing dead people all over the place. Bruce Willis is nowhere to be found, but here comes Krycek, who, despite being dead, still registers more onscreen magnetism than John Doggett. Then X shows up and later, Mulder has a run-in with The Lone Gunmen, who merrily arrive during a urination break in the desert, which makes me wonder what kind of porn Mulder's been watching during his year away from Scully.

One person Mulder will never see again is his son. Scully took care of that in "William" by pawning him off on a couple of farmers out in the backwoods. Scully tries to explain her decision to Mulder, who says he understands what she was going through while admitting the pain he was enduring without the two people he loved.

I'm glad Mulder understands because I'm still dumbfounded by Scully's mind-numbingly stupid decision. Then again, I'm still trying to figure out how Mulder contracted a fatal brain disease he clearly never had or the reason why he would turn into a coward and abandon his family.

Oh the joys of the past two seasons of "The X-Files."

Back at the trial, Skinner gets to play Perry Mason, Kersh looks like he had a really bad burrito for lunch and a host of familiar faces arrive to try and clarify nine seasons of aliens, conspiracies and a plot device masquerading as a baby boy. Among the highlights:

*Mulder was chilling with Gibson Praise during his "I don't wanna be a dad and did you see how bad the show got without me?" phase. Hopefully he wasn't introducing young Gibson to the joys of 900 numbers.

*Scully is accused of having Mulder's "love child." Please kids, let this serve as a lesson to all of you that you should never mix massive amounts of pot and the oldies station while writing a script.

*Spender comes back to tell us everything he already told us in "William." That must've helped Chris Owens save time memorizing his lines.

*Marita testifies about her role in the conspiracy, but just as she is about to shed more light on the big mystery, Krycek appears and tells Mulder she can't be allowed to continue or she'll be killed. You know, if I can't get a Mulder-Scully love scene in the finale, I think I'd settle for watching Krycek and Marita go at it again even if one of them is dead.

*Doggett admits the series going in the toilet the past two seasons is entirely his fault and the show should've ended after the seventh season. He's also thrilled he won't be in the next movie, but hopes he'll be invited to the premier.

*We learn from Reyes that William may have been an alien implant who was a result of Scully's eggs having been tampered with. Was this knowledge the product of a late-night lingerie session at Scully's place? "Oh Dana (cooing), I can't believe what those awful men did to you. (giggle) But you sure look sexy in that black lace bra and matching thong. Turn around for me baby and let me gaze at you in the firelight."

Fortunately, the trial doesn't last as long as the "L.A. Law" reunion movie, but the verdict is the same as that series without Jimmy Smits. Mulder is found guilty and sentenced to death.

He doesn't stay incarcerated for long. Skinner and Doggett (with Kersh's help) bust him out and soon he's on the road with Scully. heading to the Anasazi ruins and a meeting with a man who knows "The Truth." That man turns out to be the CSM, who looks like a cross between a hippie at Woodstock and Phyllis Diller.

The CSM reveals the big secret Mulder has been unwilling to share. We brace ourselves for the moment that's been nine seasons in the making. And the big secret? The date of colonization. Dec. 22, 2012.

Huh? THIS is the big mystery Mulder was willing to die for? THIS is what he couldn't tell Scully? Hey Mulder, you already knew the approximate date of colonization. Remember "Two Fathers/One Son?" Doesn't anybody on this show remember anything that happened before?

Oh why do I bother?

As the CSM gloats over his apparent victory at breaking Mulder's spirit, Doggett and Reyes arrive and quickly run into the back-from-the-dead Knowle Rohr. He strides toward them and that loud outburst was the sound of millions of fans around the country screaming at the top of their lungs for Knowle to wipe out the new kids - especially given how Doggett lifted Mulder's "I Want To Believe" poster after The X-Files office was shut down (again).

But alas, it's not meant to be. As he approaches the rocks, the iron is sucked out of his belly and he withers up like a poorly blown balloon at my nephew's last birthday party.

So Knowle's gone, but here come the choppers. The new kids want to stay and help, but Mulder pulls out this season's ratings chart and tells them they have to leave because if they're gone, the ratings for the final few moments of the finale will rise considerably. They leave (alive, dammit), there's an explosion, the CSM dies (again) and the ruins are destroyed.

The next thing we know, Mulder and Scully are in a Roswell motel room (a nice in-joke at the very end) and it's possible given the explosion they are now presumed to be dead. That's old hat for Mulder. He's had more "deaths" than Joan Rivers and Cher have had facelifts.

Combined.

But this is virgin territory for Scully and she responds by taking off her clothes and putting on a bathrobe. This tells me nothing gets her motor running faster than being chased by helicopters through abandoned ruins after meeting with aging, decrepit conspiracy leaders and their old Indian caretakers.

OK, so she's kinky. I dig that.

While reflecting on a similar moment in a hotel room in the "Pilot," Mulder and Scully talk about the future and whether all is now lost. Mulder admits failure, but Scully speaks of her faith in him, a reminder of the fuel which has driven him for so long. At the end, Mulder caresses Scully's cross, the ultimate symbol of her faith, and climbs into bed with her.

Holding one another close, Mulder expresses one of the most prominent themes of the series when he says "Maybe there's hope." And with that, the series ends as it began, with two people drawing upon the hope that a better future awaits them as long as they continue to believe in one another and not give up the fight.

Perhaps "The Truth" we're meant to take from this finale is that the mytharc stopped making sense years ago and the only thing that really matters anymore is that through it all, Mulder and Scully will always remain together. They shall persevere.

Romance wasn't vital, but it arrived and they embraced it as powerfully as they embraced everything else they have confronted along the way. It has become another vital element in their quest, one that has served to further strengthen their collective resolve.

Ultimately, "The Truth" told us nothing of significance about the big picture, but did serve as a reminder of why many of us have cared so much about this series. We care about Mulder and Scully's journey because we care about them no matter how much silliness goes on around them.

For me, the Mulder and Scully relationship was never about sex, so I'm not terribly disappointed we didn't get a love scene at the end. What we did get was an incredibly intimate moment, likely a prelude to sex, that showed us how devoted these two characters are to one another in a deeply moving and significant way.

It was an exquisite Mulder-Scully moment.

"The Truth" didn't give me everything I had hoped for, but it gave me something wonderful at the end. A moment between Mulder and Scully where the strength of their union and the essence of the series were in full display. Given the numerous mistakes made the past two seasons, that was a tremendous present I wondered if I would ever be given again.

So now I can walk away without anger. Like Mulder and Scully, I can look to the future confused about much of what just transpired, unsure of what lies ahead but confident knowing that whatever occurs we'll see it through together.

And if there is no future, if this is truly all that there is of "The X-Files," I can always look to the past where so many wonderful memories remain. I can look back to the basement and hear the words that set so many sensational events into motion and relive every one of them whenever I desire.

"Sorry, nobody down here but the FBI's Most Unwanted."

Fade to black.

THE TRUTH IS STILL OUT THERE

"The Truth" ended with Mulder and Scully holding one another in bed, contemplating an uncertain future. The date for colonization had been set, the aliens were still afoot and the two heroes clung to their love for one another as the fuel to empower their continued quest for a better life to come.

But is that really the end of the story? That remains to be seen..

Carter has long envisioned turning "The X-Files" into a movie franchise, much the way "Star Trek" evolved over the years. Whether Carter gets his wish to have a cinematic franchise is uncertain. But well-placed industry sources believe at least one more film is quite possible.

A potential film series remains an enticing proposition for 20th Century Fox. Although the studio has the "Star Wars" films in its movie stable, it doesn't receive the type of cut from those astronomical profits as it would from an "X-Files" film series or what Paramount receives from the "Star Trek" films.

One factor that could help a second film come to fruition is the fact "The X-Files" remains big business in terms of DVD sales. The first film made more than $180 million, including international box office, but more than twice that figure (and counting) in VHS and DVD sales.

The ability to provide future DVD sales is a huge attribute for a film to have in today's cinematic climate. "The X-Files" is one commodity that could deliver on that count, not to mention generate plenty of additional revenue from other merchandising and collectible items.

If a second film is made, it will likely occur no sooner than 2004. At that point, the television series will have ended for the international viewers and all of the money that can be milked from the seasonal DVD releases will have been.

One factor in Fox's favor is the knowledge that audiences apparently are very eager to see Duchovny on the big screen. A recent focus group was conducted that asked avid television viewers and filmgoers which TV personality they would most like to see in the movies. Duchovny was among the top three performers with the highest scores.

Duchovny's creative input may also be part of the movie package. He is expected to demand story and script approval before signing on to do another film, but his involvement with the story may not end there. Although Carter has said in several interviews that he will be writing the script (possibly with Spotnitz), sources close to 1013 and Fox said Duchovny was interested in being involved with the scripting of a second film at one point and may be interested again.

His input with the story isn't considered trivial by any means. Many television insiders consider Duchovny's sense of narrative and story ideas to be significant reasons why the show became such a success.

Duchovny has long maintained he'd be interested in doing another film version of "The X-Files." According to sources close to the actor, the idea of a film franchise is something that also has piqued Duchovny's interest.

Anderson has also expressed interest in reprising the role of Scully on the big screen. However, in recent interviews, she's expressed some reluctance about doing a long-running series of films, saying the idea of playing Scully at the age of 50 isn't something she finds terribly appealing.

Interest in a second "X-Files" film isn't confined to the show's stars. Many fans of the television series believe a second film will be made and are eagerly awaiting the return of Mulder and Scully on the big screen.

"The X-Files franchise still has a lot of life left in it," said Matthias Zucker, a fan from Germany who began watching the show late in Season 1. "Fox knows that. The ratings for the series finale proved it in a way. More than 4 million viewers returned for the show's ending, evidence to the theory that 'The X-Files' works best with Mulder and Scully, which is what they want to do in future movies.

"It's my firm belief that after several years of reruns, 'TXF' will continue to find new fans in syndication, while old fans will find their interest renewed by the same reruns and DVD releases. Come 2004 or later, people will be hungry again for new M&S adventures."

Other fans aren't so sure. Frustrated by what they perceive as the lack of character and story development in the show's final years and having witnessed the deterioration of the fan base in that same time frame, they wonder if a second film will generate enough interest among moviegoers.

If there is a second film, Carter has said in numerous interviews it will be a stand-alone story and not a continuation of the show's mytharc. Many fans do not believe that is possible, or logical, given how the series finale ended with the alien threat of colonization still in the picture.

"Chris Carter's reluctance to deal with the unresolved issues presented in 'William' and the series finale may well be the last straw for what's left of the show's original audience," said Konrad Frye, a viewer since Season 1 from the Canadian province of Manitoba. "A stand-alone story that ignores the looming colonization and fails to reunite Mulder and Scully with their son is something I'm not personally interested in. Time will tell if others feel the same."

Even if there isn't another film, the principals involved with "The X-Files" have major plans now that the television series has reached its conclusion. As part of the deal Carter signed at the end of Season 7, he reportedly has a first-look, right of first refusal deal for a movie with Fox that he would write and possibly direct, but would not be "X-Files" related. He also reportedly has a first-look, right of first refusal deal for a new TV series on Fox to be delivered no later than the 2003-04 season.

Carter's primary collaborators since the sixth season will also be keeping busy. Spotnitz has a feature pact with Dimension Films and also signed on to be the executive producer for Michael Mann's new police drama for CBS. Shiban will serve as a writer and executive producer for "Enterprise," the "Star Trek" spinoff that airs on the UPN network. Gilligan has been keeping a lower profile although he reportedly has been working on film scripts.

As for the two stars, Duchovny has several film projects in the works, including starring in "My Dark Places," an upcoming adaptation of crime novelist James Ellroy's *My Dark Places*. The film follows Ellroy's search to resolve the unsolved murder of his mother in 1958. Anderson plans to bust her acting chops on the English stage, starring in Michael Weller's new play, "What The Night Is For."

As for me, my days as an online reviewer of "The X-Files" have come to an end, barring another film or two. The show, however, will live on. Such is its powerful legacy among all of us who watched it.

One of the greatest strengths of "The X-Files" was its ability to inspire long-running discussion about the meaning of its episodes and the twists and turns Mulder and Scully's relationship endured over the years. This was a show that demanded its audience pay attention as it carefully crafted an episodic puzzle of intriguing proportions.

Unlocking the many mysteries of the series was one of the greatest joys of my participation in online fandom. When the show was really clicking, it sparked intense and exhilarating debate about its wide array of "truths" and where Mulder and Scully were headed next. I dove right in, offered my own thoughts and analysis and found myself fascinated and often in awe by the level of intelligent discourse this show inspired.

The television series may have come to an end, but such discussions will last a lifetime.

But if there are no more stories to be told, if this is indeed the end, I can't help but think about the words Dana Scully spoke in a Roswell motel room in the series finale. She told Mulder that despite all she had lost and all that had happened to both of them in their nine years together she wouldn't hesitate to "do it all over again."

I think about those words and how they pertain to my time as a fan of this series. They lead me to reflect upon how this show moved me so powerfully and how it resulted in a wonderful experience, the likes of which I may never see encounter again. When Scully told Mulder she would "do it all over again," I think about those words and the past nine years and I come to one simple conclusion.

So would I.

THE TOP 25 EPISODES OF ALL TIME

Compiling "Best Of" lists is never easy since so many variables and preferences often factor into the decision. And when it comes to singling out the best episodes for a television series such as "The X-Files," which told so many wonderful and diverse stories in its tenure, the task becomes even more difficult.

As I sat down to compile this list, I realized numerous episodes that I loved wouldn't make the cut. There was no scientific process used to determine this list. I merely went with the Top 25 that my head and heart told me stood out above the rest during the show's nine-year run.

In some instances, I counted multiple-arc episodes as "one" episode since I consider them to be a singular story. So here is one fan's look at The Top 25 "X-Files" episodes of all time in reverse order.

25. "Field Trip" (Season 6) Feeling the effects of an hallucinogenic mushroom, Mulder and Scully trip out and provide an engaging look at their evolving relationship and changing characterization after six years together. The final scene which shows Scully reaching out for Mulder's hand sight unseen is one of the most effective visual examples of their union as any the show produced.

24. "Never Again" (Season 4) Scully faces a crossroads in her life personally and professionally. Feeling as if she has lost her sense of self to the all-consuming intoxication of Mulder's quest, Scully rebels against her nature which leads her into the arms of Ed Jerse and his rather talkative tattoo (with a voice supplied by Jodie Foster). Morgan and Wong's original script featured Scully and Jerse having sex. Carter altered the final version to show only a kiss, leaving the rest of Scully and Jerse's encounter ambigious, much to the chagrin of Gillian Anderson, who had lobbied for a sex scene for Scully.

23. "Irresistible" (Season 2) Mutilated corpses bring Mulder and Scully face-to-face with Donnie Pfaster, arguably the most frightening "monster" the show ever created. Displaying a wonderful sense of continuity with its references to Scully's abduction and providing yet another layer to the Mulder-Scully relationship, the episode ends with a pivotal moment - Scully letting her guard down and tearfully embracing Mulder after Pfaster is apprehended after kidnapping Scully. By allowing herself to be seen emotionally naked in front of her partner, Scully opened herself up to him in ways she had been reluctant to do before.

22. "Conduit" (Season 1) The disappearance of a teen-age girl on a family camping trip brings memories of Mulder's sister's abduction boiling to the surface. Mulder's personal quest is deepened as he not only seeks to find the answer to Ruby Morris' disappearance, but attempts to confront the demons from his past. The final scene where Scully listens to Mulder's recount of his sister's abduction while Mulder weeps in a local church is one of the series' most powerful moments.

21. "Anasazi/The Blessing Way/Paper Clip" (Season 2-3) The second season finale and the first two episodes of Season 3 find Mulder returning from the dead only to learn a terrifying secret about his past. The conspiracy grew by leaps and bounds in these episodes and not only does it greatly impact Mulder, but Scully suffers a personal loss as well when her sister is murdered in a case of mistaken identity.

20. "Requiem" (Season 7) The seventh season finale brings Mulder and Scully back to where it all began - investigating more alien encounters in the Oregon woods. The episode ends with Mulder's abduction and Scully uttering the two words that would serve to change the series forever: "I'm pregnant."

19. "Bad Blood" (Season 5) An investigation into possible vampiric activity leads to Mulder and Scully recounting drastically different versions of the event. An episode that not only supplies plenty of laughs, but also provides exquisite insight into each character and their unique relationship. "Bad Blood" is a satiric X-File at its finest.

18. "Deep Throat" (Season 1) The second episode of the series introduces a mysterious ally for Mulder and thrusts him deeper into the alien conspiracy that has become his life's work. The fundamental elements of Mulder and Scully's partnership are set into motion in this episode as Mulder rushes wildly into the unknown in search of the truth while Scully attempts to protect him at all costs.

17. "Wetwired" (Season 3) Rarely has the element of trust between Mulder and Scully been more powerfully displayed than in this under rated third season episode. In a nice twist, here it's Scully who is overcome by paranoia as she begins to doubt Mulder's allegiance to her and their joint quest. Mulder conveyed more in terms of characterization with one sentence ("Scully, you're the only one I trust.") than many dramas do in an entire season.

16.. "Small Potatoes" (Season 4) A baby with a tail and visions of Luke Skywalker are only the beginning in this wonderful Vince Gilligan-penned episode. Former series writer Darin Morgan plays Eddie Van Blundht, whose shape shifting ability not only enables him to woo the women in his local town, but also brings him oh so close to Dana Scully.

15. "Little Green Men" (Season 2) A personal favorite and a wonderful reminder of when the mytharc was still rich with opportunity and inventiveness. Mulder and Scully are split up by The Powers That Be, but are never really apart. The strength of their relationship is evident when Mulder heads off to find aliens, but takes Scully with him via the tape recorder. Mulder comes face-to-face with aliens (or does he?) and is powerless against them. Arguably the best season opener in the series history.

14. "Squeeze" (Season 1) The episode that proved "The X-Files" wasn't just a show about UFOs. The liver-eating Tooms remains one of the series' most unforgettable "villians" and the prominent theme of trust is on display yet again. Also, we get Scully making a conscious choice to stand alongside Mulder despite the potential damage it could do to her credibility and standing in the FBI.

13. "Amor Fati" (Season 7) The CSM offers Mulder "the road not taken," but Mulder soon finds it to be filled with lies (including a false marriage to Fowley, a life in the 'burbs with his "father" and reunions with people he'd lost such as Samantha and Deep Throat). Scully is absent from the dream until the end, when she serves as a symbolic representation of the truth and snaps Mulder back to reality. The Duchovny-penned final scene is exquisite in showcasing the beauty and power of Mulder and Scully's evolving relationship.

12. "Ice" (Season 1) A first-season gem. An homage to "The Thing" finds Mulder and Scully among those stranded in the great white north, where a creature of possibly alien origin is moving from host to host. Confined in closed quarters with a mounting body count, paranoia is the word of the day as Mulder and Scully are forced to question whether they can truly place their trust in one another.

11. "Paper Hearts" (Season 4) A Vince Gilligan masterpiece. A pedophile (superbly played by Tom Noonan) somehow taps into Mulder's memories of his sister's abduction and puts a personal spin on them, leaving Mulder to question what he thought was the truth about Samantha's disappearance. Filled with some wonderful continuity (note Scully's reference to Mulder's comment about dreams from "Aubrey") and a powerful moment from Scully during the last prison interview with Roche, we see Mulder pushed to the edge of his own sanity (again) before reclaiming the truth he has always known.

10. "Redux/Redux II" (Season 5) While many people don't care for "Redux," I think it does a good job of preparing us for the second hour (although it invalidates Gillian's emotional context from the S4 finale). That said, "Redux II' is the standout hour of the two without question. With Scully on her deathbed, Mulder meets his sister only to lose her again and is put in a position where he may deal with the devil. The final few moments, culminating with the CSM's "death" are quite simply, perfect and as good as any the show ever produced.

9. "Beyond The Sea" (Season 1) We finally get a chance to really see what makes Scully tick as she loses her father and is forced to confront the very real possibility of the paranormal. As important as "Conduit" was for Mulder's characterization in S1, I'd say this episode was just as significant for Scully. Glen Morgan and James Wong belted the ball out of the ballpark with authority in this episode.

8. "Jose Chung's From Outer Space" (Season 3) A wonderful satire in true "X-Files" fashion. From the Mulder "girly scream," to kick-ass Scully's moment in the woods to Jesse Ventura and Alex Trebeck, this remains the episode by which all other "X-Files Lites" are judged. Some come very very close, but none ever really matched it.

7. "Clyde Bruckman's Final Repose" (Season 3) Peter Boyle is magnificent as the insurance salesman who can see into the future. Again, there is a wonderful blend of humor, drama and pathos, something "The X-Files" did better than just about any other show this past decade. Plus, there is the throwaway line about Scully being immortal which continues to be a hot topic in fandom to this day.

6. "The Unnatural" (Season 6) David Duchovny's directorial debut was a grand slam home run. Not only did he deliver a wonderful "X-Files" metaphor about love and the power of humanity, he produced arguably the most sensual moment between Mulder and Scully fans were ever provided outside of fan fic. No kiss between the two has ever rivaled Mulder's "birthday present" and I doubt any ever will.

5. "Home" (Season 4) I love dark, twisted nightmarish stories and this one took the cake. The Peacock boys and their mother aren't easily forgotten. The murder of Sheriff Taylor and his wife remains one of the most chilling moments in the series run, highlighted by the fact it occurred while the bouncy "Wonderful Wonderful" was playing above the scene. That's sick, twisted stuff. I loved it.

4. "Memento Mori" (Season 4) Arguably the definitive example of Mulder and Scully's devotion for one another. Scully battles cancer, but keeps Mulder by her side via her words to him in a private journal. Mulder is off searching for the truth which can save her. Another powerful example of how the strength of their bond: Despite the fact they are rarely together in the episode, we feel as if they are never apart. "The truth will save both of us." Indeed.

3. "Pusher" (Season 3) The best MOTW in the series history. Robert Modell is hands down the most fascinating antagonist "The X-Files" has ever produced. And he finds a worthy adversary in Fox Mulder. Gilligan creates a powerful episode while serving up reminder after reminder of the deepening bond between Mulder and Scully, highlighted by a gripping finale with Scully caught in the middle of Modell and Mulder's battle of wills.

2. "Triangle" (Season 6) A witty and wonderful homage to "The Wizard of Oz" gives us a peak into Mulder's subconscious as he heads back in time and meets up with the people who populate his world. It's also a fascinating look at Mulder's unconscious battle to come to terms with his growing feelings for Scully. In the end, Scully's "belief" in him allows him to take the next step he had been hesitant to take. Mulder's final declaration also stands as the only time in the series' history that Mulder or Scully professed their love for one another.

1. "Duane Barry/Ascension/One Breath" (Season 2) To this day, this remains the defining moment in the series' run. So much sprang forth from this trio of episodes. Scully's abduction and subsequent cancer. The furthering of the conspiracy threat with the CSM as a sinister figure to be reckoned with and Krycek as a polar opposite to Mulder. And most significantly, Mulder making a significant decision to choose Scully over his quest. Sensational.

ISBN 1553698128-6

9 781553 698128

Made in the USA